Slavery in the Cities

THE SOUTH 1820-1860

RICHARD C. WADE

OXFORD UNIVERSITY PRESS

LONDON   OXFORD   NEW YORK

OXFORD UNIVERSITY PRESS

Oxford London New York
Glasgow Toronto Melbourne Wellington
Cape Town Salisbury Ibadan Nairobi Lusaka Addis Ababa
Bombay Calcutta Madras Karachi Lahore Dacca
Kuala Lumpur Hong Kong Tokyo

Preface

He moved cautiously across the stage. The plantation costume, tattered and patched, fitted badly; his toes protruded through gaping holes in the shoes. The once stylish broad-rimmed hat, now old and wrinkled, sat rakishly on the back of his head. Through the blackface he grinned brightly and began the famous ditty:

> Come listen all you galls and boys
> I'm just from Tuckyhoe
> I'll join to sing a little song
> My name's Jim Crow.

When he came to the refrain he started to dance, rolling from side to side, gesturing mischievously, turning his back to the audience, and then on the words "jis so" he leaped high and turned to the front again. For whites in antebellum America this vaudeville act represented the familiar image of the Negro —natural, graceful, musical, childlike, and, most importantly, happy and contented. Later Jim Crow would be used to describe a whole system of race relations.

Less well known to subsequent generations but equally familiar to those who frequented the popular theater of the 1840's was Zip Coon, the urban counterpart to Jim Crow. Coming off Broadway rather than the plantation, he dressed in the latest style—tight pantaloons, a lacy jabot, a *lorgnon*, and a walking stick. But most of all he sported a splendid, luxurious blue coat with long swishing tails. Strutting pompously across the boards, swinging his cane, and asserting elegantly that he was a "larned skolar," Zip Coon explained his importance in song:

> *Some have de mockazins and some haves none*
> *But he dat habs a pair of boots he tinks himself a man*
> *Wid his big Brass buttons and his long tail Blue*
> *Dem what whe call the dandies of the carolina crew.*

Of course, both figures were grotesque caricatures, but the stereotypes did indicate that a single image did not fit even the limited observation of mid-century audiences. Urban Negroes, superficially at least, had been transformed, indeed sophisticated, by their life in the city. And Zip Coon was at pains to distinguish himself from the plantation-bred Jim Crow.*

In dealing with the institution of slavery historians have generally missed the contrast that vaudeville thought to be so obvious. The important books and significant controversies have all assumed the plantation and farm to be the special setting of the institution. Yet from almost the beginning slavery was also urban. Every Southern town and city had a large complement of slaves, and contemporaries considered them as much a part of the system as those who toiled in the fields or served in the mansion. Moreover, slavery in the cities was in many important ways quite different from its rural analogue. That difference is the theme of this book.

This volume is not, however, a history of the rise of the cities in the Old South, nor is it a comprehensive history of what contemporaries called "the peculiar institution." It is rather an attempt to find out what happened to slavery in

---

* Hans Nathan, *Dan Emmett and the Rise of Early Negro Minstrelsy* (Norman, Okla., 1962), pp. 50-70.

an urban environment and to reconstruct the texture of life of the Negroes who lived in bondage in the cities. That this analysis would turn out to be relevant to the issues of our own time was an unexpected byproduct, not the occasion of the study.

The story is told as much as possible in the words of contemporaries, for in the area of race words often contain meanings and connotations which even a skilled paraphrase cannot convey precisely. Yet in these subtleties are enclosed the most important relationships between master and slave, white and black, freeman and bondsman. Since these questions lie at the center of this analysis, no shortcut seemed appropriate.

In tracing the development of urban slavery I have examined intensively the records of cities located in every part of Dixie, including border towns as well as those situated in the Deep South, cities in the older states on the Atlantic as well as newer ones in the Mississippi valley, places settled by foreign as well as by native population, small as well as large towns. It is significant that slavery in the cities was fundamentally the same wherever it existed, and that the similarities of urban life were more important to the institution than the differences in settlement, region, or age.

In writing this book, I have received help in various ways from a great many people and institutions. The Social Science Research Council, the University of Rochester, Washington University in St. Louis, and the University of Chicago generously provided financial assistance which permitted extensive travel in the South and met the costs of preparing the manuscript. Local historical societies everywhere opened their extensive collections for my use; mayors and city clerks interrupted their pressing duties to make available municipal records; state libraries and archives went well beyond the usual courtesies in assembling documents and manuscripts relating to the topic. Moreover, countless individuals, white and

Negro, let me see family papers or guided me to other little used sources.

To some people, however, I owe a particular obligation. Jerome E. Edwards helped transform a rough draft into a completed manuscript by checking notes, arranging the appendix, and giving helpful advice all along the way. My colleagues, William T. Hutchinson, John Hope Franklin, and Herbert S. Klein, and my neighbor, Joseph P. Semper, improved an earlier version by careful and critical readings. I am particularly indebted to another colleague, Daniel J. Boorstin, whose suggestions not only tightened the general thesis but also contributed to the final shape of the volume. None of these scholars, of course, can be held accountable for anything in this book, but without them there certainly would have been many more errors.

No set of acknowledgments would be complete without two special citations. My wife, Louise C. Wade, was always a partner in the project. She cheerfully went south in summer months, endured the drudgery of working through old municipal records, and read the manuscript in its successive phases. Arthur M. Schlesinger contributed encouragement, his keen editorial hand, and wise counsel to this enterprise. In dedicating this volume to him, I repay only a small portion of a very large debt.

Chicago   R. C. W.
June 1964

Contents

SLAVERY IN THE CITIES

Chapter One

THE URBAN PERIMETER

BY 1860 slavery was disintegrating in Southern cities. Forty years earlier, the institution had seemed as stable and vigorous in town as in country. Slaves comprised at least 20 per cent of the population of the major cities. In most places the proportion was much higher, and in Charleston blacks outnumbered whites. Slaves handled the bulk of domestic drudgery; worked in shops and factories; built the streets, bridges, and municipal installations; some even acquired mechanical skills. Within four decades, however, the picture had changed dramatically. In the border cities the institution had nearly disappeared altogether; farther south it had diminished in extent and vitality. Everywhere proportionately, and in many places absolutely, the number of town slaves declined. In the countryside slavery still appeared stable and successful, but wherever it touched urban conditions it was in deep trouble.

A Kentuckian observed in 1848 that "slavery exists in Louisville and St. Louis only in name," for "there are two things that always, and under all circumstances, abrogates slavery. The first is a dense population, ... the next [is] the intelligence of slaves. Both of these are silently and imperceptibly working their legitimate results." [1] A Louisiana planter, who was also a frequent visitor to New Orleans, had noticed this same process: "Slavery is from its very nature eminently patriarchial and altogether agricultural. It does

not thrive with master or slave when transplanted to cities." [2]
Probably the best Northern student of the South, Frederick
Law Olmsted, made the same point in 1857. "Servile labor
must be unskilled labor," he wrote, "and unskilled labor
must be dispersed over land, and cannot support the concentrated life nor amass the capital of cities." [3] And those
Negroes who had known bondage in both town and country perhaps understood the problem best. One of them, Frederick Douglass, stated it simply, "Slavery dislikes a dense
population." [4]

But what became clear in 1860 was not apparent forty years
earlier. In 1820, slavery was as much a part of life in the city as
on farm and plantation. In fact, some municipal officials expressed anxiety over the rapid increase in colored townspeople. And surely no one questioned the adaptability of slavery
to the urban milieu. Yet experience ultimately proved this
assumption mistaken. For, as the cities grew, they produced
conditions which first strained, then undermined, the regime
of bondage in the South's metropolises.

II

Though the South was primarily rural before the Civil
War, it did not lack important cities. Resting on its irregular
perimeter were New Orleans, Mobile, Savannah, Charleston,
Richmond, Baltimore, Louisville, and St. Louis. These seaports and river towns sent Dixie's produce to the outside, distributed necessary imports to the countryside, and formed
enclaves of cosmopolitan life in a generally agricultural society. Scattered across the interior were smaller places, usually
state capitals or trading towns, with more than local importance. Then, too, there was Washington, the nation's capital
but still very much a regional city. In fact, on the eve of the

Civil War the census listed 30 places of over 8000 inhabitants throughout the South.

Taken together, these urban centers contained only a small part of the South's population, yet their influence was much greater than their numbers. De Bow, writing in 1860, was impressed by their constantly widening significance: "Within the last forty years country life has quietly and almost imperceptibly undergone great changes." These changes consisted "in the country having become more and more dependent on the town. Whether in pursuit of business, pleasure, or information, men leave the country and visit some neighboring city." "Our bodies," he concluded somewhat wistfully, "are in the country, our souls in town." [5]

New Orleans was the largest city of the deep South. It also seemed to many the least American. Founded by the French in 1718, it retained an intensely European flavor even a half century after the Louisiana Purchase. The "old quarter" in 1860 still reminded people of parts of Paris, with its "French noises and French smells, [and] French signs." [6] But beyond Canal Street, dubbed by residents "the Rubicon," was the newer and American section. There Southern architecture suggested native dominance; but the large number of Germans, Irish, and Spanish gave the area a cosmopolitan complexion. "It is unlike any other city in the Union, being foreign in air, in customs, and mainly in population," wrote one visitor.[7] Or, as an early gazetteer put it, "it is a world in miniature." [8]

New Orleans's initial growth under the American flag had been modest, but by the late 'twenties it began an extraordinary expansion. In 1831 William Gilmore Simms could observe that it had "grown prodigiously—perhaps its increase in wealth, population, and business generally, since 1825, is without parallel in the United States." [9] The census figures confirmed this enthusiasm as the population surged from nearly thirty thousand to over one hundred thousand. A decade later, an exhilarated De Bow could predict that New Orleans "will be indeed to the Father of Rivers, 'as London to the Thames, and Paris to the Seine.' " [10] On the eve of the war, the city counted 168,675 residents.

New Orleans owed its success to its location at the foot of the great river system that drained half the continent. From this strategic spot it handled most of the sugar from Louisiana, cotton from the Southwest, and grain and livestock from the interior. To its wharves came goods from the North, from Europe, Latin America, and the Orient. At the busy season the docks seethed with activity. "The very air howls with an eternal din and noise," a visitor remarked with wonder in 1847. "Drays and wagons of all descriptions, loaded with the produce of every clime, move on continually in an unbroken chain. Ships from every nation, whose masts tower aloft in a dense forest for five miles. . . . Steamboats, and crafts of every make and shape, from every river which empties into the Mississippi are here mingling in the strife of commerce." [11] Another Southerner rhapsodically pronounced the scene as without historical parallel. "Tyre nor Carthage, Alexandria nor Genoa," he wrote, "those aforetime imperial metropoles of merchant princes, boasted no quay like the Levee of New Orleans." [12]

By the late 'twenties the town's exports were second largest in the nation, and for a few years in the late 'thirties and early 'forties it actually surpassed New York. "No city in the world has ever advanced as a mart of commerce with such gigantic and rapid strides, as New Orleans," wrote De Bow, the town's leading booster, in 1846. "In 40 years she has become the fourth city of the world . . . for the magnitude and value of her commerce." [13] And the future seemed unlimited. George Washington Cable, who grew up there in these years, remembered how this development bred "an overweening confidence in the ability of the city to become speedily and without exertion the metropolis of America, if not eventually of the world." [14]

These expansive dreams, however, were dashed in the next decade. The rate of growth slackened, and though population and trade continued to rise, New Orleans could not match the pace of its competitors across the country. Nevertheless, on the eve of the Civil War, the city ranked sixth in the nation's urban sweepstakes.

One hundred and fifty miles to the east was Mobile, a few years older but considerably smaller than New Orleans. Situated on a bay between the mouth of the Alabama River and the Gulf of Mexico, it had been transformed by cotton from a drowsy little town into a bustling port. French and Spanish at the beginning, it remained so for almost a century, and despite its transformation a visitor occasionally could be struck by the colonial legacy. "The names of the streets are Frenchy," a visitor from Ohio wrote in his diary in 1858. "Dauphin, Royal, Conti, St. Joseph. St. Louis, St. Michael and plenty of other saints." [15] Continuity, too, could be found in a few old families and a sprinkling of creoles and in the "mingled traces of the manners and language of the French and Spaniards." [16] But fundamentally Mobile's population, appearance, and spirit were thoroughly American, if not peculiarly Southern. [17]

The Alabama port's progress dated from its annexation to the United States. Watching its advance, *Niles' Register* asserted in 1822 that "*Mobile* is becoming a place of great importance" and "may soon be one of the most populous of our Southern cities." In just nine years it had grown from "less than 300 inhabitants" to 2800. [18] "We have never witnessed such an influx of strangers as is now pouring into our city," boasted the *Commercial Register* in 1833. And the people kept coming. Two years later, the same editor reported that "the

city is at this moment one-fourth larger than it was twelve
months since." [19] In 1840 the census showed over twelve thousand residents, and two decades later it had reached nearly
thirty thousand.[20]

The city's ante-bellum boom sprang from the immense pro-
ductivity of the cotton hinterland. "The great business of the
town," Olmsted observed, "is the transfer of cotton, from the
producer to the manufacturer, from the wagon and steamboat
to the seagoing ship." [21] Indeed, the crop seemed to command
every aspect of Mobile's life. A sojourning Briton spoke of
the port as a place where "people live in cotton houses and
ride in cotton carriages. They buy cotton, sell cotton, think
cotton, eat cotton, drink cotton, and dream cotton. They
marry cotton wives, and unto them are born cotton children.
. . . It has made Mobile, and all its citizens." [22] The crop, another visitor asserted, was "the mighty pivot upon which the
business of this city of 30,000 inhabitants revolves." [23]

Built on commerce, too, though facing the Atlantic rather
than the Gulf, was Savannah, Georgia's major port and one
of the South's most enterprising entrepots. Founded in 1733
by James Oglethorpe, it stood sixteen miles up the river from
the ocean, and was English in background and experience. A
unique plan had fixed the development of the city around
a series of charming little parks which gave the place "a
curiously rural and modest aspect." [24] Its sandy streets, kept
unimproved presumably for reasons of health, fortified the
impression. But the small-town flavor could not conceal the
intensely commercial character of a people who prided themselves on their industry and aggressiveness. Occupying, as a
traveler noted, "the primal and efficient seat . . . of the energy
of Georgia," they advertised themselves as "plain, old fashioned, hard working men and women, who . . . transact business before 8 o'clock a.m." [25]

Though an old city, Savannah rose to importance in Dixie

in the years just before the war. In 1820 Savannah had only 7523 residents, very gradually increasing in the following decade. But by 1840 the figure climbed to over eleven thousand, moved beyond fifteen thousand at the next census, and reached over twenty thousand by 1860. While this growth seemed modest by the lusty Western standards of the time, it nonetheless was a notable achievement to triple population within forty years.

In fact, its aggressiveness had brought it early fame. In 1818 Savannah sent a steamship bearing the city's name on a pioneer, if unprofitable, trip to Liverpool. Fifteen years later, the city started a railroad venture into the uplands. A visiting New Yorker who watched this project remarked years later that it demonstrated "a spirit of enterprise that could honor any place in the country. While containing less than eight thousand people, black and white," he concluded, "it projected and completed ... a railroad 190 miles in length, to Macon, at that time the longest railroad in the country." [26]

This mercantile audacity paid off. Not only did it sustain a growing population, but the inland trade strengthened every aspect of the city's economy. By 1860 the value of cotton exports alone amounted to over $17 million.[27] Manufacturing, too, felt the stimulus, but without the fanfare of commerce. A municipal official observed in 1848 that "this increase of steam power has been so noiseless" that most residents "will be surprised to learn that of the *eighteen* establishments propelled by steam, *fourteen* of them have been erected within the last ten years." Nearly every indicator carried good news. "Her growing population—the great increase of the mechanical arts—the extended use of steam as applied to mills, presses, and other useful employments—" the same source asserted, "are all evidence of a healthful state of the body politic." [28] "She has both the power and inclination," a visitor contended, "to maintain her position in the struggle for commercial supremacy now going on among Southern cities." [29]

Savannah depended on cotton no less than Mobile. The great staple came to the docks from nearly every direction and in every kind of conveyance. The river, of course, brought most, but by the 1850's other carriers shared the commerce. "Daily," said one observer, "nine trains came down the Central Railroad . . . with from twenty to thirty cars in each train, loaded mountain high with this article. The depots and plank yards, covering several acres, were groaning constantly under the immense burden, while long trains of horse teams" moved to the commission houses. The "spacious and elegant" homes of successful merchants and factors combined with "large and well filled" stores to demonstrate that many Savannahians profited considerably by this activity.[30] Indeed, as cotton-growing moved to the interior, mercantile leaders chased the trade with railroads and river steamboats.

One hundred miles up the coast was Charleston, oldest and proudest metropolis in Dixie. By 1860 it was no longer the largest or richest, but it still claimed to be the "capital of the South." Acutely conscious of a colonial past that stretched back to 1680 and of earlier days when it ranked among the nation's most important cities, Charleston sought to preserve its supremacy through political and cultural leadership. This was no easy task, for the competitors, old and new, proved many. Yet Charleston had substantial assets. Set on a tongue of land between the Ashley and Cooper rivers, it had easy access to the back country. Its spacious harbor could accommodate most of the Atlantic's shipping at one time. Its climate and beauty, moreover, made it the favorite resort of the rice and cotton planters, who built expensive and tasteful town houses on the blue bay and gave a special polish and sophistication to Charleston society.

The celebrated ease and leisure of aristocratic life, however, could not conceal the growing difficulties of the city. De Bow, who had lived in both Charleston and New Orleans, could not help but contrast the development of the two places. "When the Crescent City consisted of a few huts on the low lands of the Mississippi, her sister of the Palmetto State was reveling in the riches of foreign commerce, and in all affluence and prosperity," he wrote in 1846. "But now the vision is changed. The noble city on the banks of the Cooper and Ashley looks back to the past with lingering regret," as the Louisiana port forged ahead.[31] From being the nation's fifth largest metropolis in 1810, Charleston dropped to twenty-second in 1860. Its supremacy in the South, moreover, slipped away with the rise of other urban centers.

This descent was relative, not absolute. In the forty years after 1820 the city nearly doubled its population, reaching forty thousand by the Civil War. By 1850 it had annexed the "Neck," a suburb on its only land boundary, which opened up possibilities of further expansion. Yet the growth was never substantial or sustained.[32]

This record of modest growth in a period of immense national urban expansion hurt both the pocketbooks and pride of the people. "Civis," writing in the *City Gazette* in 1824, drew a portrait that would be familiar to a generation of ante-bellum residents: "Charleston and neck present at this moment, a most gloomy and desponding picture; where scenes of industry, activity and growing prosperity were of late so apparent; where once reigned wealth and happiness, nothing now is to be found, but indolence, apathy, poverty and misery."[33] In 1835 another wrote with irritation that "the South alone, and Carolina and Charleston in particular, appear to be standing still, slumbering in a sleepy hollow, or 'going ahead' in such small movements as scarcely to be perceptible."[34] The changes were so slight during the next decade that one resident asserted that "but for two conflagrations which swept off many of her old houses" the city even looked the same.[35] The 'fifties proved generally no better. When war came in 1861, the economic memory of most Charlestonians revolved around stagnation and hard times.

The "capital of the South" did not submit tamely to this "premature decay."[36] In the decades before the Civil War business leaders experimented with manufacturing, merchants sought markets in the Ohio Valley, and local officials tried to improve commercial contacts with Europe and the Caribbean. In fact, for a period Charleston's railroad to Augusta was the longest such enterprise in the world. Yet these projects were only partially successful, for the economic tides of the time were running away from the Carolina entrepot. Cotton moved westward, upcountry agriculture languished, and the mountains shut off the transappalachian trade. By the 1850's it was no longer possible to hide the decline. "I was disappointed," a British traveler wrote candidly, "by the general appearance of this capital of the South. On the whole, it has a somewhat poverty-struck look."[37]

Richmond was the only state capital among Dixie's major cities. It was also the only major industrial one. Located on the James River at the head of navigation, it had centered its early hopes on trade. But gradually manufacturing and political affairs became the more important interests. Factories and warehouses crowded along the river bank, their dull brick shells at once ugly and impressive. Farther back from the water stood the Capitol building, "an imposing Grecian edifice, standing alone, and firmly placed on open and elevated ground, in the center of town." Generous private mansions downtown attested to its wealth, but Richmond seemed less Southern than the coastal towns, and reminded visitors of Northern and British cities. "It is a metropolis," Olmsted wrote, "and, of course, the tide of modern life elsewhere reaches it, stirs it, and here and there possesses it."[38]

The strong manufacturing emphasis fortified this impression. As the nation's tobacco center, it stored and processed immense quantities every year. Its Tredegar Iron Company was renowned not only because of its success, but because it employed black labor, which permitted local enthusiasts to proclaim that it was possible to have slavery and industry too. And just beyond the city's edge were extensive coal fields, ready to feed Richmond's furnaces as well as to provide fuel for New York, Baltimore, and Newark.[39] Olmsted first saw the town "through a cloud of bituminous smoke," and recalled "the sensation produced by a similar *coup d'oeil* of Edinburg." [40] Commerce still played an important role in the life of the Virginia capital, but townspeople and visitors alike preferred to think of it as the manufacturing heart of Dixie.

Yet Richmond shared many of Charleston's problems. As the focus of Southern life moved westward, Virginia, too, suffered. The Old Dominion increasingly felt its economic and political power and its national prestige slipping away. "My pride has been humbled by her decline," one "patriot" confessed in 1828, "and I could weep for her fallen greatness." [41] The fears were worse, however, than the facts. The city continued to grow even during depressions, though the pace was not dramatic. From some twelve thousand residents in 1820, the population increased four thousand in the next decade and reached twenty thousand by 1840. Local boosters usually included the suburbs in their estimates, thus adding considerably to the official figures. In 1839 the newspapers claimed 26,000 for the metropolitan area, leading a friendly neighbor to write that "she is going ahead with accumulating velocity," which he thought especially remarkable because until recently "she was in that lethargic condition so characteristic of Southern cities in the same period." [42] On the eve of the Civil War the population had jumped to nearly thirty-eight thousand.[43]

On the northeast corner of the South stood Baltimore and Washington—the former a thriving port and commercial center whose phenomenal rise after its incorporation in 1782 had threatened Philadelphia and concerned New York; the other growing steadily if not spectacularly as the national capital. Both were essentially Southern in population and institutions. Indeed, in 1860, the Maryland port's 212,000 people made it the largest in Dixie and the country's fourth city; and Washington's 61,000 thrust it ahead of the older cities of the South Atlantic states.

On the upper periphery of the South were two other large urban centers, Louisville and St. Louis. Just across the river from each lay free territory, areas connected with the city in every important way but one—the institution of slavery. Indeed, in settlement and growth the two places were Western not Southern. It was only after the emergence of slavery as a divisive issue that the perspective changed. And, ironically, the shift took place at the very time when slavery itself was virtually disappearing from both towns. Yet in 1860 each had some Negro slaves, and as a Louisville editor put it, their "prejudices, interests and feelings" were "extremely Southern." [44]

Louisville grew up at the Falls of the Ohio, the spot where the water strikes irregular shoals that force a break in transportation. The city early provided the facilities for moving goods and people around the hazard. From its founding in 1778 until the opening of the Louisville and Portland Canal in 1830, nearly all the riverborne commerce of the West passed through its hands. [45] Even after the canal broke the initial monopoly, the town's strategic position permitted a generous prosperity. [46]

Louisville's early interest was trade. In fact, in 1836 Gabriel Collins's *Directory* observed that the town depended "almost entirely upon ... commerce." "No other city perhaps in the world," he continued, "with such a large commercial business, has a population so small, or employs as little capital in other occupations." [47] This mercantile concentration later proved to be a liability, however, for when the panic of 1837 struck the Kentucky entrepot it did real damage. The census figures which had recorded constant gains in 1820 and 1830 suddenly dropped by five thousand. [48]

Yet soon the old pace was renewed. By 1850 the population had reached over forty thousand, and ten years later it increased to nearly seventy thousand. [49] "It has grown withall at a Western rapidity," Olmstead noted, having "great business, both as an entrepot and as itself, a manufacturing producer." Though "without the whirr of Cincinnati" or the charm of New Orleans, Louisville represented "a good specimen of a brisk and well-furnished city." [50]

St. Louis was both a northern and western outpost of the ante-bellum South. Born in 1764 of French fur-trading activity, it was situated just below the confluence of the Mississippi and Missouri. Set aside the great waterways of the central continent, it early thrived on an almost imperial commerce. The coming of the steamboat greatly enhanced its growth and importance. Nearly every hour, the *Missouri Republican* observed in 1855, "some gallant steamer" plows "the waves of the Mississippi, bringing from the North, as far as St. Paul— from the West, beyond the Yellow Stone—from the South, almost to the Gulf, and from the Ohio to the very confluence of the Allegheny and Monongahela, the products of the richest and most improved country in the world." On the levee "the genius, enterprise and diversified interests of the nation" were represented. "The sugars of the South lay mingled with the cereals of the North, and the manufactures of civilization contrasted with the peltries of the Indian." [51]

Nor was this merely parochial enthusiasm. *De Bow's Review* was at least as buoyant, claiming that "St. Louis is des-

tined to become commercially more than Venice ever *was*—
and in manufactures what *Lowell* is!" [52] Local boosters never
tired of chanting the statistics of metropolitan growth. Population increased from ten thousand in 1820 to seventy-eight
thousand in 1850, and then jumped to over one hundred sixty
thousand ten years later.[53] Steamboat arrivals nearly doubled
between 1840 and 1860,[54] while the value of real estate increased more than tenfold in the same period.[55] Nothing, it
seemed, could halt the town's inevitable rise. "If vegetation
should fail; if sunshine and rain should withhold their accustomed offices; ... if our mighty rivers ... should cease to
flow," wrote one editor, "then will St. Louis be arrested in
her upward march to greatness,—but not 'till then." [56]

III

Southern cities would have grown even more rapidly if the
Negro population had kept pace with the white. But the proportion of colored residents declined, and by 1860 most of the
major towns were actually losing blacks, both slave and free.
In each case the experience was the same. The number of
slaves mounted as the city became larger, often increasing
faster than whites. At some point, however, the ratio shifted.
Negro populations leveled off as the others continued to rise;
soon a gradual reduction set in. Every Dixie metropolis went
through at least the first two phases of this cycle by 1860,
and most had completed all three.

Travelers often did not notice this attrition in the number
of urban blacks. Arriving by ship or train, they first saw town
life at the dock or station where colored porters, stevedores,
and draymen handled baggage and freight. At the hotels,
boarding houses, or fashionable homes they saw slaves as
waiters, chambermaids, and general domestics. A trip to the
market place would find Negro vendors, hawkers, and main-

tenance men. Even a casual stroll on the street during the day or early evening was likely to exaggerate the size of the black population, for bondsmen could be seen running errands, driving wagons, and doing much of the unskilled outdoor work. These contacts, coupled with an intense interest in the South's system, obscured for most visitors the proportionate decline of Negro residents in the cities.

"The vast proportion of blacks in the street soon struck me," an Englishman wrote about New Orleans. "I should think they were five to one of the white population." [57] In fact, the ratio in the Crescent City at that time was nearly the reverse. Likewise, Fredrika Bremer, visiting Charleston in 1850 when whites outnumbered colored, could assert that "Negroes swarm the streets. Two-thirds of the people one sees in town are negroes." [58] Still another contended in 1857 that "Richmond was at this time literally swarming with negroes." [59]

Yet the facts ran the other way. In Charleston, for example, though initially both groups increased together, the proportion of blacks substantially declined in the two ante-bellum decades. In 1820 the total black population exceeded 58 per cent. But in 1840 the relationship began to change. On the eve of the war less than half the Charlestonians were Negroes, and only slightly more than a third were slaves. [60]

The same pattern emerged in New Orleans, except that the number of free colored was always much higher. In 1805 more than half the city's residents were Negroes, the bulk of them slaves. The immense growth of the next fifteen years did not alter the proportions between the races significantly, though free blacks nearly equaled slaves. The 1830's, however, brought an almost revolutionary increase in population and an important change in the racial complexion of the city. Now over half of the hundred thousand or so inhabitants were white, though the blacks still numbered almost forty-three thousand.[61]

New Orleans's expansion slowed but did not stop during the following twenty years. But colored residents declined both proportionately and absolutely. Indeed, in 1860, only one in every seven inhabitants was Negro. This trend, of course, ran sharply against the tendency in rural Louisiana, where the slave population rose markedly each year.

In Richmond the decline of bondsmen was relative not absolute by 1860. The decisive decade had been the 'thirties. Until then the blacks had a slight edge over the whites. In the next ten years the ratio changed slightly, then the gap soon widened. At the end of the period Richmond's slaves and free colored comprised less than 40 per cent of the city's population. And the increase in slaves in the last decade was modest—less than 2000—representing a reduction in the rate of growth and presaging a future reduction.

Mobile and Savannah enjoyed their greatest growth later than the larger places, hence the comparative decline of their Negro population did not appear as early. Nonetheless the story was the same. In 1830 the races were almost evenly divided in the Alabama port. By the 1860 census the percentage of blacks had fallen to just over a quarter of the total. Slaves still outnumbered free Negroes nearly ten to one, and while both continued to increase slowly, they lagged far behind the white advance.

[In Savannah over half the population was colored in 1830.] Within ten years, however, supremacy in the city shifted, the whites having a slight majority. But by 1860 the familiar difference appeared. The Negro population had dropped below 40 per cent, and the number of slaves to approximately a third.

The northeastern cities had a lower proportion of slaves in 1820 than other places, but they, too, conformed to the experience elsewhere. Baltimore's slave population was reduced by half in four decades, while Washington dropped slightly during the whole period. In both towns, however, the free Negro residents rose continuously but at greatly reduced rates in the 1850's. The combined black population, moreover, comprised a much smaller percentage of the total than before.

Dixie's northwestern cities revealed the pattern even more clearly. In St. Louis and Louisville the numerical distance between white and black was widest, and the Negro descent most precipitous. In both places colored people constituted nearly a quarter of the population in 1830. Yet within thirty years that proportion dipped to about 10 per cent in Louisville and to slightly over two per cent in St. Louis. Indeed, by 1860 there were more free blacks in St. Louis than slaves. And each year found fewer slaves in Louisville. These two towns, then, illustrate best the full cycle of slavery in the cities—early dynamic growth, stagnation, and finally decline.

The broad lines of this development could be conveniently traced in the decennial censuses of the federal government and in occasional local counts by municipalities. But in any given period slave populations varied considerably from year to year. The number of blacks might increase rapidly as masters brought coffles to town for sale, or be depleted as high prices elsewhere drew off urban Negroes. Some whites coming to the growing cities carried bondsmen with them, while others did not. In short, slave populations in the city were changing constantly. Rural statistics, on the other hand, show much more stability, with fewer variations and with steadier growth through the ante-bellum period.]

IV

The fluctuations in the number of urban slaves, then, contrasted with rural patterns. Significantly, too, the distribution of bondsmen among city masters differed from the practice in

the countryside. In towns, conditions seemed to foster a broad
diffusion of ownership, with a large proportion of white families having at least a few Negroes. Indeed, for most of the
period the percentage of slaveholders in most towns was
higher than the surrounding areas. Of course, the number in
each household was usually small, but the practice was widespread enough to give many a direct involvement in the "peculiar institution."

The 1820 census demonstrated the breadth of early urban
slaveholding. In Charleston, of the 2100 "heads of families"
listed, over three-quarters owned at least a single Negro.[62]
The Richmond figures reveal that about two-thirds of the
households had blacks, while in Savannah and Mobile over
one-half fell in this category. Even New Orleans, which had
an extraordinary number of free colored in 1820, recorded
owners as over a third of its white population. More remarkable, in Louisville over 50 per cent of whites held slaves.
Clearly, in 1820 the city dwellers in Dixie had a substantial
stake in slavery.

By 1840, however, the ratio of slaveholding to nonslave-
holding began to change. To be sure, this did not happen in
static cities like Charleston, where more than three-quarters
of the white families still had colored bondsmen, nor in towns
enjoying their first real expansion such as Mobile, where the
proportion actually rose. But Richmond saw the percentage
dip to about fifty; in New Orleans it fell below thirty. The
most precipitous decline occurred in the border cities, Louisville showing fewer than a quarter of the family heads with
slaves, while in St. Louis only one in seven owned any.

This tendency accelerated during the last two ante-bellum
decades. A new system of scheduling by the federal census
bureau in 1850 and 1860 makes comparison with early figures
difficult, but local tax ledgers disclose a continuous decline
in the incidence of slaveholding. Richmond's experience was

typical. The city's personal property levy hit only a portion of white families, since it applied to just a handful of items. But it included slaves over twelve years old. In 1840 all but a small fraction of the residents paid on Negroes. In 1860 more than 60 per cent of the returns were without taxable slaves.[63] In short, by the Civil War most inhabitants in the Virginia city had no direct financial investment in the system.

During the forty-year period, then, the extent of urban slaveholding can be traced in the census returns and tax ledgers. Until about 1840 the percentage of ownership was higher in the cities than in the countryside. In the 'forties, however, the trend changed, first slowly, then rapidly. Initially the proportion of masters declined as the total population of each community grew. Later the decrease could be measured in absolute terms. By the end of the period most of Dixie's metropolises were shedding slaves, and each year fewer of the residents had a monetary stake in the system.

V

The high incidence of slaveowning through most of the ante-bellum decades meant that, by and large, individual holdings would be modest. A few blacks was the normal unit, though each locality had some masters with more than a score of Negroes. This distribution again set off slavery in the cities from the rural institution, where the plantation, large or small, with its cluster of slaves around a white household, was more characteristic. This pattern of ownership was present almost from the beginning of each town, and it became more distinct as communities grew and populations expanded.

Charleston, with the highest percentage of slaves, provides a good illustration. The 1830 census listed 2873 "heads of families"; 379 had no bondsmen; and 401 had at least ten. A few had more extensive holdings, 87 owners with 20 or more and 19 with over 30. Yet the great majority of Charlestonians in this year owned some slaves and the number usually was not large. Three decades later there were fewer masters and fewer slaves in the South Carolina metropolis; and the proportion of those with big holdings dropped substantially.[64]

New Orleans had the same experience. The number of large slaveowners was never impressive, but even those few diminished as the decades passed. In 1830, 215 residents had over ten blacks and 22 listed more than 20. On the eve of the Civil War the city listed only 83 "heads of families" owning at least ten Negroes and but 20 with better than a score. In short, substantial holdings had almost disappeared in Dixie's largest urban center.

Though border-city statistics followed the same trend, the Richmond picture was more complex. Over the forty-year period the number of large units increased. Those of ten to twenty rose from 14 to 47 and, more importantly, those of 20 and more jumped from 7 to 93.[65] But this growth was almost exclusively in corporate ownership, representing a widespread use of Negroes in manufacturing. Individual holdings, on the other hand, showed the normal curve, with substantial holdings becoming scarcer as the decades passed.

Though the small unit characterized urban ownership, there were some masters in every city with extensive holdings. Any census of New Orleans, for example, would contain such listings as I.A. Blanc, 69, James Higgins, 155, J.M. Wilson, 45, Walter Campbell, 59, or Isaac Cubrer, 59.[66] Charleston's tax list in 1860 included several entries, like J.W. Bennett, 77, Eliza Ball, 40, Abraham Wilson, 37, Jacob Barrett, 46, Mrs. M.A. Mathews, 36.[67] A similar levy in Richmond in the same year furnishes further examples: R.A. Blackburn, 44, James J. Dorwin, 48, A.W. Taylor, 40, William Graener, 60, William H. Grant, 60.[68]

Increasingly, the large urban slaveowners were business

partnerships or corporations. Working the blacks in shops and
factories, they could utilize many more than most individual
masters; and some accumulated great numbers. For instance,
on Charleston "Neck" two mills, Canonboro and Chrisolus,
each had over 70 Negroes in 1840. The Louisville firms
Crutchfield & Company and William A. Richardson Bagging
Factory both possessed over 40 a decade later. And Factor's
Press Company ranked among the largest of Mobile's slaveholders in 1860 with 95 Negroes.

The most spectacular figures, however, were always in industrial Richmond. On the eve of the Civil War, over 54
corporations owned at least ten slaves each. The Virginia Central Railroad held as many as 274, but several others had 75
or more.[69] The possessions of many others, moreover, easily
outstripped all but the most affluent individual masters. In
New Orleans the incidence of corporate holding was never
as high, yet firms like the New Orleans Canal and Banking
Company, the Fireproof Cotton Press, and L. A. Garidal
& Company could generally be found among the more substantial owners.[70]

VI

⌐Urban slavery increasingly contained an imbalance between
male and female Negroes. As early as 1820 women had begun to outnumber men; by 1860 the difference was striking.
In the later decades owners began to sell their younger males
to planters, especially into the cane and cotton country. Left
behind in the cities was a growing surplus of women. Hence,
on the eve of the war almost every Southern town had a
greatly distorted population distribution, with a glaring shortage of men.*⌐

* See tables in the Appendix, p. 325.

Richmond alone seemed exempt from the trend, but conditions there were so special as almost to prove the rule. It was the place which most widely employed young male slaves in manufacturing, and it was the only city with a significant majority of Negro men. Indeed, the population figures reflect the increasing industrial utilization of this class. At the beginning of the period there was a slight excess of females; by 1860, 57 per cent of the town's slaves were male. No other urban center developed an economy that absorbed this kind of labor, hence other Southern cities saw women in the majority in Negro life.

The sex distribution among urban free colored also followed the same trend found in slave statistics. New Orleans, for example, had 1750 more females than males in this category in 1860, while Charleston developed a large imbalance, the census listing 2000 free Negro women and only 1200 men. Even Richmond, where the slave figures ran the other way, had a 10 per cent surplus of females in the free group on the eve of the war.

Smaller places displayed the same tendency. Savannah initially had more free colored men than women, but by 1840 the ratio changed. In Mobile a similar development left a disparity of more than 10 per cent by 1860. Nor did border cities break the pattern. In both Louisville and St. Louis the female margin was seldom less than in the others and usually greater. But the most compelling illustration of this peculiar urban tendency was Baltimore, which had the largest group of free Negroes in Dixie. There the female surplus was almost five thousand in an aggregate of over twenty-five thousand blacks.[71]

In the cities, the colored women, both bond and free, easily outnumbered the men. In the white population, however, precisely the reverse was true. Nearly every Southern urban center had many more males than females, a disparity that was especially great in the periods of most rapid municipal growth. For instance, when Mobile enjoyed its first important expansion, it had twice as many men as women. As the pace of development slowed, however, a more normal distribution appeared.

New Orleans, too, showed the same imbalance in the era of its largest growth. In 1830 the census reported the division among whites as 7300 males and 4900 females. Ten years later the figures were 34,900 to 24,600. But as the city's expansion slackened during the next two decades, the numerical gap between the sexes closed substantially. St. Louis's experience brought similar distortions in the population structure, but the disparity was not so quickly reduced, remaining almost 10,000 out of more than 157,000 in 1860.

Less dynamic towns acquired more evenly proportioned white populations. Seldom did women exceed men, and often the difference was not great. Throughout the ante-bellum decades Charleston's statistics reveal no important discrepancy, and in 1860 male supremacy was barely sustained. In Richmond the sex differential among whites was never significant and was only about 5 per cent at the end of the period. At the same time Savannah's surplus of men was somewhat larger, yet it appeared to be declining.

VII

These shifting statistics suggest that in the cities slavery was never a static institution. In fact, nearly every critical aspect of the system changed constantly in the ante-bellum years. The Negro population, the number of slaveowners, the incidence and size of slaveholding, and the sex differentials all varied considerably in each decade. Furthermore, the towns themselves also changed, altering the conditions in which bondage functioned and forcing institutional adjustments to meet new situations. This flux was less conspicuous on the countryside. There the rural setting promoted a stability seldom found in towns. Indeed, a recent historian has asserted that by the 1830's "Slavery had crystallized; its form was fixed. In 1860 the peculiar institution was almost precisely what it had been thirty years before." Hence, he continues, it is possible "to examine it institutionally with only slight regard for chronology." [72]

These generalizations were perhaps too sweeping even for slavery on the plantations, but they are clearly inappropriate for the cities. In fact, urban slavery developed through two distinct phases in the ante-bellum years. It is hard to find a single dividing point that would fit all places because of the variations in the speed and the extent of growth of Southern towns. Yet a rough watershed can be established between 1835 and 1845. Before that period slavery was an integral part of urban life. As the cities grew, so did slavery. But at some moment the system began to lose ground in the metropolis, and though still present it played an increasingly less important role. That "moment" usually came in the late 'thirties or early 'forties. But whether earlier or later its appearance was common in all Dixie's cities.

In the earlier period urban slavery resembled the plantation system. The incidence of ownership was high, the size of the holdings often substantial, and the presumption of permanence widespread. While slavery encountered difficulties in the city, no one predicted, much less advocated, its abandonment. And the statistical indices in 1820 and 1830 apparently pointed to further steady and substantial growth.

Yet within a decade or two there were many indications of change. The number of urban Negroes declined, fewer whites owned any, and the size of holdings dwindled. In addition, the sale of young bondsmen to the countryside produced an increasing surplus of female slaves remaining in the towns.

New people meanwhile swelled Dixie's cities, which further reduced the importance of the blacks. Clearly the vitality was gone from the system in the urban centers, and each year witnessed a further waning. The transformation was never uniform, but every city experienced it.

No such development occurred in the rural South. "If anything," writes Kenneth Stampp in *The Peculiar Institution*, "the chains of bondage were strengthened, not weakened, in this ante-bellum period." [73] It may be, as some contemporaries and historians have contended, that slavery contained a residual weakness and its vigor in 1860 was largely illusory. Yet, as a Virginian put it, it was "a fixed fact" in that year, and few indices suggested an early collapse. And certainly few Southerners were of a mind to overturn it themselves.

The contrast, then, between urban and rural slavery was marked. Whether the comparison be made of the proportion of slaves to the general population, the distribution of bondsmen among whites, the size of the holdings, or the sex ratio among the blacks, the statistical differences are striking. These figures, however, merely outline a deeper antithesis. Behind the census returns, tax ledgers, and official reports lies a sharper cleavage between ways of living. The city had created its own kind of world, with a pace, sophistication, and environment that separated it from rural modes. In the process it transformed Negro no less than white, slave no less than free man. Hence it is not surprising that slavery as an urban institution differed greatly from its rural counterpart, and that the city slave was often quite unlike his country brother.

Chapter Two

———

BONDSMEN AND HIRELINGS

WELL BEFORE DAWN "reveille" called the slaves from their sleep. At five o'clock the drum roll or church bells sounded across the city, announcing the beginning of another day to the bondsmen. Slowly the Negro quarters came alive. Families were roused, fires started, and breakfasts readied. Soon the men who worked outside their owner's place headed toward the shops, docks, or plants. "The tobacco factory men are by this time astir, and you see them one after another, each with his own provision pail, proceeding to his labors," one observer wrote, describing "Richmond before Daylight."[1] Carts and drays began to move noisily through the streets, a stray Negro hurried back home with bread or milk, and some country slaves strolled lazily toward the market with foodstuffs. Before the darkness was dispelled, the slave part of the town was at its chores.

Most of the womenfolk were domestics engaged in a constant round of household tasks. These ranged from nursing and tending white children to the most menial toil. Well-to-do masters with palatial homes and spacious grounds often had crews of servants, each member of which was carefully trained for a single responsibility—cooking, baking, washing, sewing, gardening, personal service, etc. But most commonly a few slaves cared for a modest middle-class estate and the whites who lived on it. In any case, the bondsmen performed nearly every chore, large and small, around the house. Whether it be waiting on a formal dinner party or indulging the tiniest whim of the master's boy, constant service was part of the expectation, if not always the fulfillment, of slavery. No white woman, "however humble in the scale of society," would touch this domestic work if she could avoid it, for, as De Bow observed, she "considers such services a degree of degradation to which she could not descend." [2]

And duty extended beyond the master's house. Errands to the neighbors, to the store or shop, and even into the nearby countryside were part of it. In the morning especially, slaves, both men and women, young and old, could be seen going about their owner's business. The most common target was the market, where, as a New Orleans resident noted, "almost the whole of the purchasing and selling of edible articles for domestic consumption [is] transacted by colored persons." Here the bondsmen would find other blacks at their work. "Our butchers are negroes; our fishmongers negroes, our vendors of vegetables, fruits and flowers are all negroes," the same observer wrote, and "the only purchasers that frequent the market are negroes; and generally slaves." [3]

The men handled most of the heavy outdoor work. On the docks and piers of the ports they loaded the ships, carried cargo to warehouses, and repaired vessels in dry dock. A traveler remembered Baltimore's harbor as so crowded with colored people "that it seemed, at first, as if I had been transplanted to some unknown land." The blacks were "yelling and shouting to one another from numerous fishing vessels at the wharf, while others—driving teams, carrying loads—" set up "such a din in their nigger tongue" that the scene seemed wholly foreign. [4] Away from the landing slaves could be seen, often in gangs, repairing streets, digging sewers, and, wherever construction was underway, performing routine tasks and arduous labor. Indeed, a building site was likely to resemble "a rookery," as one unhappy white mechanic put it, "with so many blackbirds around it." [5]

Shops and factories also employed slaves though usually in unskilled capacities. In tobacco manufacturing, rope-walks, and cotton presses blacks did simple but wearisome tasks. Railroads, too, claimed their muscle along the tracks or in the city yards. Negroes tended the horses in the livery stables and drove most of the wagons and drays. Yet some could always be found where skills were needed. Negro painters, plasterers, carpenters, and coopers were common, and occasionally a slave would become a typesetter, a bookkeeper, or a foreman. In the last ante-bellum decades, however, whites pushed the colored out of many of the less onerous jobs and left them largely menial work. "From the nature of our society," the Charleston City Council explained, "menial occupations are necessarily confined to coloured persons." [6]

II

The great bulk of urban slaves were domestics, living in the master's house and doing the household chores. Preparing food, washing and cleaning, making clothes, and rendering personal service to the master or mistress comprised the core of the job, but there were endless other tasks. Children had to be tended, visitors cared for, and the elderly comforted. Since whites had come to look upon even the smallest domestic exertion as demeaning, everything was left to the bondsmen. Even where there were many servants, the amount of work for each seemed boundless.

And the hours were long. Formally the day began at five in the morning and ran until curfew at nine or ten at night. But domestics were on call at any time, and a crisis in the master's family would bring additional demands. "Southern women, when they are ill," observed Charles Lyell, "have three or four female slaves to sleep on the floor of their sick room." [7] Even lesser emergencies, though, could claim the presence of personal servants. Nor was Sunday exempt; in fact, in some homes it was the most active day. Considerate masters tried to minimize the work of their blacks after the regular routine, but it was never possible to eliminate this "overtime" altogether. In short, domestic slaves had steady jobs.

The household contingent included men as well as women. Some were valets for the master; others cared for the grounds and gardens; still others handled the horses and carriages. But in more modest residences one bondsman usually managed all these tasks. And the duties of the male servant often took him away from the premises. Driving for his owner, picking up or delivering packages, running errands in the city or surrounding area sometimes kept him away for hours at a time and on some occasions overnight. Like female slaves, he found the work more than full time, involving a kind of stand-by readiness to answer his master's voice at any moment. "They are ever at the elbow," a New Orleans doctor explained, "behind the table, in hotels and steamboats; ever ready, brush in hand, to brush the coat or black the shoes, or to perform any menial service which may be required." [8]

Slave children were brought into domestic service while still very young. Taught simple tasks and habituated to servitude, they became an important part of the household's work force. Newspaper advertisements for selling or hiring Negroes or for returning runaways testify to the many employments of the young. "Girls suitable for Chambers, Nursing, &c.," ran a typical item in the *Louisville Daily Democrat*.[9] In New Orleans an owner offered to sell or hire "a young boy" who was a "good waiter." [10] "My employment was to run of errands," wrote Frederick Douglass of his youth in Baltimore, "and to take care of Tommy; to prevent his getting in the way of carriages, and to keep him out of harm's way generally." [11] By the eighth or ninth year the bonded youth entered the world of slavery, initially at least, as a house servant.

Indeed, most were destined to remain in that capacity as long as they lived in the city. Every census indicated that the majority of urban bondsmen were domestics. This was especially true in towns with few industries. In Savannah, for instance, a local inventory in 1848 found only a small minority in other jobs. Eighty-three appeared as skilled workmen, while manufacturing, commerce, and transportation accounted for a few hundred more. Yet the total slave population was 5686. Significantly, too, women outnumbered men by over 1000, and, of course, nearly all were household servants.[12]

Charleston conducted an even more detailed employment survey the same year. Local officials referred to it as "the first time that an attempt has ever been made ... to obtain positive information relative to the occupations of the inhabitants." The census included all but 318 slaves out of a total of more than 12,000. Of these 7355 were adults with identifiable duties, and 5272 were listed as "house servants." In this category women again predominated, 3384 to 1888. The inventory also demonstrated again that domestic service was almost a colored monopoly, with only 100 whites, mostly Irish girls, competing.[13]

Exact statistics are lacking for other cities, but throughout the urban South owners customarily used their slaves in first instance in the home. Generally, too, the ratio of domestics to masters was extremely high. In Charleston there were 5272 black servants at a time when the white population barely exceeded 14,000. And that figure did not include children performing household chores. Yet residents often complained of a shortage. "It is not surprising," wrote "Broadstreet" to the *Courier* in 1850, "that there are not servants enough for menial offices in families in Charleston ... nothing is more *difficult* than getting any servants, and nothing more impossible than getting a good one." [14] Every town knew the familiar lament. "We are constantly hearing of complaints of the scarcity of servants," wrote the *New Orleans Daily Picayune*, "and the great difficulty families experience in procuring the most necessary household service." [15]

III

If a shortage existed it was in part because many masters found other and more profitable employment for their slaves. Proprietors of hotels and factories, for example, were among the large holders in every city; some found it feasible to train blacks as mechanics or clerks; others put their bondsmen on wagons and drays. In addition, business corporations often bought their own for use as the basic labor force in manufacturing or in gangs on railroads and canals. Occasionally, municipalities acquired some for work on public projects, and in rarer instances institutions like hospitals or even churches would purchase a few for maintenance. In a word, bondage extended to a wide variety of enterprises.

The most conspicuous use of blacks in non-domestic labor was in Richmond, where the two key industries, tobacco and iron, depended on the Negro. Both operated with slaves either owned by the proprietors or hired from other masters. In tobacco the processors owned more than half of the workers through most of the period, though the proportion dropped below half during the last ante-bellum decade. Indeed, they were among the town's largest holders. In 1860 such well-known concerns as James H. Grant & Co. had 110 bondsmen, T. & S. Hardgrove 108, and Talbott & Bros. 78. Smaller firms, too, employed the same system. The *Richmond Directory* of

that year listed 55 "tobacconists," 42 of which appeared on
the tax rolls as possessing ten or more Negroes.[16]

Whether owned or hired, however, slaves did nearly all
of the work, simple and skilled, in the tobacco industry.
From the time the leaves arrived at the plant until the moment the finished chewing plug headed for market, the product was processed by black hands. William Cullen Bryant,
visiting a factory in 1843, stood amidst the "narcotic fumes"
and watched the older slaves "separating leaf from leaf" while
farther along "others were arranging the leaves in layers and
sprinkling each layer with the extract of licorice." In another
room "about eighty negroes—boys they are called, from the
age of twelve years up to manhood— ... rolled the [leaves]
into long, even rolls, and then cut them into plugs of about
four inches in length." When the pressing was finished, the
product was ready for store shelves.[17]

These factories, demonstrating the feasibility of slave labor
in manufacturing enterprises, became a Richmond trademark
and a necessary part of travelers' itineraries. The most celebrated tourist attraction was the singing of the Negroes as
they processed the tobacco. Not every visitor was fortunate
enough to hear this, since the blacks sang of their own accord.
"Sometimes they will sing all day long with great spirit," one
of the managers told Bryant, "at other times you will not
hear a single note." The poet, however, came at a good moment, catching a "murmur of psalmody running through the
sable assembly, which now and then swelled into a strain
of very tolerable music." [18] Alexander MacKay, even more
impressed, found the "solos, duets, glees, etc., ... truly surprising," especially "considering that they were entirely self-
taught." [19]

Compared to other slave employments, the tobacco laborers undoubtedly had something to sing about. An "over-
work" system permitted both owned and hired bondsmen to

earn some cash, which in some cases ran as high as ten dollars a week.[20] Hours on the job were formally set between ten and eleven a day, and plants shut down on Sunday.[21] Yet actual conditions were less pleasant. Much of the work was difficult, especially during humid summer days. Charles Weld recalled visiting a press room in 1825 and finding at each of the machines "some dozen slaves, stripped to the waist (it was very hot) ... tugging and heaving at long iron arms, which turned screws, accompanying each push and pull by deep-drawn groans." [22] And slaves generally testified that the hours were much longer than publicized. One told Frederick Law Olmsted of "workin' might hard too—up to 12 o'clock a night very often." [23] Another, a runaway, asserted that "we were obliged to work *fourteen* hours a day in the summer, and *sixteen* in the winter." [24]

The bulk of tobacco hands were men. In fact, the census of 1860 disclosed that corporate holding and hirings were almost exclusively male. Christian and Lee, for example, reported 89 slaves, and only one was female. Turpin & Yarborough had no women among its 97, nor did J. H. Gentry & Co. among its 65.[25] This pattern held throughout the industry, though in the 1850's one firm brought in white girls to make plugs.[26] If women were spared, children were not. Where an operation required nimbleness and dexterity rather than strength, young people were used. Collin MacRae's advertisement for "fifty boys from 12 to 10 years of age" in 1825 reflected the customary demand of tobacco manufacturers in the ante-bellum years.[27]

Richmond's iron enterprises were only slightly less famous than its tobacco factories. Joseph R. Anderson's Tredegar Works, though not the only producer, was particularly celebrated because it became a kind of test case of the adaptability of slavery to heavy industry. There the blacks did the skilled work such as puddling, heating, and rolling as well as the usual common tasks. The proprietor kept costs low and quality high, and until the war he competed successfully with Northern producers. Though Anderson hired many of his slaves, he preferred to own them, and the core of his gang was a picked lot of 35 men and boys he had specially trained to handle key operations. A ten-hour day was prescribed, but those who wanted to earn some extra money could do so by overtime. In 1860 the company paid such bonuses to 62 bondsmen. By this time, too, the utilization of blacks in manufacturing seemed less an experiment than a settled fact.[28] "The principle ... is not confined to Mr. Anderson or the Tredegar Works alone," wrote the *Enquirer*, "but to all kinds of business." [29]

In no other field were slaves used as prominently as in Richmond's iron and tobacco enterprises. But other cities had similar successes. Even in the Virginia capital, cotton and flour mills had profitably employed blacks for decades. The same was true of the ropewalks of Louisville and Lexington, and in the cotton ports bondsmen traditionally operated the presses. New Orleans Levee Steam Cotton Press, for example, owned 104 slaves in 1850, and it was only one of several firms.[30] A newspaper editor, writing about the Sugar Refinery of New Orleans, asserted its good fortune proved "the extent to which" factories were feasible where the "work is done chiefly" by Negroes.[31] A visitor to the same place was surprised to discover colored labor running the town's gas works, and even more surprised to find a black superintendent who could explain the whole process "with striking precision and clearness." [32] Charleston, Savannah, and Mobile also used slaves in industry, the former two in rice mills, Mobile in its important cotton presses.

Most Southerners hoped for greater success, however, and they carried on a lively campaign for more manufacturing. Though some believed that more extensive industrialization would have to depend on white workers, others felt that slave labor provided Dixie with a great advantage. "The South can manufacture cheaper than any part of the world," wrote the *New Orleans Daily Picayune* in 1859, about the industrial argument. "With raw material growing within sight of the factory; with slave labor that, under all circumstances and at all times, is absolutely reliable"; and with low transportation costs, "manufactured fabrics can be produced so as to compete successfully with the world." [33] Since there was evidence enough to support both views, the controversy remained inconclusive.

There was no doubt, however, that slaves could be used on railroad construction. "This is the way to build railroads," the *New Orleans Daily Crescent* exulted as slaves began to toil on an Alabama project. "These eighty-eight negroes will probably do more work, and for one-fourth the cost, than double the number of hired laborers." [34] This conviction was widely held, and in almost every city railroads could be found among the largest slaveholders. In New Orleans the Pontchartrain R. R. Company, whose line connected the city with the lake, had over 30 blacks.[35] The South Carolina Railway owned 103 in Charleston in 1860, and in the Virginia capital the Richmond and Fredericksburg, the Richmond and Petersburg, the Danville, and the Virgina Central paid taxes on 597 bondsmen in the same year.[36] Many of these slaves spent a good deal of time in the countryside, but they were nonetheless part of the city's economy and life.

In addition to manufacturing and railroads, there were less orthodox uses for bondsmen. In New Orleans a visitor ran across a bookseller "whose principal clerk was his slave," who "knew all the current literature." [37] A Mobile master trained one of his blacks to examine cotton on the docks. "Will any Southern man say that an intelligent slave cannot Sample Cotton as well as any white man?" he asked.[38] Charleston horse-racing enthusiasts bought Negroes who showed promise as jockeys as well as experienced grooms for sporting stock.[39] In Louisville, they tended the sick in the Marine Hospital.[40] And Edward Abdy found churches among the owners in New Orleans. In short, slave labor could be found nearly anywhere there was a task to perform.[41]

IV

The development of the hiring-out system, moreover, greatly broadened the opportunity for the use of slaves. Under this practice masters who owned more blacks than they could utilize either at home or in their business hired some to short-handed employers. This custom greatly lessened the rigidity of slavery, allowing a constant reallocation of the labor supply according to demand. The cities required some arrangement of this kind if the institution was to survive amid the shifting needs and increasing complexities of urban economies. "Hiring out" seemed to combine the fluidity of the wage system with the restraints Southerners felt necessary to maintain bondage. Two variations of this device grew up. One was simply the binding over of a Negro to another white. The other, more complicated, allowed a slave to work for different masters at different times. The first technique was not peculiar to the cities, though most widely practiced there; the second was almost exclusively urban.[42]

"Hiring out" in its plainest form generally involved a contract which included the price, length of service, some assurances on treatment, and the nature of the work to be performed. Arrangements varied, some lasting only a week or for the duration of the job, others for five years. Usually, though, they ran for nearly twelve months, leaving a short holiday around Christmas.[43] Money terms also differed greatly, depending on the market price of slaves, the prevailing wage levels, and the skill involved. A Louisville document signed on January 1, 1832, contained most of the normal provisions. C.W. Thruston and his brother promised "to pay James Brown Ninety Dollars for the hire of Negro Phill until 25 Dec. next. And we agree to pay taxes & doctor bills. Clothe him during said time & return him ... with good substantial cloth or Janes shoes and socks and a blanket." [44]

In most cities this kind of transaction accounted for a large portion of the hiring. Yet this simple exchange did not fully meet the needs of urban economies. The annual contract might be appropriate for a house servant or even a factory hand, but other work in the cities was more irregular, taking only a few weeks or perhaps just a few hours. An employer might want a couple of men today but not again for some time. "It would be impossible to have this sort of slave labor," wrote a South Carolina legislative committee, "if there must be a contract with the owner for every specific job—as, for instance, the transportation of a load in a wagon or dray, the carrying of a passenger's trunk to or from a railroad, &c." [45] Clearly the complex division of labor in a metropolis required some technique which would utilize blacks more freely, yet, at the same time, not imperil the institution.

In place of the annual agreement the towns therefore developed a method for short-term employment. Owners with Negroes they wanted to hire could purchase badges from the municipality which permitted the slave to work by the day or even the hour. No contract or additional document was required. If the master could find an employer, a bargain could be struck without further formality. To smooth the exchange, some cities furnished a public place as a sort of hiring hall. These devices greatly eased the movement of Negro labor without the cumbersome use of the written agreement.

This flexibility, however, presented a new problem of control. In this looser arrangement the slave was released from the management of his master but bound out only casually to another. To fill this vacuum of private responsibility, local governments carefully constructed a public system of supervision. A series of regulations surrounded the whole process, governing both employer and black and invoking the city's full enforcement powers. Municipalities licensed hirelings through badges; some provided a central rendezvous for the two parties of the exchange; others set by law the length of the working day; and a few even established wage levels. Smaller towns and border cities did not resort to such extensive restrictions, since their difficulties were not so acute, but everywhere officials exercised broad supervisory power.

V

As early as 1808, New Orleans's Police Code required a badge for slaves "hired out by the day." [46] Eleven years later, an ordinance tightened the regulation, forcing owners to register each hireling with the mayor, giving "name, age and size." The city then issued a numbered brass badge for the worker to wear "on some conspicuous part of his dress." [47] A Charleston law of 1818 contained the same provisions, but its "ticket" carried the occupation as well as the number of the slave. Its permits fell into three categories, the first applying to "every handicraft tradesman," the second to "every carter, drayman, porter, or day labourer," and the third to "every fisherman or fisherwoman." [48] Mobile and Savannah developed similar schemes. The upper South, with fewer slaves, had less need for such elaborate organization.

Prices for the badges varied, but officials kept them high enough to discourage owners from putting old or poor workers in the market and to provide enough revenue to meet some of the costs of enforcement. By 1843 Charleston's fees ran from seven dollars for the most skilled to two dollars for the least.[49] Savannah's charges were generally steeper, the categories more refined. Masters had to pay ten dollars "for any slave to exercise the trade of cabinet-maker, house or ship carpenter, caulker, bricklayer, blacksmith, tailor, barber, baker or butcher"; eight dollars for "pilots, fishermen, boatmen, grass cutters and hucksters"; four for a porter "or other daily labor" but only two and a half for females in the same job.[50] Mobile collected a flat five dollars for every badge without regard to the kind of work.[51]

Municipal income from this source never proved very great, but it tended to grow. Savannah's receipts, for instance, rose from $1,311 in 1820 to $3,197 in 1840, and to $9,381 in 1860.[52] Charleston's collections for this item came to nearly $14,000 in 1849.[53] Yet the real purpose of the system was control, not revenue; and fines and punishment reflect the intent better than proceeds. Whites who hired slaves illegally ran the risk of losing up to $50, and the bondsmen involved might suffer a severe whipping. Charleston's regulations on this question were not unusual. A black picked up without a badge received "at the public market twenty stripes on the bare back" or his owner paid $20. An employer who used a Negro without the proper identification was assessed twice the price of the badge plus costs.[54] In Savannah the penalties were heavier, running up to thirty-nine lashes for the slave and $50 for the master.[55]

Badges were merely the first phase of municipal supervision. The second consisted in providing a central place where employers could find help when they needed it. In New Orleans the mayor appointed "several places on the quay . . . whither slaves . . . may repair to find work."[56] The city marshal in Charleston fixed "proper stands for porters and day laborers" where they waited to be called.[57] Mobile's chief officer had the same responsibility, and he furnished facilities where hirer and hired met.[58]

Some cities went even further by fixing the hours and

wages of their hirelings. The official length of the work day
generally conformed to local practice. New Orleans's ordinance defined it as "from sunrise until sunset, allowing . . . half
an hour for breakfast, and an hour and a half for dinner."
During the summer the meal period was extended thirty minutes.[59] Mobile had the same provisions, and Charleston's differed only in unimportant details.[60] Wages, however, were
more arbitrary. The South Carolina port pegged pay for slaves
at 81¼ cents a day in 1817 and did not raise it to one dollar for twenty years.[61] New Orleans kept the latter figure
throughout the period. These levels were maximum as well
as minimum, and usually applied to all unskilled workers. It is
hard to know if the scales were enforced, but the attempt
suggests the range of formal restrictions on the hiring-out
process.

Not all municipalities developed such a highly organized
system. The border cities and Richmond relied more on private agencies to bring employers and available bondsmen together. Brokers for the purpose grew up, much like the "Intelligence Offices" in the North, and even appeared where
public facilities were available. In St. Louis in 1821, for example, "Mr. Jacobs" was hiring "at the Sign of the Green
Tree." [62] During December in any year or in any city the
newspapers listed many opportunities for the coming season.
"An experience of many years business with the citizens of
Louisville and vicinity," ran a typical notice, "renders us competent of judging and picking good homes and masters for
your negroes," and those who needed blacks "had better apply
. . . in time," if they wanted "the pick and choice of many
good reliable servants." [63] In Richmond there were "several
hiring sections" where employers could find "crowds of servants, men, women, boys and girls, for hire" even in a slack
period.[64] These outlets together probably placed more slaves

than municipal stands; they played an important role in the constant redistribution of labor resources in Dixie's towns.

Hiring out, then, whether publicly organized or privately facilitated, sprung urban bondage out of the narrow confinements of the master-slave relationship, permitting a greatly extended use of colored labor. Under this system the blacks moved into many kinds of jobs. A white too poor to own a Negro could rent one. Large employers anxious to avoid the problem of housing workers could engage them by the day, month, or year. Industrial concerns which owned steady crews could take on additional hands at the busy season. And municipalities themselves could find men for public projects without assuming the responsibilities of slaveholding. It was thus possible for urban economies to maintain a flexible colored labor force without disturbing, legally at least, the institution of slavery.

VI

The broad demand for hirelings which resulted was steadily reflected in newspaper advertisements. N.B. Hill, proprietor of the Bell Tavern in Richmond, for instance, wanted fifteen men and "three or four boys"; [65] the Coach Smith Shop needed "six strong, active, intelligent, coloured boys, for a term of not less than five years"; [66] and Sam. S. Myers & Co., one of Virginia's leading tobacco manufacturers, called for 150 to 200 hands to become "Twisters, Stemmers, Screwmen, Jobbers, &c.," but for only twelve months.[67] In the same city Jacob Barnes sought "four or five boys as apprentices to learn the blacksmith business." [68] And the Richmond, Fredericksburg and Potomac Rail Road, one of the largest slaveholders in the capital, advertised for additional help, assuring masters that their Negroes would be "well fed, well clothed and well treated." [69]

The same pattern appeared in New Orleans newspapers. One notice asked for twelve "able bodied Negro Men and Women" to work in a saw mill.[70] The Southern Shoe Manufacturing Company needed "several slave boys" for apprentices,[71] and a "healthy watering place across the Lake" could use fifteen or twenty "likely colored waiters." [72] The New Orleans Planing Company was more inviting in its search for "12 negro boys," promising that "the work is easy, being principally in the house. They are wanted by the month, and if suitable, . . . for years." [73] The railroads, much less personal, asked for groups around a hundred and hired "in gangs of five or more." [74] Masters, too, used the columns of the papers to place bondsmen. One offered an 18-year-old "good second rate Engineer" with experience in a cotton press.[75] Another listed a "first class hotel or steamboat Man cook." [76] Less valuable probably was "an honest and faithful Negro Man, used to attending horses, a good drayman and cart driver; in a word, fit for any purpose." [77]

The same diversity characterized the early decades in the border cities, but as the number of bondsmen declined they were increasingly confined to domestic work, often on a hiring basis. W. E. Woodruff's notice was typical for Louisville. He announced that he had "numerous applications" from "excellent homes" for slaves and urged "persons having servants they wish to hire out for the coming year" to turn their names in quickly.[78] Another agency listed "No. 1 Cooks, Washers, &c.," [79] and still another handled "Good Chamber maids— from 16 to 20." [80] Yet the demand continued in other lines. Hotels, taverns, coffee houses, and confectioners often hired and sometimes owned colored help, and slaves kept their jobs on steamboats and around the docks until the war came.[81]

Municipal works depended heavily on slave labor. Gangs of Negroes graded, paved, and cleaned streets, built bridges, collected garbage, dug canals and sewers, and generally provided the muscle for city projects. Some blacks were put on this work as punishment, but probably most were hirelings. In New Orleans the council authorized the mayor in 1820 to use jailed slaves "to cleanse the gutters of the foot-ways, and the crossing bridges of the streets." Women prisoners could also be assigned, "if their masters or mistresses agree to their going . . . without being chained." [82] Two years later the mayor hired additional hands to help "the chain negroes" construct sewers, and a year later 50 more were put on "urgent works that the corporation must do before the rise of the waters." [83] For each bondsman local authorities paid owners between 25 and 50 cents a day. The fact that the First Municipality alone paid out over $30,000 annually for this labor indicates that New Orleans relied heavily on this system.[84]

Other towns, except the border ones, where slaves were scarce, adopted similar policies. Negroes not only did heavy work but odd jobs as well. As early as 1806 Charleston's municipal scavenger took on three colored hands; in 1820 Richmond paid three dollars a month to George R. Myers for his "black man," who cleaned the mayor's office and made fires "since the cold weather commenced." [85] Public employment for bondsmen was generally much less profitable than private placing, and some masters dumped their less productive hands there. "It is an entire mistake," complained Savannah's Committee on Streets and Lanes, "to suppose this work can be performed by super-annuated negroes, or by those who are unfit for ordinary daily labour." [86]

The most unusual public use of slaves, however, was as firemen. In Savannah they comprised the crack engine teams as well as the axe and bucket brigades and were, indeed, the pride of the town. "We suppose that there are no more efficient or well managed fire companies in the United States," crowed the *Republican* after watching the annual "turn out." [87] Every Negro with a badge between 16 and 60 years became liable for service, and the city chipped in twelve and a half cents an hour to those on duty. As a spur to greater enthusiasm a bonus of one dollar was given to the first to arrive on the scene of a blaze, and the second and third received fifty cents apiece.[88] Charleston's fire-fighting fleet was, of course, larger. There the bondsmen worked sixteen engines, but whites increasingly took over other functions as volunteer organizations became popular.[89]

VII

Masters and employers arranged the wages for hirelings. In some cities pay for the unskilled was set by ordinance, but generally local conditions determined the scales. Hiring time came in late December, and owners bargained for the highest prices. Skilled slaves brought the best returns, but shortages in any line could raise price levels. Occasionally, the offered wage was not enough, and slaveholders stayed out of the market to force a change. In 1858, for example, Richmond's tobacco manufacturers fixed their rates so low that one master urged others to hold "your servants . . . in reserve till the Spring, when they will most assuredly command higher prices." [90] Farther south, Mary left John Berkley Grimball because he paid only six dollars a month, and she claimed "all Nurses in Charleston got 8 dollars per month." [91] And in some instances the haggling developed over fringe problems rather than money. Robert Russell, visiting Richmond in 1854, recorded with amusement the hitch in one agreement, "the grand obstacle" being that she refused "to work in the garden, even when she had nothing else to do." [92]

Pay for hired slaves varied so much from place to place, job to job, and time to time that it is difficult to find meaningful figures. In fact, the most significant feature of the statistics available is the diversity they reveal. The long-range tendency of wages was upward, but variations remained marked. The experience of the Tredegar Iron Works in the 1850's was perhaps typical. The first year of the decade it had hired 23 men for $100 and three others at $75. Though the general level remained the same for the next two years, the company paid as high as $160 for one the next year. At the same time, however, other factory hands brought over $200.[93] In 1859 prices of labor seemed to have continued to rise. Hiring rates, the *Richmond Enquirer* observed, "are about 20 per cent higher than last year, though no very satisfactory causes can be given why such should be the case."[94]

James Rudd's account books in Louisville tell the same story. In 1838 he placed Harriet in the Marine Hospital for $76, but James brought $100 for the same period. A decade later, Arthur hired out at $60 and Albert at $100. Yet in 1849 Rudd received $200 from McGrain & Brother for Thornton.[95] In the 1830's the Thruston brothers of the same city obtained the yearly use of "old man Daniel" for $60 and picked up Phill for $90. And while taking on slaves in Louisville the Thrustons let out another to John O'Fallon in St. Louis for $75.[96]

One generalization that can be made about wages is that white pay in the same jobs was significantly more than that for hired blacks. A booster in 1817, for example, tried to attract workers to St. Louis, and in so doing gave the going rates, which showed "laborers" receiving $1.50 a day and "negroes" $18 to $25 a month, while "female slaves" hired out at $5 to $50 per month.[97] Over twenty years later the New Orleans Commissioner of Public Roads and Streets recognized a similar differential. White wages began at $1.20 a day and ran up to $3 for carpenters; the top for Negroes was $1.[98] In many cities employment became so segregated that comparisons are difficult, but wherever statistics are available they reveal a wide spread.

VIII

The hiring-out system gave slavery the flexibility it required in the urban milieu, but it also bred problems that many Southerners thought struck at the very heart of the institution. Once the bond between master and slave was loosened by the addition of an employer, a further extension quickly developed. Soon owners found it easier and usually more profitable to permit their bondsmen to find their own employment. "In the cities, the slaves—excepting the household slaves—are generally allowed to 'hire their *own* time,' as, with hidden sarcasm, the negroes term it: that is to say, they give their master a certain sum per month; and all that they make over that amount they retain." [99] This created a new dimension of independence for the Negroes, since it circumvented the elaborate controls municipalities had placed around the hiring process. Under this arrangement, masters told their Negroes to locate a job, make their own agreement on wages, and simply bring back a certain sum every week or month. The slave, moreover, could pocket any profit he made. "At the Christmas holidays," wrote a visitor, "some of the Southern cities and towns are alive with negroes, in their best attire, seeking employment to come, changing places, and having full liberty to suit themselves as to their employers." [100]

Often the owner did not know where his blacks worked; no contract bound master and employer; and no special public supervision governed the arrangement. "Hiring their own time," as this was called, brought the slave into a new relationship with his owner, more like that of tenant and landlord than bondage in the usual sense. Even this connection broke down in many instances when hirelings began to rent housing away from the old premises. This development was everywhere illegal, but it was extensively practiced in the cities. "A species of *quasi* freedom has been granted by many masters to their slaves," complained the New Orleans *Picayune*. "They have been permitted to hire their own time, and with nominal protection of their masters, though with none of their oversight, to engage in business on their own account, to live according to their own fancy, to be idle or industrious ... provided only the monthly wages are regularly gained." [101]

The ambitious slave welcomed the chance to get on his own. Frederick Douglass remembered the sense of freedom that came to him on acquiring a skill and being allowed to hire his own time. "After learning to calk, I sought my own employment," he wrote in his autobiography, "made my own contracts, and collected my own earnings; giving Master Hugh no trouble in any part of the transactions to which I was a party." "Some slaves have made enough, in this way," he added, "to purchase their freedom." [102] Under the system it was even possible for one bondsman to become the employer of another. Seeking work in Savannah, Charles Ball found it with a Negro who "hired his time of his master at two hundred and fifty dollars a year, which he paid in monthly installments. He did what he called job work, which consisted of undertaking jobs, and hiring men to work under him." At that time "he had seven or eight black men, besides me, all hired to help him remove the cotton in wheelbarrows." [103]

Douglass and Ball were not isolated cases, for "hiring one's own time" became an inseparable part of urban slavery. In 1820, when Louisville was still a small town, one observer contended that "there are at least 150 slaves of the above description in this town—some of whom pay their 'owners' twenty dollars per month ... female slaves pay from four to six dollars and support three or four children each." [104] Thirty years later a Charlestonian mentioned, probably with exaggeration, "thousands" hiring their own time in that city. [105] There is no way of knowing how many slaves actually acquired this privilege, but the extent to which each town struggled to stop this practice is a good index of how widespread it was.

A grand jury in Savannah, for instance, declared in 1845 that "the practice of slaves being permitted to hire their own time or labor for themselves" was "an evil of magnitude" and that "it is not to be denied that it is striking directly at the existence of our institutions." "It is but the beginning of the end," the presentment concluded solemnly, "and unless broken up in time, will result in the total prostration of existing relations." [106] In the same year the South Carolina Committee on Colored Population admitted that the question "has for several years in succession been brought to the notice of the legislature in presentments of Grand Juries" sitting in Charleston.[107] The resultant statute, toughening the restrictions, became a dead letter, however, within a few years, and a local newspaper could write in despair that "not one slave less hires his time than before." [108]

In St. Louis complaints began very early. A local editor in 1824 endorsed legislation against the custom. It called it "one principal source of the irregularity and crimes of slaves in this place." A fellow townsmen agreed, contending that "the prime source" of their "bad habits is the liberty, . . . of hiring themselves out." "While they remain *slaves*," he counseled, "they must, for their own good, as well as for the public benefit, be held under very rigid constraint." [109] Nine years later, the city, finding that law unequal to the task, added its own ordinance because, as the *Missouri Republican* put it, "the evil is a very serious one." [110] Yet in 1835 a public meeting could call the practice "one of the greatest evils that can be inflicted on a community" and urge the appointment of a "permanent committee" to stamp it out.[111]

But no city was able to halt it. States continually strengthened legal prohibitions and cities passed additional ordinances to improve enforcement and increase penalties. Charleston's efforts were typical—as was its failure. In 1806 masters were fined $20 for each Negro caught hiring himself out.[112] The state legislature in 1822 made a slave who did so subject to forfeiture.[113] Actually this seemed too harsh to some, and a grand jury two years later asked that some discretion be allowed to local authorities in its enforcement.[114] In 1849 South Carolina included the employer as well as the owner in the punishment by assessing violators $50.[115] But legislation seemed helpless in the face of custom. In 1858, 184 Charlestonians repeated the familiar lament, declaring law on this topic "a dead letter," and spoke of the continuing "baneful evil" of blacks hiring their own time.[116]

The basic fear was not economic, although some whites were often eager to prevent Negroes from encroaching on their jobs. The great anxiety was the degree of freedom conferred upon the slave if he was permitted to find his own employment. The slave not only slipped away from the supervision of his owner, but also, despite all kinds of public restrictions, had the liberty of choosing his employer, acquiring a little money, arranging his own hours, and, in some cases, providing for his own room and board. So long as he made his payments to his master and kept out of the way of the police, he enjoyed a wide margin of liberty. Though no less a slave legally, he was in reality less so. In fact, in the Richmond census of 1860 beside the names of over 400 hired slaves was the simple notation: "owner unknown."

The practice "has weakened the close connection of master and servant," said the editor of the New Orleans Daily Picayune, "producing the most serious change in the latter." "The ties which bound together the master and the slave" are "gradually severed," it continued, and the hirelings "become intemperate, disorderly, and lose the respect which the servant should entertain for the master." And, just as important, "their example is contagious upon those who do not possess these dangerous privileges." [117] Making the same point, a Savannah editor asserted that, "more than any single cause," this custom was destroying "in fact, if not in name, the relation of master and servant." [118]

"The evil is he buys the control of his own time from his owner," a South Carolina committee declared. "He avoids the discipline and surveillance of his master and is separated from his observation and superintendance." To those who believed that the trouble stemmed from the kind of work bondsmen did under this system, the committee contended that the danger came from the fact that "slaves are permitted to go at large, exercising all the privileges of free persons, making contracts, doing work and in every way being and conducting themselves as if they were not slaves." "It seems . . . that the evil is the same," the group added wisely, "whether the slave so working out on his own account, is mechanic or handicraftsman, a stevedore, a laborer, a Porter, a drayman or anything else." [119]

The peril was thus widely understood in Southern cities. Few topics produced so much local and state legislation, and so much concern among municipal officials. But the system had convenience and usage on its side. "We are a slaveholding people habitual to slave labor," the South Carolina committee explained. "Yet we have towns and villages where ordinary labor is to be performed . . . by either white or negro hands. We are accustomed to black labor and it would create a revolution to drive it way." In cities it "would be impossible to have this sort of labor" without some arrangement that would facilitate the constant redistribution of workers required by an urban economy. Hence no amount of law or declamation could stop an expedient, if dangerous, practice. "The subject is therefore fraught with difficulties," the same report observed. "Until you can change the direction of

the public prejudice, presuppositions & habit, you can never
enforce a law which conflicts with them." [120]

Profit, moreover, reinforced the "public prejudices," for
masters often found it financially more rewarding to let Negroes find their own jobs rather than to use legal channels.
Though exact statistics are meager, the evidence is conclusive. The available records reveal that owners received more
from slaves hiring themselves out than they did by leasing
them through annual contracts. James Rudd's experience with
"Yellow Jim" in Louisville is illustrative. Jim was allowed to
be on his own, the only proviso being that he give $5 a week
to his master. Rudd's account books record that payments
were steady and prompt: $262.10 in 1847; $235.55 in 1848;
$245.60 in 1849; $202.35 in 1850; $211.05 in 1851; $231.45 in
1852; and $271.55 in 1853. Over eight years Rudd collected
nearly $1900 on the ingenuity of a single bondsman. At the
same time the prevailing hiring rates ranged around $100 an-
nually, and seldom reached $200. A simple notation in the
ledger, however, suggests that the whites' fear of allowing
slaves to hire their own time was not entirely unfounded. It
read: "Dec. 11, 1853. Ranaway." [121]

But even with this danger, other records support the notion that master and slave found the system mutually profitable. Thomas Jones testified that he gave his owner $150 a
year while he found work on the docks.[122] A Charleston
couple, Jungo and Betty, paid $670 for the privilege, and
they still saved enough to "feed, clothe and house themselves." [123] In Mobile, $180 was enough to satisfy an owner,
with "the slave's supporting himself and saving a little money
besides." [124] Frederick Douglass's agreement with "Master
Hugh" called for weekly installments of $3, though the hire-
ling had to provide his own clothes and calking tools. When
the ante was raised to $9, Douglass found that he could not
make ends meet.[125] A "Carolinian" summed up the situation

to a traveler in the 1850's by observing "that the practice of sending out slaves to earn money . . . , has been in vogue from time immemorial, and that it was such a profitable" arrangement that "it was followed more extensively in the state now than formerly." [126]

"Hiring out," then, in either its legal or extended form, was an attempt to adjust slavery to the economic demands of urban life. Coupled with the more orthodox use of bondsmen by their masters in the home, shop, or factory, it allowed towns to maintain a Negro labor base through most of the antebellum period. Yet this complex system never proved very satisfactory. Loosening the restraints on the hirelings aroused apprehensions that the "peculiar institution" itself was in jeopardy, and the proportionate shrinkage in the colored population in pre-war decades created shortages which had to be made up by white workers, especially by immigrants. But slavery's difficulties in the city were not wholly economic; even if the hiring custom had worked more smoothly, other urban forces would have seriously strained the fabric of slavery.

Chapter Three

THE QUARTERS AND THE HOUSE

HOUSING SLAVES in the city required facilities quite different from those in the countryside. A dense population, town lots of limited size, and relatively high land values all precluded the arrangement of the plantation. Instead of cabins strung together in a colony well beyond the big house, cities produced a more compact system with Negro quarters located on the same plot as the owner's residence. Indeed, the buildings were often adjacent, or at most a few yards separated the abodes of master and bondsman. If the urge in rural areas was to keep the slaves at a distance, the enforced conditions of the city induced proximity. Great spaces in the cane and cotton country might permit the isolation of each planter's property and make possible a relatively thin sprinkling of buildings on each, but no such leeway existed in the towns. There, hundreds of people, black and white, had to be fitted into every block. Furthermore they had to be placed in such a way that social distance between the races was maintained even under conditions of close physical proximity.

For planters there were many choices in the location of slave housing. "My first care has been to select a proper place for my 'quarters,'" wrote a Mississippian, "well protected by the shade of forest trees, sufficiently thinned out to admit a free circulation of air, so situated as to be free from the impurity of stagnant water, and to erect comfortable houses for

my negroes." [1] Ideally, a single or double row of cabins
headed by the overseer's residence comprised these quarters;
ideally, too, the cluster would be removed from the master's
place, yet within sight. On the other side of the colony, and
easily accessible, were the fields which the slaves worked. Of
course, the quality of the quarters varied greatly, but it was
never very good. The "common run," a later historian could
assert, was "cramped, crudely built, scantily furnished, un-
painted, and dirty." [2] Designed basically as sleeping rooms
rather than centers of family life, bivouacs rather than homes,
they provided shelter and little more.[3]

The larger spaces of the rural areas moreover assured a
kind of semi-isolation for each plantation. This detachment
meant, of course, that slaves had few contacts with neighboring slaves, and only seldom saw whites from the outside. Even
blacks on small farms had something of the same experience
because the population was scattered and communication difficult and irregular. Hence the life of the rural Negro was
shaped by relatively few forces—the master and his family,
perhaps an overseer, other slaves on the same plantation, the
nature of his daily tasks, and in a broad but compelling way
the customs of the "peculiar institution." An occasional visitor, the addition or the sale of a few blacks, or perhaps some
natural calamity could alone alter the texture of things or
the pace of his life.

The city, however, offered quite a different setting. Housing blacks there was a more difficult matter. Small lots left
little choice in locating slave quarters; master and bondsman
would share a plot usually not larger than 50 feet by 150 feet
and often smaller. The comfortable distances of the plantation were no longer available. And owners found it hard to
isolate their Negroes from nearby ones. With a couple of
hundred people in the same block, regular contacts were
inevitable. And, of course, beyond the block was the great

congestion of the town, with its incessant mingling of people, bond and free, of all colors. So special arrangements were needed for slave quarters.

The most common design placed the main residence on the street or nearly so; behind stood the yard and the slave quarters. The Negro buildings, long and narrow and usually two stories high, either adjoined the master's house at right angles or stood at the back of the lot overlooking a small open area. Only the second floor had sleeping rooms; the first generally contained the kitchen and store rooms, and in some instances a stable. Usually constructed of brick, they were sturdy, compact, and well-built. In fact, a great many have outlasted the owner's place, and in some cities like Charleston and New Orleans remodeled slave quarters are now fashionable apartments. This system easily accommodated a white family and a few Negroes, as long as the number of children remained manageable. Owners with more blacks often built larger barracks—occasionally three stories—or merely had them double up in existing facilities. Variations of this "model" existed, of course, but the basic pattern involved master and slaves sharing the same plot.

Because of the proximity to the main residence, slave quarters were generally much better than those found on farms or plantation. But even so they were barely adequate. The rooms were small, typically about 10 feet by 15 feet, usually without windows and poorly ventilated. In most cases three rooms in a row ran off a narrow balcony; in each a single door provided whatever light and air entered. Sometimes a fireplace furnished heat, but this was not the rule.[4] Furniture was scarce and crude. Many blacks slept on the floor, not in beds. No doubt the South's balmy climate made the outdoors a pleasant alternative to these Spartan facilities, and the many duties of the slaves kept them away from their quarters most of the time. Yet these accommodations were not much of a home.

Part of the problem was crowding. As long as the slave complement was small the space was adequate. But beyond a few there was trouble. Since the number of bondsmen fluctuated greatly, it is impossible to know precisely how many occupied these quarters at any time. Yet cumulative figures convey something of the congestion characteristic of pre-war Southern cities. Savannah's situation in 1840 was perhaps typical. Its more than 11,000 inhabitants were nearly evenly divided between the races. About half the whites had no Negroes; hence, in most slaveowning families bondsmen outnumbered masters.[5] In such instances, though slave quarters were much smaller than the main house, they held many more people.

Charleston's statistics reveal the same situation. A local census in 1848, which included the number of dwellings as well as the total population, showed an average of more than ten people to a plot. Two thousand two hundred and sixty-six of 2666 were single family units, indicating that not many whites doubled up.[6] But 601 of these had at least ten slaves in addition to the master's family.[7] These were bound to be tight quarters. And other sources suggest this was the case. A physician, for example, put heavy blame for the epidemic of 1857 on "houses crowded, or rather packed, from basement to attic with human beings," [8] and a grand jury just a year before complained of some spots where "from twenty to fifty male slaves live together in one house." [9]

Travelers occasionally commented on the crowding. Carlton Rogers, for example, noticed that in "first-class residences" in Montgomery "the yard literally [was] swarming with these human chattels; frequently a dozen or more in sight, of both sexes, and comprising at least three generations." [10]

Congestion, however, on the scale of later urban concentrations was unusual. City conditions in general discouraged large slaveholding, thus precluding sustained overcrowding. Limited facilities on town lots further inhibited the accumulation of Negroes by a single owner. The common arrangement found a white family living in the central house on the street with a few blacks in the rear quarters. The danger of severe congestion did decline as the number of slaves dwindled. The peak of pressure probably came in the 1830's when the cities themselves grew most rapidly and before the attrition on the colored population had set in. During these years Negroes in most cities lived at close quarters; in the later decades the problem was to find room for the white newcomers.

II

Overcrowded or not, the important thing about slave housing was the social view it embodied. Its basic objective was to seal off the Negroes from outside contacts. Not only were the bondsmen's quarters placed close to the main building, but the plot itself was enclosed by high brick walls. The rooms had no windows to the outside and were accessible only by a narrow balcony that overlooked the yard and the master's residence. The sole route to the street lay through the house or a door at the side. Thus the physical design of the whole complex compelled slaves to center their activity upon the owner and the owner's place. Symbolically, the pitch of the roof of the Negro quarters was highest at the outside edge and then slanted sharply toward the yard—a kind of architectural expression of the human relationship involved. The whole design was concentric, drawing the life of the bondsman inward toward his master.[11]

In this arrangement, the walls had an extraordinary significance. Sometimes more than a foot thick, almost always made of brick, generally very high, they transformed a residential complex into a compound. The very smallness of the yards and gardens at the center of the lots seemed to magnify the commanding size of the walls and emphasize the calculated

isolation of the slave quarters. The relentless masonry en-
circlement was broken only by the stark escarpment created
by the rear of adjacent buildings—the backs of kitchens,
stables, or neighboring Negro quarters. Standing in the middle of the plot the bondsman could see only a maze of brick
and stone, the forbidding reminders of his servile confinement.

Enough of these enclosures still stand to convey the sense
of isolation embodied in the design. Occasional fire insurance
maps of the period moreover furnish some precise information on the exact dimensions of the walls. A sketch of New
Orleans, for instance, discloses that the city was honeycombed
with brick barriers dividing each block in dozens of individual parcels. The inside of the squares bounded by Bour-
bon, Conti, Dauphin, and St. Louis streets provides a convenient sample. It had 38 lots, three quarters of which were
residential and contained the familiar slave quarters. In every
case the back yards were sealed by adjoining buildings; and—
in the cool notations of the fire map—"wall 12'," "wall 10',"
"wall 20'," "wall 16'." All exits led into the house or onto the
street through a side door; there were no openings in the middle of the block.[12] Other areas of the city showed the same
pattern. Even the "American section," where lots were more
generous and homes larger and where space itself afforded a
certain detachment, adopted the system of brick enclosures.[13]

A Charleston map of 1851, though lacking the precision of
the New Orleans one, reveals the same arrangement.[14] Walls,
at times nearly 20 feet high, skirted the boundaries of each
plot and produced the characteristic privacy and confinement.
If the documents for other places are scarce, additional evidence is not. In the old parts of every Southern city, buildings constructed in the slave period remained as late as 1958.
To be sure, urban renewal programs had marked nearly all
of them for extinction. Yet in Louisville, St. Louis, and
Richmond, and more obviously in Mobile or Savannah, the

massive walls still surrounded a small yard or garden. Later alterations or additions usually obscured the original design, and garages pierced the brick enclosures, but it required little imagination to reconstruct the old complex. And in St. Louis a topographical survey of 1875 preserves the outlines of the older sections.[15]

Urban housing in the South also omitted alleys. Local officials felt they would upset the basic scheme embodied in the enclosure system. To cut through city blocks would have broken into each lot, required rear entrances to the residential unit, and induced interior traffic somewhat removed from public view. But, most compellingly, whenever alleys were opened they created an alternative center for slave activity. Soon Negro life in the neighborhood gravitated to the middle of the block and away from the supervision of slaveowners or white authorities. The isolation of the compound could no longer be maintained, and the bondsman's orientation moved away from his master in the yard to his contacts in the back street. Municipal officers found this competing focus annoying, and slaveholders thought it dangerous. Unlike the thinly sliced commercial and residential areas, elsewhere, the city blocks in the South remained solid.

The characteristic housing arrangement, then, was the single dwelling unit for the master, with the Negro quarters behind. High walls and buildings hemmed in the slaves while on the premises, and drew the lines of life around their owner. This "compound" was the urban equivalent of the plantation. Like its rural analogue, it provided a means of social control as well as of shelter; it embodied the servile relationship between white and black; and it expressed a style of living appropriate to its setting. "They are divided out among us and mingled up with us, and we with them, in a thousand ways," a Charleston minister said while describing slavery in his own city. "They live with us—eating from the same store-houses, drinking from the same fountains, dwelling in the same enclosures." [16] This constant proximity meant that slave housing in the towns, though cramped, crude, and uncomfortable, would seldom be as bad as that commonly found in the countryside.

III

The compound system was the "model," and in the early years of most places it accounted for the bulk of Negro housing. But cities bred diversity in this as in other matters. Soon this neat arrangement started to break down. Masters with too many blacks to keep on their premises, commercial and industrial owners whose bondsmen were not used as domestics, and, increasingly, slaveholders who found it profitable or convenient to let their slaves seek lodging for themselves permitted a gradual loosening of the common arrangement. Negroes started to "live out," finding a room here, renting a house there, and in other cases simply disappearing into remote sections of town. In fact, this process had developed so rapidly that when taking a local census of Savannah in 1848, Joseph Bancroft adopted the technique of "enumerating the slave population in their places of abode without recourse to owners." "Some objections may attend this mode," he admitted, "but under the system, so much in vogue at the present time, of permitting this class of our population to live in streets and lanes by themselves, it has proved more reliable than the old system of depending upon owners for returns." [17]

Though widely practiced, this device was never sanctioned by law. At most, state statutes and local ordinances allowed slaves to reside outside of the owner's enclosure only with written authorization and for limited periods. In some cases the prohibition was complete. As early as 1740, for example, Charleston regulations forbade bondsmen "from sleeping and

living out of his master's premises or of those of some white
person appointed by the master." [18] The restrictions written
into the 1806 municipal legislation were more precise. "No
slave or slaves within the city shall have, hold, occupy, reside
or sleep in any house, out-house, building or enclosure, other
than his or her owner's or his or her owner's representative,"
except after "first obtaining tickets" from the master "expressly describing the place . . . and specifying also the time,"
during which permission was granted. Penalties for violation
fell on both bondsmen ("twenty lashes on the bare back")
and white ("fifty dollars for each and every such offense"). [19]
A Charleston contract of December 21, 1834, illustrates the
approved form: "This is to certify that Diana has my permission to reside in a house belonging to Holyway in College
Street. This ticket is good for three months from date."
Thomas L. Ogir, the master, signed the document.

New Orleans's ordinances included a similar injunction. As
required by an 1817 law, a slave must live on his master's
premises, or on that of "his owner's representative, or of the
person whom he is . . . serving for hire." He needed a "ticket"
before he would be allowed to "occupy, reside, or sleep" in
some other place. In addition, New Orleans further tried to
discourage "living out" by prohibiting renting to bondsmen
"even with the permission" of his master. This was designed
to break up the practice of hirelings finding their own accommodations on a long-term basis. The same legislation gave
broad powers to the police to search any house when it had
"cause to suspect" violations existed. [20]

Every city passed similar laws, often using the same language. Mobile's 1837 ordinance, for instance, asserted that no
slave "shall have, hold, occupy, reside, or sleep in any house,
outhouse, building, or enclosure, other than his . . . owner's,
or his . . . owner's representative." If he did so, he was committed to the guard house and given 25 lashes "on his bare

back." Written authorization, however, could provide the usual exception.[21] But St. Louis tried to remove even this limited permissiveness. A public committee in 1835 urged the adoption of legislation which insisted "that no slave should be suffered to live or dwell in this city or county, at any place other than the same lot or parcel of ground on which his . . . owner, or the white person having control over him . . . , shall reside." [22]

Richmond's large industrial slave population presented particular difficulties of housing control. Corporate owners only occasionally tried to accommodate their hands on their own premises; rather they would place them among residents around the city. This added a new dimension to the problem, and it was never satisfactorily resolved. An ordinance of 1857, however, summed up the hope, if not the actuality, of municipal officials. It provided that "every owner, hirer, or other employer" must "provide food and lodging . . . upon his own premises, or by engaging board and lodging for them with some free person and paying the price thereof, except when the slave has a wife living in the city and he stays with her at the house of her master." To ensure supervision, owners who "boarded out" slaves had to submit a list of his bondsmen to the mayor with "the place where each one is boarded." In case of any change, it had to be recorded at city hall within a week.[23]

Despite the clarity of local law and the severity of its penalties, enforcement seldom proved effective. Residents and officials alike constantly complained that slaves lived almost everywhere in the city and not always with the knowledge, much less the consent, of the owner. Louisville's councilmen, for example, found bondsmen "renting houses, and residing therein" as early as 1828 and declared it "a great public nuisance." [24] A St. Louis newspaper, lamenting that "the evil has been a very serious one," observed that "there is a statute law upon the subject; but it might as well never have been passed, as it is not enforced." [25] Similarly a Savannah editor claimed that Negroes allowed "to live apart from their owners" were a "great source of all the corruption and discontent of our slaves." [26] "How many of us retire on a night under the impression that all our servants are on the premises, and will continue there until morning. And how often is it quite the reverse, especially with our men servants, who are wandering to and fro all night, or are quietly ensconced in some dark retreat of villainy, exposed to all sorts of vices and temptations, alike destructive of their morals and usefulness. It is thus that some of our best servants become *cast-aways*." [27]

Mobile encountered the same common difficulties. The slave code there always included a prohibition against "living out," yet the daily proceedings of the municipal court reveal continual violations. For instance, on November 4, 1851, two slaves were picked up for sleeping "off-premises" and saved from a whipping only because their master paid a fee.[28] The next day "Negro Alfred and his wife Mary were brought before the mayor, charged with living and keeping house by themselves, without a permit from the mayor as required by law. Their owners were fined ten dollars for their neglect." [29] On November 8, the court fined a white, J. H. McIhenny, $50 for keeping a slave in his house "without the knowledge and consent of her owner." [30] This week was typical, and it is significant that it followed only by a few years a major effort at tightening the regulations.[31]

In fact, "living out" not only increased, but it became so embedded in urban custom that local authorities found great resistance to any attempt to stop it. When Mobile's council passed an ordinance in 1856 designed to alter fundamentally the permit system, a lively debate ensued in the town's newspapers. "Owner and Taxpayer," writing in the *Evening News*, pointed out that the arrangement was so widespread that if abolished the city would lose $4000 now collected in fees for the tickets. He doubted moreover that simple legislation would overcome what many had found convenient.[32] A little more than a year later, four items indicated the accuracy of his prediction. "Three persons of color, quasi free, were severally fined $20 for living out without the usual permits"; "Mary, a slave, was found living out without a pass; her master was fined $20"; "Aaron, a negro, was living out without a permit. His master was fined $10"; "Henry was found living out without the regular documents, but under mitigating circumstances. His master, at the Mayor's request, dropped a V ($5), and nothing more was said."[33]

Though efforts to stop the practice were never successful, city officials could not afford to give up, and this system was just as dangerous to slavery as "hiring out." Indeed, the two devices were often connected. As soon as the slave began to earn wages, he was in a position to pay his own rent; and owners whose blacks worked away from home were often lenient in granting permission for sleeping out. Both arrangements weakened the normal tie between master and bondsman, for they reduced supervision and complicated the problem of control. A Mobile editor summed up these relationships clearly in 1847. "One of the most fruitful sources of crime and licentiousness ... among our slave population," he wrote, "we think may safely be traced to the great liberty and freedom of restraint allowed them to hire their own time, and to rent premises on which to live, where they are entirely free from restraint imposed upon them by the presence of their owners or employers."[34]

If "living out" created a dilemma for the white community, it brought opportunity to the blacks. Every year more sought the relative freedom afforded by renting away from the master's premises. Some did so legally through the permit system; others had no more than oral consent; and not a few simply acted on their own. Though slave populations in Southern cities grew more slowly—or even declined—in the ante-bellum decades, the number residing outside the enclosure increased. In short, the basic housing arrangement was breaking down. Negroes could be found living in all kinds of buildings in all parts of town, and the residential supervision thought so crucial by officials diminished each year. By the 1850's so many variations existed that it is only broadly accurate to speak of any "pattern" at all.

IV

Exact information on the housing of urban slaves outside of the master's compound is scanty, but enough remains to permit at least a rough sketch. Scattered around the city, in sheds, basements, attics, small houses, and single rooms, bondsmen improvised shelter. Never very elegant and usually quite shabby, it nevertheless provided a privacy and independence seldom possible at the owner's place. But Negroes "living out" were always transients, since their master or the police might at any time remove their privilege. Hence it is difficult to document with any precision the numbers or location of these people.

Travelers stopping at hotels and boarding houses found Negroes in almost every place. C. G. Parsons, for example, lived at the Marshall House in Savannah and ran across three "male servants sleeping on narrow boards placed on chairs, the floor being sanded, without a pillow or blanket." In the "boot room," he stumbled on two blacks "in a room too short for them to lie down at full length, and nothing but boots for pillows." [35] James Stuart discovered the same conditions in a Charleston hotel, where he returned one evening to find "the male servants of the house ... already laid down for the night in the passages with their clothes on. They had neither beds nor bedding, and you may kick them or tread upon them (as you come in) with impunity." And in New Orleans, though he thought slaves better treated there than elsewhere, "they had no beds . . . to sleep on,—all lying, like dogs, in the passages of the house." [36]

Other bondsmen, however, rented rooms by themselves. For male slaves this usually involved merely sleeping privileges in some shed or building; for females it was something more, since they often lived where they hired out. And sometimes several Negroes with different masters would share quarters on the same premises. A Richmond court case, for instance, revealed that a Mr. Hunter employed four girls, only one of whom he owned, as domestic help. One slept outside his door, another in the passageway, and two others in "a room in a lower story." [37] In many instances, too, the man stayed with his wife, even though the couple had different masters. In fact, this became so common that local ordinances increasingly sanctioned the practice. [38]

A growing number of slaves in each city either lived in single rooms or had a makeshift arrangement, but the main tendency was toward renting a dwelling of their own. Like so many other aspects of urban slavery, this practice had no standing in law, and it greatly complicated official efforts to maintain control. Terms with landlords differed, some involving money and others work; and, of course, there were no written leases. In one case, however, Henry Box Brown, who worked in a Richmond tobacco factory, paid $72 a year for a place. [39] Though such precise information is scarce, there are other clear indications that renting single houses was widespread.

Fire reports often yield important housing data. Charleston's safety engineer, for example, noted a minor mishap in a "small two story wooden house, on the West side of State-street, . . . occupied by a slave named Rebecca Hamilton." [40]

Four years later, a serious conflagration destroyed three Negro dwellings as well as many other structures: ". . . in Ellery-street, one story and a half wooden building, owned by R. Martin Esq., and occupied by colored persons, was consumed. A one story wooden building at the north east corner of Anson and Ellery-street, owned by T. N. Gadsen, and occupied by Albert Quash, a free man of color, as a barber shop, was blown up. A tenement wooden building, occupied by Negroes, and owned by T. N. Gadsen, was considerably damaged." [41] In that same year a "small wooden building, at the lower end of Tradd-street . . . owned by L. H. Kennedy Esq. and occupied by a colored woman, belonging to Mrs. Lowndes" caught fire.[42]

Police reports reveal another order of slave housing. A complaint in Mobile about "a little shanty in the immediate vicinity of the old 'wood pile,'" turned up a Negro family "living out." [43] Earlier, an editor in the same city urged local officials to watch the "little sheds and shanties" which "became the rendezvous of the idle and dissipated of their own color." [44] In Richmond a scuffle took place between slaves who occupied "cabins in the neighborhood of the residence of the late Mrs. Bullock"; the fight followed some "grand entertainment" at the residence of William Sherman, "the property of Mr. J. D. Quarles." [45] In Savannah, a dangerous growth in the dog population was traced to slaves who "reside in their own, or rented houses, severally situated in the remotest sections of the city." [46] "A Citizen" of New Orleans recorded a similar lament about "Negro slaves, who hire their time of their respective owners, and by various means, contrive to pay a few dollars for the rent of a back tenement in the back parts of the city." [47]

The process in Charleston was clearer, because very early the population there spilled over the town line and thus created a kind of low-income suburb. The distinction, though artificial in many ways, had great significance for housing. In 1838 the council prohibited the construction of brick buildings within certain limits, with the result that the Neck became "rapidly filled with small cheap wooden houses." [48] Slaves seeking quarters away from their masters found them easily here. Indeed, in the decade following the passage of the "brick ordinance," Charleston proper lost people to its northern appendage. "This decrease," observed the local census takers in 1848, "can be accounted for only in this way, that the slaves and free colored have removed to the Neck ... where the class of houses suited to their condition are numerous, and obtained at moderate rents." [49] Others complained of the "very denseness of population and the closely contiguous settlements" of Negroes at the city's upper edge.[50]

This area, which had always contained a large number of blacks, soon attracted more. Some whites even built shacks to house them. In 1856 a grand jury appealed to the state legislature to stop the practice. Calling these tenements a "nuisance," the presentment asserted that "rows of buildings" were constructed "expressly for and rented to slaves and persons of color." In these barracks "as many as fifty to one hundred negroes or persons of color are sometimes residing shut out from the public street by a gate, all the buildings have but one common yeard, and not a single white person on the premise." [51] Other places in town had similar complaints. "Many neighbors," to cite but a single case, could grumble about the behavior of Negroes "both free and slave, who infest that part of the city called Jones' lot," where they lived with "a number of low white men." [52]

Though the initiative for "living out" most often came from the slave himself, there were masters who also found it convenient. Owners using blacks for industrial or commercial purposes required accommodations near their establishment yet removed from their own residences. To these whites the need for such quarters seemed compelling. "Does anyone suppose," asked someone in Mobile, "that the man who owns or is agent of 50 or 100 negroes, hired at the presses or engaged in draying, could or would have them in his yard, sleeping and eating on the premises where his family resides?" "Such numbers of slaves would produce disease," he said in answer to his own question. "It would be intolerable." [53] Hence, many of the largest owners not only permitted but encouraged the practice.

Richmond's heavy commitment to the tobacco and iron industries imposed a special burden on that town's facilities. Manufacturers generally preferred to keep out of the housing business, since it meant accommodating large numbers of male slaves on the company's property. Though a few, notably the Tredegar Iron Works, tried it, the others developed a variation on the "living out" scheme.[54] Called "board money," it entailed the payment to slaves of small sums in lieu of food and shelter. The bondsman then found his own meals and lodging. Whether the concern owned or hired its slaves, it adopted this method of caring for the men while off the job. "Board money" also presumably discharged the basic responsibility of the master, leaving only medical care and clothing to be provided by slaveholder or agent.

With this freedom Richmond's industrial Negroes scattered every year across the city looking for shelter. Many struck good bargains and found a room or small house. Some lived with their "wives" in her master's enclosure; others found a place for their own "family." But large numbers drifted, spent the "board money," slept in shacks, alleys, and attics—and got into trouble. Free blacks took in many; a few located a spot outside the city. Yet even these diverse categories make an inadequate inventory of Richmond's Negro housing, since "board money" led to all kinds of makeshift arrangements.

It also compounded the difficulty of supervising the slaves

involved. Receiving their pay directly from the employer and put on their own for food and lodging, the blacks spread out haphazardly through the town. While many discovered in this an opportunity to establish an area of independence, others contrived a much less settled life, often floating from door to door and scrape to scrape. Residents complained that they became beggars, gambled, drank too much, and generally escaped the restrictions commonly applied to bondsmen. Other owners contended that the freedom granted to one group roused envy and emulation in those without it. Police officials, too, found their problems of control greatly complicated by a transient slave population which was always hard to locate.[55]

By the mid-'fifties the mayor moved to tighten up the system. He proposed closer supervision over "board money" and irregularities arising from the spread of "living out," as well as breaking up the relations which had resulted between slaves and free Negroes.[56] The final ordinance put greater responsibility on "every owner, hirer or other employer of a slave in the city of Richmond." Either the master must furnish "food and lodging for such slaves on his own premises," or "engage board and lodging for them with some free person and pay the price thereof to such a person, except when the slave has a wife living in the city and he stays with her at the house of her master." The law further required that the slaveholder "mark out a list" of bondsmen "boarded out by him and the place where each one is boarded." Any changes had to be reported within a week.[57] The measure hoped to re-establish control by preventing money from going directly to the blacks and forcing masters to locate the housing. Doubtless, too, local officials expected that these requirements would discourage the practice altogether.

Some of Richmond's colored "problem" centered in its alleys. Though the Virginia capital, like other Southern cities, generally preferred not to cut up its blocks, it did so in some instances. In residential areas this was done within the framework of the familiar enclosure system, with high walls shutting out intercourse between plots and with slave quarters facing into the back yard. Yet to get any use out of the alley, a rear entrance was necessary. The stable usually provided this opening, though heavy doors were also common. Despite precautions, this design proved even less successful than the compound. Supervision was difficult, contacts among the blacks developed, and an informal social life grew up. Most of Dixie's cities had a few areas like this, but it was more characteristic in the border towns than farther south.[58]

Even more troublesome for municipal authorities, however, were the alleys in the mercantile districts, which spawned warehouses, stables, utility sheds, and all sorts of out-buildings. Serving commercial purposes by day, by night they attracted transients—white and Negro, slave and free. Along these dark passageways accumulated much of the city's flotsam and jetsam; here, too, slaves out after hours illegally could find sanctuary. Mixed in with free Negroes, runaways, hirelings, and some whites, bondsmen could spend a night and often longer in the ramshackle facilities available in the alley. Not many buildings could really be called housing, but they were places to sleep away from the eyes of the master. Local officials never ceased urging the police to clean out these areas and break up the settlements. Their attempts were never very successful, but they did serve to confirm the urban South's prejudice against alleys.

Savannah inherited housing problems from its original plan. The design divided the city into small oblong blocks, each of which was split lengthwise by a lane. The two sections were then divided into regular plots. On each side the big house fronted on the street and the slave quarters occupied the rear. The high walls sealed off neighbors and connected the master's residence with the slave quarters behind. But the lanes offered an exit for the blacks through the stables and sheds. Very soon these walkways came alive with Negro activity, and the chances of control were greatly complicated. Thus, the greater looseness of Savannah's housing system stemmed from its initial city plan and what visitors called its charming lanes.[59]

No matter which variation developed, off-premise housing was usually physically inferior to the enclosure. And it is easy to see why. Seldom did anyone have a permanent interest in the buildings. Slave tenants were necessarily transients, and landlords had little incentive to maintain very high standards. Those who found rooms with free Negroes probably fared better than those who rented from whites, because they often shared the same house. Nonetheless, conditions were never very good. Testimony on this is conclusive if not extensive. Traveler's accounts generally ignore Negro shelters in the city, though they often describe plantation cabins; residents commented only when trouble stirred in these spots; slave reminiscences are almost silent on the problem. But, whenever noted, the words used—"sheds," "shanties," "hovels," "shacks," "dens"—all convey the poverty, barrenness, crowding, and inadequacy of these accommodations. Parsons's picture of "the low, dingy, dirty, squalid, cheerless negro huts" of Savannah embodies the harsh facts of the bondsmen's shelter away from the enclosure.[60]

Yet, for all this, most slaves still preferred to "live out" if they could, not because they liked inferior housing, but because life in the master's place was a constant reminder of their enslavement. "The negroes appear to think," a Charleston woman wrote, with some surprise and belated insight, "that even if they receive wages, besides their old privileges, they are not free as long as they are with their old masters, and you see them leaving their comfortable homes and living in miserable shanties, often seeking a day's work for food." [61] To rent a modest house or room, or indeed simply to steal a night out anywhere, provided an area of independence and discretion denied those staying on the owner's lot. Hence the character of the shelter was much less important than the freedom to get away from the enclosure.

V

During the time of the South's "peculiar institution," Negro housing was mean but it was usually not geographically segregated. In every city in Dixie, blacks and whites lived side by side, sharing the same premises if not equal facilities and being constantly in each other's presence. Even those who owned no slaves resided next to or near some who did. Nor did slaves who "lived out" escape white neighbors, even though they might elude the supervision of their own masters. Free blacks, too, were sprinkled through most parts of town and surrounded by people of both races. The purpose of this residential mixture was not, of course, to integrate the community but rather to prevent the growth of a cohesive Negro society. Local authorities used every available weapon to keep the blacks divided; housing was simply the physical expression of this racial policy.

This system was a fundamental part of urban slavery. To be sure, toward the end of the period a measure of segregation in housing appeared. But this development was a symptom of the general sickness of the institution in the cities, not the conscious choice of the slaveholders. The typical pattern, especially when the proportion of Negroes was greatest, provided for a virtual mixture of white and black in each section of town. And later changes in the ratio of the races did not alter the character of most neighborhoods.

The pattern of every city was very much the same. Savan-

nah's statistics, however, are most illustrative, because its ward
system divided the town into thirty small units which permit
closer analysis. Slaves lived in every ward; moreover, in each
they constituted a substantial percentage of the population.
The 1840 census, for instance, counted 5888 whites and 5326
Negroes (632 of whom were free), the blacks comprising
between a quarter and a half of every neighborhood.[62] Eight
years later, a local directory which listed bondsmen from
their place of residence rather than from the home of their
owner found the composition only slightly altered.[63] Free
blacks, too, appeared in every section. In short, a typical block
in the Georgia port contained people of both races, with the
colored diffused throughout.

Charleston's figures disclose a similar situation. An 1824
census showed more slaves than whites in three of the four
wards, and the difference was negligible in the other.[64] In 1848
another local count found a decline in the proportion of colored, but every section still had large numbers. In addition,
free Negroes also resided in all areas of the city.[65] The national census in 1860 demonstrates the persistence of this
pattern.[66] Now there were eight wards and the municipal
boundary included the Neck. Yet slaves were found in every
neighborhood.

New Orleans, especially in the old quarter, often seemed
to travelers to be a collection of irregular racial concentrations. But these clusters obscured the more important fact that
every area of the city had some blacks, and that slave housing
everywhere conformed to the usual practice.[67] Outside the
"French" section, the Negro population was much smaller,
but not segregated. The Second Municipality, comprising the
newer and "American" part of the city, had only 6250 slaves
among over 35,000 people in 1847, yet they were fairly evenly
distributed over its seven wards.[68] Even on the eve of seces-

sion, when New Orleans's colored population had dropped substantially, the broad pattern remained.[69]

In Mobile, slaves were likewise widely dispersed, ranging in 1833 from 30 per cent in the Middle Ward to nearly half in the rest of the town.[70] And tax records in 1854 demonstrated that this residential composition continued.[71] A Richmond census in the same year again reveals the familiar pattern, with Negroes spread throughout the entire city.[72] Even in Baltimore, where slavery was rapidly disappearing in the pre-war decades, the arrangement prevailed. In the 1820's all twelve wards had a significant scattering of slaves, and the distribution persisted, though with much reduced numbers, into the 'fifties.[73]

Other border towns had similar experiences. Jegle's Louisville directory of 1845 listed the population by race and wards, and once more the absence of segregation or even important Negro concentrations was revealed. Though the slave population had dipped to less than 15 per cent by that date, these figures are representative of the kind of distribution found in every Southern city.[74]

Ward	White	Slave	Free colored
1	3225	249	21
2	3448	289	37
3	5323	599	63
4	5178	636	75
5	6035	685	122
6	3745	875	102
7	2718	504	79
8	2930	219	61

With an even smaller number of bondsmen, St. Louis presented the same picture at least to 1860.

The basic housing custom in Southern cities, then, was to

keep the Negroes divided; to require that slaves live with their masters or their agents; to spread the blacks throughout the town; to prevent concentration of colored people free from the control of whites. This objective was seldom directly expressed, but it was everywhere understood. Any practice which altered this arrangement was opposed; any tendency which weakened those restraints was resisted. The logic of this residential scheme was usually argued only when some threat to its effectiveness appeared, yet every day it could be seen in the heavy brick walls of the enclosures and the broad windowless backs of buildings and slave quarters still standing in most of Dixie's cities.

This housing policy, though embedded in custom, logic, brick, and mortar, encountered increasing trouble. Its effectiveness required the substantial isolation of slaves and continual supervision of their every activity, day and night. Urban pressures, however, made this difficult. City life maximized human contacts; employment, even as domestics, often took slaves away from their master's place; "hiring out" weakened further the ordinary restraints of slavery; and "living out" provided a still wider area of independence. A significant number of free Negroes also resided in cities, where they enjoyed privileges denied slaves even while they shared many of the same inhibitions. As time passed, these developments tended to alter significantly the residential patterns in Southern towns. Small Negro sections appeared, a mixture of bond and free, usually at the edge of town and always shabby in appearance.

A Savannah editor, for example, found these clusters "in the remotest sections of the city, at the extremities of the Fort, Yamacraw, or Springhill." [75] And a traveler could later refer to these spots "in the suburbs," where squalid Negro houses "remind the Northern visitor of the fearful price paid by one class to support another." [76] Charleston's Negro concentrations grew up in the Neck and stretched northward beyond the built-up areas. In Richmond, William Chambers ran across little enclaves where "the dwellings occupied by the lower classes of coloured people are of a miserable kind, resembling the worst brick-houses in the back-lanes of English manufacturing towns." [77] And a resident of New Orleans identified these areas as "suburb sheds" in the "back parts of the city" and "dens" where slaves, free Negroes, and runaways gathered.[78] Alleys, too, stimulated the growth of colored neighborhoods, and wherever blocks were cut an informal life among the blacks appeared. In every city the tendency of Negroes, both slave and free, to withdraw toward the periphery accelerated in these last ante-bellum years.

This development was more significant for what it portended than for its importance in this period. The great bulk of slaves lived on their master's lots or in accommodations furnished by their employer. Some had the opportunity to choose a landlord under the "living out" custom. And some others found housing on their own. Yet the situation was changing. Each year it was more difficult to keep the old ways; each year some blacks slipped out of the owner's yard into a new dimension of independence, if not freedom. Though the policy did not change, the practice did. This gradual breakdown of the characteristic housing habits in Southern cities reflected the wider problems of slavery in an urban context. For other forces at work in cities helped make the maintenance of slavery more arduous each succeeding year.

Chapter Four

THE WEB OF RESTRAINTS

"Over the sparsely settled *country*," a Charlestonian remarked in 1845, "where gangs of negroes are restricted within settled plantations under the immediate control and discipline of their respective owners," slaves were not permitted "to idle and roam about in pursuit of mischief." In these rural regions "the mere occasional riding about and general supervision of a patrol may be sufficient." But, he continued, "some more energetic and scrutinizing system is absolutely *necessary*" in cities, "where from the very denseness of population and closely contiguous settlements . . . there must be need of closer and more careful circumspection." "A few active officers" there, the same writer concluded shrewdly, were even more effective "than all the patrols together." [1] This observation summed up both the special problem of police control over urban slaves and the remedy adopted by Southern municipalities.

State law laid down the broad outlines for policing bondsmen. Though masters constituted the primary authority and any white person might discipline any slave, more formal power rested in the "patrol." Usually connected in some form with the militia, the patrol took over day-to-day supervision of Negroes who were away from their owner's premises. States organized this force in different ways, but each had some system of routine vigilance. When on duty, squads of men rode the district, stopping any blacks away from their plantations, picking up runaways, or simply overwhelming the slaves by their presence. It was probably less important whether the system proved effective on a day-to-day basis than that most localities had ready at hand a force powerful enough to quiet Negro unrest and police the countryside when needed. If whites stressed the laxness of the patrols, the slaves generally considered them pretty formidable.

The system was designed to meet rural conditions, where chattels only infrequently left their master's place and where colored people might outnumber whites. "This law may be well adapted to plantations," "T.R." wrote to a Charleston newspaper in 1827; "that it is ill calculated for a town or thick population, the many complaints made against it, prove." The constant mobility of urban dwellers obviously raised new problems which made enforcement difficult for the police and often irritating to masters. For example, one of the "objectional clauses" in the legislation, the same observer contended, "makes liable every Negro seen out of his owner's lot to be taken up, nor can a servant be sent on the most trifling errand, without a ticket, or they are subject to be (and very often are) taken up by either the Patrol or others." And when the slave had instructions to buy things, each article had to be specified on his pass to be countersigned later by the storekeeper.[2]

The inconvenience of permits was only one of the problems of managing urban slaves. The city also presented its colored population with numberless opportunities for contact, meeting, and even organization. No sooner had the slave left his residence, with or without a permit, than he bumped into all kinds of people—white and black, bond and free. Quickly there were acquaintances and friends; next informal gathering and meeting places; then, inevitably, a more stable associational life. Sometimes the center of this activity was a church, sometimes the neighborhood grocery store or grog shop, sometimes the home of a free Negro. But no matter how it grew up or where its locus might be, it was always a sort of underground world, its very existence being illegal and nearly all its actions considered subversive of the accepted system of slavery.

In addition, it was hard to break up this kind of intercourse, because the city itself created the conditions out of which it sprang. No master could isolate his slaves totally, and not even substantially, if they were to be of any use to him. "Hiring out" and "living out" undermined normal control most obviously. But domestics, too, left the residence in the course of their duties. Even slave children spent much time outside the compound. In short, these contacts were an inescapable component of urban bondage. To prevent them would have required a system of surveillance so extensive and so expensive in both money and manpower as to make the institution itself unfeasible. The result was a persistent struggle to minimize Negro fraternizing and, more especially, to prevent the growth of an organized colored community. Such policy made it necessary to pay particular attention to certain kinds of slave activity.

II

The churches provided the most acceptable opportunity for blacks to come together. Slaveholders were vaguely committed to the religious instruction of those in their care. In addition, many masters believed that Holy Writ, rightly interpreted, sustained the institution of slavery and confirmed the subordination of Negroes. Yet the whites were never very happy about church meetings. There was less hesitation where the church itself encouraged master and slave to worship together; but churches which held separate services often encountered acute problems. Congregations grew rapidly, and, as authorized preachers were scarce, colored leaders emerged as influential figures in colored activity. This development produced exactly the conditions which the white community feared.

In 1847 "Many Citizens" in Charleston expressed their forebodings in a debate over the "religious instruction of the black population." Arguing against local practice, they asserted that separate congregations tended to "diminish the influence and authority of the master" by vesting "either presently or prospectively, ecclesiastical authority in the slave." They thought such autonomy gave Negroes "the plenitude of freedom of thought, word and action in the church" that would establish an "organized community." Soon the blacks would get "excited by the privileges they enjoy, as a separate and to some extent independent society." "To this end," the Charlestonians warned, "not only may it come, but to this end it must come!" Nor would mere formal white supervision do, for experience demonstrated that "it is not the white minister who is really the responsible instructor in any one of our churches which has a large black membership—the black [Bible] class leaders are the real wire pullers." [3]

"For years," wrote a New Orleans editor in 1839, on the same question, "we have been trying to induce our authorities to put down that greatest of all public nuisances and den for hatching plots against their masters, the church on Gravier street." [4] A year later, another journalist complained of a meeting house where Negroes gathered "in large numbers—every Sabbath evening, where a black fellow in black holds forth in the loudest kind of manner," and where "the vicious and designing" imbued them with "pernicious doctrines." [5] By 1846 the issue had not changed. The police in New Orleans arrested a dozen blacks in a makeshift church, and charged that they "as well as other colored persons, have been in the habit of repairing to this place for the purpose of joining in singing hymns and cantiques which was followed by sermons, the subject of which was of the most inflammatory character." [6]

Even when Negro churches were attacked for making noise and disturbing the peace, the real concern, it can be assumed, went much deeper. For instance, a petition of 74 citizens to the Mobile City Council in 1840 covered the usual range of formal complaints. "From a very early hour in the morning until after dark," the document declared, "those residing in the neighborhood of the meeting house are annoyed and disturbed by the noise and outcries of the assembled negroes—so that it has become a perfect nuisance." But the white ministers of the church who were charged with supervising the services contended that the petitioners' objections were much more fundamental. "If we are rightly informed," they countered, "*other* and *graver* reasons have been assigned *verbally* by those who have become active in this matter." [7] The fear was insubordination or, worse still, insurrection. To exert some kind of control over the religious activity of slaves, then, became a persistent objective of municipal authority in Dixie.

III

City life also bred other dangerous practices. Though the law prohibited trading with slaves except under highly restricted conditions, enforcement proved almost impossible. No shopkeeper could deal with a bondsman unless he carried a written request from his master. If blacks had any of their own garden produce, they could sell it at the market only during fixed hours. Yet exchanges took place all the time. In a cash transaction no questions were likely, and barter flourished everywhere. Whites contended that these opportunities encouraged Negro stealing, and they constantly insisted that the police crack down. "The habit of buying things from slaves or dealing with them, unless they have the permission of their owners, is dangerous," the *Richmond Enquirer* observed, "although it is a habit very extensively practiced." [8] "Hiring out" and "board money," however, put money in slave hands and to some extent institutionalized the custom at the expense of the law.

But the real fear of illicit trading was more substantial. Grog shops grew up to exploit the situation. Negroes with a little money—no matter how they got it—were limited in what they could buy. Presumably their owners provided them with food, clothing, and shelter. To turn up with an expensive or unusual item would raise suspicions. Yet who would know if a slave slipped into a nearby spot for a drink, perhaps a hand of cards, and a little conviviality? Or at night the visit might be a little more elaborate—a good deal of liquor, some serious gambling, and perhaps a few prostitutes. And often the gatherings were mixed, colored and white, bond and free, men and women. These places were "distinguished for the equality which reigned . . . between the blacks and whites—all is hail fellow well met, no matter what the complexion." [9] Slaveowners considered these rendezvous extremely dangerous; the public consistently attacked them; the police tried every expedient to suppress them. Yet they multiplied and apparently prospered.

Every city had many of them. "Not a street, nor a corner can be passed without encountering these magazines of degradation," wrote the *New Orleans Bee* in 1837. "They spring up in all directions with inconceivable rapidity; within the last few years they have augmented in almost an unparalleled ratio, and are fostered and sustained by the thousands who flock to them, . . . either by invitation, or impelled irresistible

habit." [10] Nor were things improved fifteen years later. "The
law against selling liquor to slaves is broken oftener than any
other, we suppose, on the statute books," the *Daily Delta* observed, "and the violators are a class that are less frequently
brought to justice than any other lawbreakers. For candidly,
we believe there are hundreds of liquor shops, located in different parts of the city where liquors are retailed as freely to
the bond as the free." [11] A Savannah grand jury found the
same situation in 1836. "The great number of Retailers of
Spiritous Liquors within the City, whose intercourse with
slaves has a most ingenious tendency, presenting an inducement to theft and intoxication" were "a grievance of great
and growing magnitude." [12]

By 1854 the problem in Mobile had become so acute that
the mayor devoted a large portion of his annual message to
it. After noting the spread of "dissipation and vice, and, as a
necessary consequence, insubordination" among the blacks,
he traced the "fruitful source" to "the numerous drinking
houses kept by white men, that are to be found in all parts
of the city. Here the slaves are invited to assemble, encouraged to gamble, steal and practice every species of vice, and
all in spite of law and in defiance of public opinion." [13] A
Louisville judge said that on Broadway alone "there are a
good many groceries ... where negro slaves can obtain liquor
without the consent of their masters," and this in the face of
a "very stringent law." [14]

A court case in Richmond disclosed that one of these shops
had even been set up in the rear of the stylish Exchange Hotel.
In keeping with its fashionable surroundings, it boasted "marble tables where the 'gem'men of color' did constantly congregate, day and night, to indulge in games at cards, dominoes,
dice, et cetera." In addition, witnesses testified that "ladies
(of a certain class) rustling in silks and odoriferous as pinks
and honeysuckles, occasionally honored the establishment

with a visit." [15] No city managed to control, much less stamp out, these spots, which remained a part of urban slavery to the end. Indeed, in 1859 a Charleston grand jury lamented that "the greater portion of the time of the Jury has been occupied by the rendering of 'true bills' against those who have been charged with unlawfully selling spirits to slaves." "It is to these dens of iniquity," the presentment asserted, "that our slaves resort at night and on Sundays, with stolen property to be exchanged for poisonous strychnine whisky." [16]

This problem was, of course, present to some degree on the plantation, but cities greatly magnified the opportunities open to slaves. Probably no other question caused so much comment or roused so much anxiety. "A Slave Holder," writing in the *Savannah Republican*, summarized whites' fears in all their dimensions. Noting that the Georgia port was "one of the largest towns in the state, where more slaves are necessarily congregated together," he catalogued the dangers of grog shops: "Because the passions of slaves ought not be inflamed by ardent spirits. Because it injures their health and their worth as well as their morals. Because it demoralizes both seller and buyer. Because the sale of spirits increases the duties of our Police." Then, to wrap up the indictment, he added: "Because it makes our streets more noisy than they ought to be—desecrates the Sabbath—pollutes our children by pernicious example—crowds our jails—increases our city expenditures—increases the danger during epidemics—annoys the sick, and is not pleasant to those who are well." [17] And beneath was a deeper apprehension. "Should a servile outbreak ever occur in the city of New Orleans," warned the editor of the *Daily Delta*, "we shall have to thank the keepers of these Negro cabarets and club houses for it, within the precincts of whose damned halls, at the dead hour of midnight, heaven knows what plots are hatched against our peace." [18]

IV

Tippling houses were not the only focus of this wide-spread, though illegal, traffic with Negroes. Whites used private homes for the same purpose, and police found these even more difficult to control. Once again the court records suggest the range of the operations. Patrick Maxfield's brush with Richmond's officialdom in 1853 was characteristic. His house on Main and 25th Street had become a notorious center, with "sailors, negroes, lewd women and 'spirits' of all shades and complexions indiscriminately meeting there, drinking, dancing, quarreling and creating a noise and confusion" that was "annoying and alarming to all the quiet citizens." [19] The judge fined him, but if the amount was no greater than the usual $5 to $15, then Maxfield was doubtless at it again very soon.[20] At the same time a Louisville newspaper carried a similar account. Arnold Still was picked up for gambling with a slave; they had been caught "sitting on the bed with a quantity of money before them, and cards in their hands." Still claimed he was "telling the Negro's fortune," but the judge thought otherwise.[21]

Negroes, too, both bond and free, flouted the law against trading with other blacks. Their homes often became convenient meeting places where a little conviviality could be found, some new friendships made, and a little temporary privacy secured. Like the grog shops and other white establishments, however, these spots were not always innocent. Sometimes stolen goods changed hands, liquor frequently flowed in abundance, and petty crimes—even violence—was common. The fact that these gatherings included free as well as enslaved Negroes deepened the anxieties of local officials and complicated detection. The dockets of municipal courts indicate that suppressing these assemblages was a continuing problem.

"Two negroes were arrested (in company with several others)," the *Mobile Evening News* reported in 1854, "at a house near Geldin's blacksmith shop, where they had been gambling all day on Sunday." [22] Again in the same year: "H. Strong, f(free). m(man). of c(color)., for entertaining and trafficking with slaves, fined $50." [23] "Two Negroes," the *Richmond Enquirer's* police reporter wrote in the same routine way, "were ordered yesterday . . . to be duly punished for forming part of an unlawful assemblage . . . in a house . . . on Broad street." [24] At 26 Gerod Street in New Orleans, a free colored residence was "nightly thronged by slaves and free negroes from all parts of the city for the purpose of gambling." Fights broke out continually, the newspaper counting six on the previous Sunday night.[25] Every city administration tangled with this covert activity; all found it impossible to put down.

If the laws against stealing were broken everyday, the restrictions on Negro assemblies were disregarded only slightly less often. Local ordinances and state laws, designed to prevent any concerted Negro action, prohibited any gatherings of over five—or sometimes seven—persons unless by written permission from their masters. Yet the city threw people together. Bondsmen would loiter on the street to chat; others would join. Youths would get up a game; others might stop to watch. A vacant lot could draw a large number of colored neighbors for an outing on Sunday or socializing at night. And, of course, slaves would drop in at each other's places, or visit at the home of a free Negro. Most of this was innocent conviviality, but the whites could see only the danger. Here, consorting together, often concealed from the outside world, they might plan an escape or plot an insurrection. In the countryside the occasions for assemblages were few and usually easy to control; in the city they were many and seldom supervised.

Whites in the towns suspected that illegal gatherings took place all the time, but their only certain knowledge came from the frequency of public complaints. These usually centered on meetings in public or semi-public spots. In 1851, for example, the *Mobile Daily Advertiser* quoted a familiar entry on the police docket: "Six slaves, being part of some fifteen or twenty, who had congregated at the intersection of St. Joseph and St. Francis streets, were arrested Saturday evening for forming an unlawful assemblage." [26] Again, two months later, the court reporter noted that "some ten or a dozen negroes" had been picked up "while indulging in music and dancing without leave or license, in the vicinity of the up-town cotton presses. . . . The mayor caused them to dance to the tune of ten lashes each." [27]

Richmond newspaper readers were also accustomed to stories where "Peter and William, slaves to George Mills were caught by the Police, on Sunday last, in the company of six other blacks, pitching coppers. . . . They were taken to the cage" and given 15 "stripes." [28] A Charleston resident put the problem more generally. Noting that the law was "peremptory against the disorderly gathering of negroes," he asked, "yet are we not constantly annoyed, especially on Sundays, with the most unruly and profane mobs, setting all law at defiance, and, if dispersed from one vicinity, re-collecting with increased numbers, at another?" [29] In short, urban conditions so augmented the points of human contact that regulations and ordinances could not keep people apart.

V

The same conditions which made control so difficult also created one fundamental problem. Urban slaves had all around them the inducements and the opportunities to learn to read and write. Many whites thought nothing was more dangerous.

"To be able to read and write is certainly not necessary to the performance of those duties which are required of our slaves," the Charleston City Council wrote to the South Carolina legislature in 1826, "and on the contrary is incompatible with the public safety." Why? Because "this knowledge" will enable bondsmen "to carry on illicit traffic, to communicate privately among themselves, and to evade those regulations that are intended to prevent confederation among them." [30] Put another way, slaveholders felt that the whole system of servitude would collapse if blacks picked up the rudiments of learning. "To prevent the general instruction of negroes in the arts of reading and writing," thus became in the words of the *Southern Literary Messenger*, "a measure of police essential to the tranquility, nay to *the existence* of Southern society." [31]

The fear was genuine and logical, and state law everywhere forbade such instruction. The comparative isolation of the plantation permitted a limitation of the spread of literacy, though it certainly was never complete. In the cities, however, supervision and control were never strong enough to stop it. Speaking of Southern towns, a traveler asserted that "many slaves have learned to read in spite of all prohibitions." Indeed, he found "the very prohibition has stimulated exertion." "In Richmond," he continued, "I am informed, almost every slave-child is learning to read. Even in Columbia, the capital of South Carolina, hundreds of slaves can read." [32] Lyell found the same situation in Charleston, even after the regulations were tightened and more "rigorously enforced." "The negroes are often taught to read, and they learn much in Sunday schools, and for the most part are desirous of instruction." [33]

The testimony of former slaves also abounds with such evidence. Frederick Douglass, for example, wrote that "I used to carry, almost constantly, a copy of Webster's spelling book in my pocket; and when sent of errands, or when play time was allowed me, I would step, with my young friends, aside, and take a lesson in spelling." [34] Another, Henry Morehead in St. Louis, received a little formal schooling before his master stopped him, with the remark that " 'niggers' going to school would only teach them rascality." [35] Urban whites understood this fact, and an anxious Charleston resident despaired of ever stamping out literacy among the bondsmen. "As it is easily communicated," he observed, "it is probable that, in spite of all endeavors to the contrary, the evil will increase rather than diminish." [36]

The white community thus felt and understood the problem of maintaining discipline among the slaves. Yet the nature of urban life undermined traditional devices of control. City dwellers, lacking any alternatives, could only continually call for new legislation or stricter enforcement. "Indeed can any plausible reason be given," wrote an exasperated New Orleans editor in 1839, returning to the elementary question, "why slaves are permitted to be roaming about the streets, lounging about grog shops, or meeting at and in front of the theatre, and other places of amusements, idling away their time, concerting mischief, or ruining their morals and health by drinking and acquiring various habits and disease, and disgusting the eyes and ears of passers-by with their filthy talk and indecent actions?" [37]

Discipline seemed so persistent and intractable a problem that, when the cases on the docket declined, the judge was likely to suspect the police force rather than acknowledge any improvement in the basic situation. The mayor of Mobile, who presided over the city's municipal court and had a lax day in 1858, immediately blamed it on the men on the beat. "The Mayor could not understand how it was that there were so few arrests of negroes," a newspaper reported. "He was satisfied . . . from his own observation" that "they were living and conducting themselves in direct contradiction of the city ordinances.... Was it that the police were getting lazy? or the negroes getting more watchful?" [38] But if authorities were sometimes skeptical of solving the problem, they never ceased working on it. They organized patrols, tightened enforcement procedures, and passed new legislation.

VI

The broadest method of discipline was also the subtlest. "The only principle upon which any authority over them can be maintained is fear," wrote a Charleston man in 1822. "When there is this principle in the bosom of a slave, coupled with a strong sense of inferiority, he is happy and contented, and that is almost universally the case among the *country* Negroes." [39] This fear and the sense of inferiority were manifested in many ways—in the deference of the bondsmen and the habitual arrogance of the whites, in the different dress of the races, in the calculated separation of housing arrangements, in the division of work, in the casual etiquette of the street, and, of course, in an armed police and militia. These customs created an atmosphere which sustained the subordination of the blacks and gave slavery a conducive climate no less in the cities than on farm and plantation. "The security of the whites," wrote Olmsted, "is in a much less degree contingent on the action of patrols than upon the constant, habitual, and instinctive surveillance and authority of all the white people over all the black." [40]

But discipline on the slave in the specific instance was first exercised by the owner. Fundamental authority, a British traveler observed, "as far as the Blacks are concerned, is usurped, or, at all events, is virtually delegated by the laws to the masters, who, in most cases, are obliged to act as judge, jury and executioner." From their action, "the slave has no appeal, except in cases of rare enormity. Thus the masters, in point of fact, possess almost the exclusive administration of the laws, as far as concerns their slaves." [41] Legislation on this matter was even more sweeping. "The condition of the slave being merely a passive one," a Louisiana statute asserted, "his subordination to his master and to all who represent him, is not susceptible to any modification or restriction." He "owes to his master and to all his family, a respect without bounds, and an absolute obedience." [42] Hence, in the application of public law as well as private rules, the owner constituted the primary agent of enforcement.

In 1826 an appalled Jared Sparks saw what this might mean. While staying at a Georgia hotel, he heard the "cries and screechings of a man in distress." Hurrying into the market place he found a small crowd watching a man "with his coat off, whipping a negro." A rope passed through a pulley and tied around the slave's wrists held his arms above his head. The master wielded "a very heavy teamster's whip" and beat the black "with all the strength he could command." Sparks calculated that "nearly one hundred lashes" were inflicted. "I have never witnessed so shocking a scene," he continued, "and it was rendered doubly aggravating from the obvious fact that the negro suffered rather from the master's caprice and sudden anger than from any just cause of punishment." The owner contended that his bondsman had been caught in a grog shop, where he had "ventured some remote hints that he should run away." Sparks thought the laws "ought not suffer such exhibitions in public." [43]

Cities, of course, could not alter the system, but urban masters did rely more heavily on public agencies for discipline than was possible in the countryside. Ordinances provided that a master could send blacks to the local prison for "correction." He simply made out a slip for the number of lashes, gave it to the slave to be whipped, and sent him off to jail for punishment. Planters, of course, had the same option, but distances made its use impractical. Increasingly, however, urban owners found the system convenient. It was easy and quick; it saved the master the grim experience of wielding the whip himself. While visiting Charleston, Basil Hall summed up both the importance and mechanics of the arrangement: "It seemed indeed, an essential part of the system of slavery, that the lash should be used as a means of enforcing obedience. But as the disagreeable nature of this discipline prevents the master from administering it at home, the offending slave is sent to the workhouse with a note and a piece of money, on delivering which he receives so many stripes, and is sent back again." [44]

Negroes and outside observers felt that beyond convenience there were other reasons for the wide use of this public system. In the city, an owner's treatment of his slave often was no private matter. What happened on a plantation was not general knowledge, but in an urban neighborhood news traveled quickly. And the handling of blacks was part of that news. Masters therefore preferred to avoid a reputation for harshness by relying on the jail or workhouse. "The general sense of decency that must pervade" towns, wrote Frederick Douglass, "does much to check and prevent . . . atrocious cruelty . . . and . . . dark crimes . . . openly perpetrated on the plantation." "He is a desperate slaveholder," the former slave continued, "who will shock the humanity of his non-slave-holding neighbors, by the cries of the lacerated slaves; and very few in the city are willing to incur the odium of being cruel masters." [45] James Stirling found this view shared by other Negroes, who believed that the "control of public opinion, natural to a large city" had tended to minimize private "correction." [46] "Owners who affected culture and refinement," another former slave recalled, "preferred to send a servant to the yard for punishment to inflicting it themselves.

It saved them trouble, they said, and possibly a slight wear and tear of feeling." [47]

The result was that every city furnished a public alternative. Characteristic was Charleston's ordinance of 1807, which made it "lawful" for any owner to send his Negroes to the workhouse "to be corrected by whipping." It cost 25 cents a trip, and the number of lashes was limited to twenty. No slave could be punished more than twice a week, and then only with a three-day interval.[48] The same treatment cost the master only 12½ cents in New Orleans, though the jailor could apply up to 25 stripes.[49] Elsewhere variations were minor. And the evidence suggests that business was often brisk.[50] In Charleston, for example, "corrections" at the two workhouses averaged over 150 a month in the immediate pre-war decade.

In some places the master could substitute time on the treadmill for whipping. The 1825 law establishing one in Charleston explained its function as "meliorating corporal punishment" as well as "improving prison discipline." [51] But an additional argument was also persuasive. "A City Rustic" observed that while "every owner of town Negroes" would find a "Stepping Mill" useful, "female owners of slaves, whose humanity too often stands between the Negro and the well-merited visit to the Work-House," would find in "this excellent invention" an alternative to the cowhide.[52] A traveler's account, however, throws some doubt on the humaneness of the new device. "Six tread at once on each wheel," wrote Karl Bernhard, "while six rest upon a bench placed behind the wheel. Every half minute the left hand man steps off . . . while the other five move to the left . . . at the same time the right hand man sitting on the bench slips behind the wheel." The chattels thus worked three minutes and rested three. The daily stint was eight hours. It was no wonder that the visitor could add that "the negroes entertain a strong fear of the treadmills, and regard flogging as the lighter evil." [53]

The municipal correction facilities expressed the importance of public control over slavery in Southern towns. Few things illustrate better the difference between urban and rural conditions. On the plantation discipline was almost always private. "On our estates we dispose with the whole machinery of public police, and public courts of justice," wrote De Bow. "Thus we try, decide, and execute the sentence of *thousands of cases*, which, in other countries, would go into the courts." [54] In the metropolis, on the other hand, official agencies took over large areas of control—and this was inevitable. The blacks were away from the master's premises so often that their supervision was irregular; enforcement of ordinances necessarily fell to the local police and municipal courts; the denseness of population made discipline a municipal rather than individual matter; and the concentration of large numbers of Negroes required consistent rather than sporadic attention.

Even if the transfer of some aspects of discipline to public agencies was necessary, not everyone was happy about it. The very fact of sharing control reduced the unique authority of the master over his blacks, compromising the absolute control that many deemed essential to the institution. Slaves no longer felt that there was a single focus of power, a single point of appeal, a single source of command. "They cannot distinguish why their master has no power to give them his consent to go out and spend an evening with a friend without fear of the guardhouse hanging over his head," wrote "A Slave Owner" asking for the repeal of the "Negro laws." It was better that the slave have "only his master and mistress to appeal to." "Now we have so many new *men* and measures," he complained, "and so much law and talk" that the basis of authority became confused. [55]

Despite such objections, municipalities felt their general

responsibilities were greater than the prerogatives of the owner, and everywhere they established elaborate police systems. In fact, travelers were often astonished at their extent. Olmsted, who visited nearly every Southern city, asserted that underneath the superficial "childlike and cordial" relations between the races "you come to police machinery such as you never find in towns under free governments: citadels, sentries, passports, grape-shotted cannon, and daily public whippings . . . for accidental infractions of police ceremonies." This apparatus was not simply on paper but in being. "I happened myself," he continued, "to see more direct expression of tyranny in a single day and night at Charleston, than in Naples in a week; and I found that more than half the inhabitants of this town were subject to arrest, imprisonment, and barbarous punishment." Nor was Charleston unique, for "similar precautions and similar customs may be discovered in every large town in the South," he concluded.[56]

Louis Fitzgerald Tasistro, who had traveled widely, thought Charleston had "the best organized system of police that ever was devised. . . . The colored people are permitted to be abroad till ten o'clock in the evening but no later." As soon as "the clocks strike that hour," he added, "the city suddenly assumes the appearance of a great military garrison, and all the principal streets become forthwith alive with patrolling parties of twenties and thirties, headed by fife and drum, conveying the idea of a general siege."[57]

In Richmond, William Chambers, strolling around the capitol building at dusk, happened upon an "armed sentinel" and recalled that it had "the startling effect of an apparition; for it was the first time I had seen a bayonet in the United States." He explained it by "the unpleasant reflection, that the large infusion of slaves in the composition of society was not unattended with danger."[58] James Stuart, too, was struck by the prominence of the mounted *gens d'armes* in New

Orleans, something he had not noticed in the North. "In this respect," he added, Dixie's towns "do not resemble the free cities of America; but the great number of blacks, and the way they are treated by the whites, render this precaution, I have no doubt, indispensably necessary." [59] And if visitors understood the reason for a large force, residents themselves could be just as clear. "The city guards were actively patrolling the streets day and night," Arthur Cunynhame wrote, "for the purpose, as one of them told me, 'of keeping down the niggers.' " [60]

The size of the force varied, of course, with the extent and needs of the town. Louisville, with less than 5000 people in 1820, had only a three-man watch.[61] By 1826 the trustees declared that this was "insufficient," and they added another man, with instructions "to be very particular as it regards collections of colored people . . . about the Market House and groceries." [62] This guard also included a special Sunday beat designed to break up "disorderly houses" which provided "a rendezvous for negroes." [63] Supplemented by a militia, this modest force served a population of over 10,000 in 1830.

Older and larger places had more elaborate systems. In 1837, for example, Charleston had a city guard of 100 men, maintained at an annual expense of $24,000. In addition, the state guard with sixty more was stationed at the Citadel, and a general militia of adult males was always on call. "With these means," Mayor Robert Y. Hayne said proudly, "there cannot be a doubt, that Charleston is not only placed in a condition of entire safety, but that her persons enjoy far greater security in their persons and property, than can possibly be possessed" in "any city north of the Potomac." [64] To improve its effectiveness, the corps was organized on a ward basis. An assistant marshal presided over each division in a kind of precinct arrangement. Meanwhile foot and mounted units made the rounds both day and night.[65] Twenty years later, the force had increased to 281, with at least 25 horse-men.[66] Such an extensive system was obviously expensive, and police costs generally constituted the largest single item in the town's budget.

Richmond's organization was also impressive. As early as 1833 it had 19 men on the night watch alone, "each of whom," the Common Council ordered, "shall be permanently assigned to a district or beat, and for whom a watch box should be provided." The men went on duty at "early candlelight." More significantly, however, two officers were placed "under the direction and advice" of the mayor himself "to attend exclusively to the Police of the black population of the city." [67] The organization remained the same throughout the ante-bellum decades, though in 1857 the force was increased from 30 to 40.[68] At the same time Savannah employed 56 regulars, "ten supernumeraries, two sentinels and two steeple-men" for a population of just over 22,000.[69] New Orleans, meanwhile, had a complement of 300 day and night policemen under a chief, four lieutenants, and ten sergeants. Though 184 comprised the night watch the mayor wanted to increase this number.[70]

Police departments in Southern municipalities were gener-ally more imposing on paper than in fact. Despite their size and complex structure, the public was never satisfied for long. The police were accused of everything from mere incompe-tence to all kinds of corruption. "The police are not half active enough; they have too much to do with politics. The Recorder is too lenient; the prosecutor too sleepy," ran the usual indictment.[71] In Louisville, citizens petitioned the trus-tees to fire the entire watch because it was not "vigilant or temperate." [72] Occasionally, there were dark hints that the man on the beat was "conniving" with the people he ought to have been putting in jail.[73] Even when arrests were made, some charged that the punishment was too lenient ("a small whip being lightly dropped upon the shoulders").[74]

Such attacks led to periodic shake-ups. "The City Guard has been organized and re-organized during the last ten years," the *Charleston Courier* wearily recalled in 1842, "and yet existing regulations are not found to answer." [75] Fifteen years later, local authorities were tackling the problem once more. Mayor William Niles asserted that "no subject" had "occupied more of the public attention." Before making final recommendations, he sent a committee to New Orleans and Savannah "to see what they were doing." It discovered that the Georgia port had in "successful operation a system of police which seemed to commend it to all." Like most reforms, however, it would have cost money, requiring a budget of $110,000 instead of $75,000. Ultimately, the council adopted a modified version of the "Savannah Plan," which among other things doubled the complement of horsemen. "When the Police was re-organized," the mayor reported reassuringly, "one of its earliest objects . . . was the suppression of the practice of selling liquor to slaves and of the illegal traffic with them generally." [76]

Whenever municipal officials showed reluctance to tighten up enforcement, private groups threatened to do it themselves. They set up citizens' committees, harangued the police, wrote to newspapers, and petitioned the city council. In 1827, 20 of Louisville's most prominent residents announced that, beginning January 1, they would "put into effect" the laws "prohibiting slaves from going at large and hiring themselves." These were "evils . . . much complained of, and generally admitted," the statement declared, before concluding sarcastically, "the Trustees of the town of Louisville and town officers generally will aid in carrying the above objects into effect." [77] In St. Louis the police seemed so inadequate that in the midst of rumored slave unrest, a public meeting urged the establishment of a vigilante network in each ward to enforce the Negro statutes.[78] In 1835 a public meeting in Mobile, also reacting to presumed colored agitation, set up "volunteer companies" in each neighborhood "provided with arms and ammunition . . . to protect the persons, lives and property of our fellow citizens." [79] Such sentiment was sporadic, but its recurrence reflected both the extent of the anxieties of the white and the inability to find really effective means to control the colored population.

Once picked up by the police, the slave was brought before a city court. A "hearing" rather than a trial followed. An officer presented the charge; the judge, after perhaps some conversation, passed sentence. Most cases were routine, involving violation of ordinances—out after dark without a pass, buying liquor or other goods, creating a disturbance, trespassing, smoking in the streets, etc. Occasionally more serious accusations arose. A Negro struck a white man, an illegal assemblage suggested the existence of colored organization, or, more crucially, a slave plot against the community itself was uncovered. Questions of this magnitude often came before state courts, which met regularly in the cities. But the line of jurisdiction was not always clear. When the Vesey "insurrection" shook Charleston, local authorities established their own tribunal, even though the Governor complained bitterly that the state was the appropriate authority to try the case.

Generally, however, some municipal magistrate handled violations of city ordinances and hence directed the day-to-day punishment of colored offenders. In some places he presided over what was called the "Negro Court," in others the "Mayor's Court," and in still others the "Police Court." No matter what the title, the court's function was usually the same. "The Police or Mayor's Court," an official Charleston publication explained, "is held daily by the Mayor for the trial of riotous and disorderly persons assaulting the peace of the City. This Court has the power to inflict corporal punishment, by whipping, on persons of color, for disturbing the peace of the City." [80]

Something of both the volume of business and the range of cases before these courts is embodied in the annual figures of the Charleston tribunal. Mayor H. L. Pinckney's 1839 report was characteristic: "Slaves and free persons of color were arrested for being out after the beating of tatoo without tickets, fighting and rioting in the streets, following military companies, walking on the Battery contrary to law, bathing horses at prohibited places, theft, and other violations of City and State laws." In a single year the court examined 1424 cases. Two hundred and seventy were discharged, 330 punished in the work house, 26 fined "or committed to workhouse until fine paid," and 115 runaways "disposed of according to law." Owners or guardians paid "penalties" in 398 cases, and in 252 cases slaves were "delivered to the orders" of their masters. In the same period 824 whites came before the Police Court, 545 being "discharged after examination." [81]

The daily entries of a court reporter in Mobile gave a less impersonal view of local judicial proceedings. Covering the Mayor's Court on November 4, 1851, he observed "a general revival of business" in the chambers, "though it was mostly of a *dark* order." In the first cases "slaves Jim and Harry, for engaging in a game of *fisticuffs* Sunday morning, were sentenced to receive twenty-five lashes. Mingo, for a similar offense was warmed up with twenty lashes. Two slaves were committed as runaways, and two for being out after hours were let off by their owners paying the Guardhouse fees." A little later "some ten or a dozen negroes, while indulging in music and dancing without leave or license, in a kitchen in the vicinity of the up-town cotton presses, were broken in upon by the night watch about 12 o'clock Sunday night, and lodged in the Guardhouse. The Mayor caused them to dance to the tune of ten lashes each." [82]

Some items from the court reporter's pad in 1855 indicate that the brisk pace continued and the guard house "corrector" seldom went a day without some activity. More than half the cases before the mayor came under the "Negro ordinances," and males and females both felt the sting of the law. "A Negro woman was chastised for insulting a white woman," ran an ordinary account. [83] "An impudent negro, who resisted a white man was chastised with 25. Another darkey, taken under suspicious circumstances, was served exactly as the impudent one was served," read a March entry. [84] The casual tone of another report suggests the routine handling of colored defendants and the vague charges against them, "Two negroes for being out of place were dealt with accordingly; our reporter says *accordingly*, in this connection means *whipping*." [85] The phrase "out of place" constituted the charge in nearly a quarter of the cases in Mobile in a single year.

Many indictments were, of course, more specific and some, from the standpoint of slave control, much more serious. In 1857 the mayor ordered 100 stripes on one bondsman to be given over a four-day period. "Stephen behaved badly, *cut* and *slashed* about, injured a boy and committed other excesses which were contrary to law." [86] Zack, "working without a badge," got 20 strokes; Mary "for being drunk and disorderly, 20 lashes"; and "two negroes for larceny, 25 and 39 lashes." [87] "A colored disciple of the expressed juice of the corn was sobered by twenty paddles." [88] In addition, sprinkled among the petty decisions, appeared the chilling, final verdicts: a slave hanged "for assault with the intent to kill a white man," or the death penalty for Tom who axed his master during a fight. [89]

Even in the border cities where slaves comprised a much smaller part of the population these cases crowded the dockets of the Police Court. "The number of negroes presented to the court," a reporter noted in 1858, "still continues large in proportion to the [total] number of blacks and whites." [90] December always brought the heaviest traffic, as hired-out slaves, having completed the year's contract, awaited their next assignment. "There have been from four to five 'cellud individs' before His Honor every morning for the last week." [91] But the range of violations ran pretty much the same in Louisville as elsewhere. "Mary Ann, a slave of Fry Lawrence, was sent to the Cave [jail] for hiring her own time." [92] Anderson received 30 stripes for stealing a trunk from a hack, and "Perry, slave of Frank Hyatt," was "ordered to receive thirty lashes on his bare back, well laid on, for insulting Mrs. Wolfe." [93]

Municipal courts were thus the judicial centers of urban slavery. In them lay the final power of discipline over bondsmen outside the master's premises. In the cities this authority took on considerable significance, for even domestics spent a large portion of time away from the owner's place. This meant that authority, so clearly focused on the master in the country, would be at least shared if not dominated by a public tribunal. In the violation of local ordinances the court had exclusive jurisdiction. The judge sometimes sent a black home again for correction, but he did not have to and usually did not. On the other hand, the owner had no voice in the treatment of his slaves before the bench. At most he could commute a whipping of his slave by the payment of a fine. This diffusion of power was a unique feature of bondage in the towns. Some proponents of slavery felt such fracturing of authority weakened the system. As Judge Ruffin of North Carolina put it: "We cannot allow the right of the master to be brought into discussion in the Courts of justice. The slave, to remain a slave, must be made sensible that there is no appeal from his master . . ." [94] Yet the exigencies of control in the metropolis necessarily reduced the position of the master as it raised the power of local courts.

If the whites were never satisfied with the system and its enforcement, the Negroes thought it imposing enough. "This system of police usually answers its atrocious purpose very well," wrote Benjamin Drew in introducing the testimony of escaped slaves. "It wields the lash against offenders, and instils into the oppressed the fear requisite to suppress any overt act toward gaining their rights as human beings." And "incidentally, it hinders the commission of crimes, prevents mobs (of colored persons), and keeps the street quiet, and is so far beneficent in its action." [95]

VII

Public enforcement agencies, of course, operated within laws established by local governments. The difficulties of control, the persistence of the problems, and continued public criticism prompted officials to recast their legislative framework many times in the ante-bellum period. Councils added new categories to the regulations of Negroes or altered the severity of the punishment involved. Occasionally, changes were required by modification of state Black Codes, but most stemmed from local problems and the attempts by towns to strengthen the web of restraints around urban slaves and free Negroes. The tendency was toward more rules rather than less, toward complexity rather than simplicity, toward harshness rather than leniency. And the striking feature about these "Negro ordinances" was their similarity. By the 1850's municipal codes, on this question at least, were almost interchangeable.

The omnibus "Ordinance concerning Negroes" adopted by Richmond in 1857 provides a convenient model. [96] It drew together old provisions, discarded a few that had been superseded, and included a small number of very minor new items. The legislation began by asserting that "the word 'negro' shall be construed to mean 'mulatto' as well as negro," leaving a closer definition of race to state law.[97] The first few sections dealt with the pass system, which governed the conditions under which a slave could be absent from his "owner's or employer's tenement" at night ("two hours after sunset"). The pass designated "the particular place or places" where he could go and the "purpose for which the slave may go." Richmond's law included in this instance a unique feature: if the black had the same destination each night, he might be issued a monthly pass, "provided the assent of the occupier of such house, to the slave's staying there, be signified by signing his name on the back of the pass." This variation reflected the large amount of "boarding out" and "living out" that developed in the city's tobacco and iron industries.

If picked up without the written permission, the slave "may be punished with stripes," though "the justice before whom the offense is tried may, in his discretion," commute the whipping to a fine paid by the owner or employer. A white who forged such a pass could be fined up to $20; a free black or slave caught signing a ticket was "punished with stripes." The equation of free and bonded Negroes was characteristic of all urban regulations except, of course, when the law dealt with a specific master-servant relationship. Some towns had a portion of their code devoted to free colored, but the most important sections came under the more general heading which emphasized slave control.

Subsequent sections of the ordinance prohibted a slave from riding in a "licensed hack or carriage without the written consent of his owner"; violations brought fines of $5 to $20 for cab drivers and stripes "not exceeding thirty nine at any one time" for bondsmen. Others declared that "no negro shall walk or be in the Capitol Square or in the grounds adjacent to

the City Spring, City Hall, or Athenæum" or "within the enclosures of any of the places known as city grounds" unless
to "attend to a white person, being an infant, or sick, or
infirm, or to serve their owner or employer." Likewise, colored people were excluded from "any public burying ground"
unless to "attend the funeral of his owner or employer, or
some of his family."

Some prohibitions on conduct were absolute and could not
be allowed even with the permission of the master. "No negro
shall smoke tobacco . . . on any public street or public place."
"No negro shall in the night carry a cane unless of age or
infirmity," and no more than five could stand "at the corner
of a street or public alley." Even street etiquette was carefully
governed. "Negroes shall not at any time stand on a sidewalk
to the inconvenience of persons passing by. A negro meeting
or overtaking, or being overtaken by a white person . . . shall
pass on the outside; and if it be necessary to enable such white
person to pass, shall immediately get off the sidewalk." Moreover, if any colored person "use provoking language" or "insolent or menacing gestures to a white person, or speak aloud
any blasphemous or indecent word, or make any loud or
offensive noise by conversation or otherwise, in any streets or
other public place," he was subject to the usual 39 lashes.

The restrictions on assemblage were equally explicit. Not
only did the ordinance forbid the organization of any "secret society of negroes" and declare any gathering of five
—"whether free or not"—illegal, but it also required that the
areas around churches be cleared of all colored people within
thirty minutes after "divine service." In search of these un-
authorized meetings, police could enter any lot or tenement
and arrest everyone involved of both races. A justice could
then fine the free and order the slaves whipped.

The law put some restraint on whites as well as Negroes.
They could not sell to slaves any "ardent spirits, firearms,

sword, bowie-knife, or any offensive weapon of any kind whatsoever, or any balls, shot, gunpowder, or other ammunition." And penalties were stiff: "$20 for each and every article so sold, given, lent or otherwise furnished." Half that sum was assessed for traffiicking in medicine and drugs, though this did not apply when the slave had a written order from his owner or employer "specifying the kind and amount" to be purchased. The unauthorized use of medicine by a colored person brought the heavy punishment—"not exceeding thirty-nine stripes."

This comprehensive ordinance also embraced the regulations on hiring out, living out, and boarding out.[98] Violations usually involved top penalties for both slave and master. Finally, the code contained a certain protection for the bondsman: "If any person shall unlawfully assault and beat a slave, he may—if a white person—be fined not less than one, nor more than twenty dollars; and if a free negro may be so fined or punished by stripes at the discretion of the justice."

Other problems—such as restrictions on selling any goods to slaves, certain privileges granted Negroes in the market, and the treatment of bondsmen on the job—were handled elsewhere in the municipal code, as were regulations covering the hospital, jail, and workhouse. But the normal range of controls could be found conveniently in the 1857 ordinance. By the last ante-bellum decade every city had developed a similarly detailed body of laws "concerning Negroes." The embodiment of long experience, experiment, and judicial interpretation, these ordinances provided the legal framework for urban slavery.

State governments, of course, laid down the broad definitions and general rules governing the "peculiar institution," and municipal legislation could not conflict with them. But conditions in the town required a much more complex and elaborate system of regulation than those needed in the countryside. Most especially, public agencies had to exercise much of the authority wielded by masters on plantations and farms. When the slave moved away from his owner's premises, he had to be picked up, so to speak, by local ordinances which governed his relationship with the rest of the community. To the extent that this law was uniform, predictable, and routine, he escaped the caprice of his master and in so doing lost something of his bondage. "A city slave is almost a free citizen," wrote Frederick Douglass, comparing life in Baltimore with his earlier days on the Maryland countryside. He "enjoys privileges altogether unknown to the whip-driven slave on the plantation." [99] Still much less than a citizen, lacking even the minimum rights of the free Negro, yet different from an ordinary slave, the urban slave contrived a life that had no analogue in the rest of the South.

Chapter Five

———

THE CONDITIONS OF LIFE

THE LATITUDE of the urban slave did not come from the immediate surroundings within the owner's house and yard. Indeed, here the arrangement of life was designed to remind him of his servitude. If the historic "free air" of the city existed outside, the atmosphere of slavery inside was confining. The small, windowless room in the quarters, the narrow balcony with its view of the back of the master's house, the high brick walls which enclosed the modest yard, all comprised somehow a physical statement of the slave's status. The setting was not without its charm—the enclosure usually had a garden kept green and lush by the South's long, moist growing season; the walls and tall buildings blocked out the hot summer sun, except for the brief hours at noon; during the day children, white and black, played on the paved piazza below where the master's family might later enjoy the cool evening air. Yet what might appear comfortable and even elegant to some was to the slave a constant reminder of his condition.

So long as he remained inside the enclosure, there was no escape from the demands and supervision of the owner. Of course, the job had to be done; if the bondsman worked at home the chores were understood and routine. The master, or more likely the mistress, would see to it that he was kept busy enough and that any slack time was somehow utilized. But even after the directives had ceased and a chance to re-

tire from the whites appeared, there was no place to go. The
room along the veranda was mainly for sleeping; it had, at
best, a bed, a piece of furniture or two, and a clothes trunk.
Besides it was no retreat. The owner or any of the family
could easily call, since the room was only a few feet from
the house.

The high walls around the lot played a role, too. They
heightened the sense of confinement which the enclosure conveyed. Standing in the center of the yard, the slave could see
on all sides the brick encasement. Green vines, a tree, some
shrubs, or perhaps a shed or outbuilding would break the red
monotony of the brick; irregular heights of abutting buildings
and walls created an uneven cornice on the compound. But
no matter where he turned, he found the forbidding masonry
barriers before him. This physical character of the enclosure
was the central fact of the slave's immediate environment. It
circumscribed his movement; it inhibited his contact with the
outside world; it threw him back on his master. The design
itself expressed his subordination. To the whites the walls
might suggest privacy and security; to the blacks they meant
confinement and restraint.

Many slaves usually shared the same enclosure. Sometimes
there were "couples," joined by the master in slavery's unique
way. If they had lived there together for a few years there
might be children—"a family." More likely, however, the
slave had been acquired when there was a need or had been
handed down in the white household. In either event, the
range of ages would be wide and the relationships among the
slaves vague. In the last ante-bellum decades females so outnumbered men that even the haphazard earlier balance between the sexes could not be sustained. This meant that whatever harmony developed in the yard would be fortuitous and,
except in unusual circumstances, the result mainly of the owner's judgment in handling his slaves. Coercion could at best

keep peace; it is doubtful that it produced much genuine happiness.

That tensions arose in the yard is not surprising. Sources of discord among slaves were many. Assignment of rooms, allocation of tasks, relations with members of the master's family, for example, required decisions which could not have pleased everyone. Most controversies of this kind were settled privately by the owner, but enough came into the Police Courts to indicate that the walls around a town lot contained a good deal of trouble. On a plantation the division between field hand and house servant constituted the major cleavage. In the city, distinctions among Negroes, as among whites, were finer, and so led to a larger range of differences and higher incidence of conflict. The instability of urban slavery, especially its steady numerical decline in the 'forties and 'fifties, concealed this problem to some extent. The thinning out of blacks within the enclosure no doubt reduced the pressure. Yet frictions stemming from living at close quarters were seldom absent, and where crowding prevailed the problem persisted.

For slaves who were part of modest holdings the physical surroundings were more satisfactory. A Richmond visitor found the quarters "dirty, and scantily furnished" but "the inmates looked strong and healthy. I saw no delicate, half starved mothers; no sore-eyed, sore-eared, miserable looking children; on the contrary, anyone free from the prejudice of colour, would say, they are some of the finest, and most healthy-looking children in the country." [1] The yard and the room provided ample space if not freedom of movement. A windowless room 10′ x 15′ might not be comfortable, but it could be large enough for sleeping and keeping clothes and personal items. Whenever summer nights became unbearable, it was possible to lie on the balcony and catch a little breeze. And many quarters had fireplaces which cut the edge of the winter's cold. At the outer end of the balcony was a privy for the use of the blacks. In addition, since all these facilities were but a few steps from the master's door, the servant areas were kept reasonably clean and uncluttered.

Whether the master owned one slave or a dozen, the environment of the enclosure seemed much better than Negroes enjoyed elsewhere. Certainly travelers thought so, and masters viewed urban slaves as a privileged lot. Their proximity to the whites assured them of minimum living standards, and life in the yard had at least a surface gentility. Yet, for the slave, the compound had fatal handicaps. The confinement embodied in the walls and the isolation from the outside, the constant presence of the master's family, the utter lack of privacy—all created an oppressive "togetherness" that the Negroes shunned. On the plantation, the testimony is strong that slaves preferred to be house servants, thereby escaping the heavy work in the field. In the cities, where the options were greater, they left the owner's house whenever possible.

The slave expressed this preference in many ways. If given a chance to "live out," he took it. In the last decades before the war, urban slaves increasingly managed to have this privilege. Savannah's local census taker came to terms with this fact in 1848 simply by enumerating blacks "in the place of abode, without recourse to owners," because it was "so much in vogue at the present time, of permitting this class of our population to live in streets or lanes by themselves." [2] Municipal courts discovered that a considerable part of their "Negro cases" came from slaves who had opted for the outside without permission. The difficulty of keeping blacks in the yard at night showed how strongly they felt about gaining freedom of movement, even if illegal, rather than remaining in the highly supervised life of the yard. Whites thought it strange after the war that former slaves should leave "their comfortable homes" for some "miserable shanties" even when offered new privileges and wages. But the dislike of the enclosure was deep; when given the opportunity either in bondage or freedom, the blacks left it.[3] "Almost every house servant in the city has left his or her place," wrote a Savannah physician a month before Appomattox. "They do *nothing* and are huddled up in small buildings." [4]

For those who left the yard, then, some independence was more important than modest comfort. And it had to be, because few who sought their own housing found anything as adequate as the enclosure. No doubt occasionally some bettered themselves, living as a single domestic in a white household or, probably less often, with free colored people. But most took what they could find—a room above a stable, a little space in an unused shed, a shanty converted for sleeping. As transients, blacks could ask for little; as slaves, they were expected to demand little. The living-out contract was a convenience for masters and whites, not a better housing program for slaves.

Certain exceptions to these haphazard arrangements appeared. From time to time a slave rented an entire house. To be sure it was small and generally of wood. On the Neck in Charleston the practice was most common, and it occurred in the city itself as well. The Old Quarter of New Orleans knew something of this system, and every town saw its development to some extent. The few contemporary descriptions of these buildings are seldom informative and never very flattering. Fire reports merely list them as "dwellings," and censuses mention them only in passing. But for a few slaves a "home" of this kind was the outer edge of the "peculiar institution." In these cases, then, a Negro might not have his freedom, but he had lost a considerable part of his bondage. Life on the job still involved servitude, customary inhibitions still circumscribed his movements outside of the house;

but inside, at least, he could do as he pleased surrounded by whatever furnishings he might be able to assemble.

To some slaves, home was a dormitory for ten to fifty, or sometimes as high as a hundred, others like him. In Richmond and Charleston this arrangement was not unusual, though it had probably disappeared in the border cities by 1850. Containing only males, and ordinarily younger ones, these buildings housed a portion of the slaves working in the larger enterprises such as tobacco, iron, or railroads. Probably no cooking took place on the premises, and often no whites resided there. Free from the constant supervision of their masters, these hirelings had a latitude far greater than could be found in the enclosure. But the condition of the housing disclosed that the measure of freedom was not purchased easily. Rooms were small, crowded, unlighted, probably unheated, with only board partitions separating the "tenements." A large fence generally enclosed the barracks, but discipline over the residents depended on the police. This environment bred trouble, and blacks living there were seldom strangers in municipal courts. "The neighborhoods of these rows," a Charleston grand jury asserted in 1856, "are constantly disturbed by the fights, quarrels and turbulence of the inmates." [5]

Not much more satisfactory were the conditions of those who lived out illegally. Since they had no permission from their masters, they dwelt in semi-concealment. Many paid a small rent to whites or free colored who would co-operate in the deception. Others simply used whatever space they could find. The need for secrecy governed the character of this housing. Shanties along commercial alleyways or back streets, lofts of stables, abandoned outbuildings of every kind attracted irregular tenants. Police records indicate that blacks often occupied these places for months at a time, and contemporary complaints suggest that cities were never able to stop the practice. This vagabond life no doubt attracted an order of slaves on a par with whites who existed the same way. Yet many were merely slaves who could not get permission to live out, but who wanted to escape their owner's yard.

II

For a slave, no matter where he resided, a house was never a home. Families could scarcely exist in bondage. The law recognized no marriage contract: *de facto* arrangements could be broken by any number of events; offspring became the property of the master, not the children of parents. These were the general conditions of slavery. Life in the city only amplified the unhappy consequences that flowed from them. To be sure, urban proximity permitted wider opportunity for the choice of a mate, and "living out" secured a portion of privacy to some which was almost wholly absent in rural areas. Yet the greater instability of slavery in the towns meant that attachments were seldom permanent, that promiscuity became normal, that racial mixing was common. As the number of male blacks declined in the pre-war decades, these characteristics dominated the relationships of the sexes in every metropolis.

A great deal of fiction often surrounded the connection between male and female slaves. A "marriage ceremony" might unite the two, with the master or even a minister presiding over the affair with genuine or mock solemnity. Newspapers often spoke of "husband" and "wife" as if the term had its ordinary connotations. Thus the *Mobile Daily Advertiser* could routinely report in 1851 that "Negro man Alfred and his wife Mary were brought before the Mayor, charged with living and keeping house by themselves, without a permit from the Mayor as required by law." [6] Even local ordinances gave apparent legal sanction to such connections. Louisville's central police ordinance, for example, listed the responsibilities of the watch which began: "They shall arrest all slaves found away from home without a pass or good excuse (except a slave found at his wife's home)." [7]

Day-to-day etiquette often endorsed the fiction. A man might visit his "wife" in the enclosure or even live with her. Her children called him "father." Friends considered the two a couple. Small bits of property would be shared. But these conventions masked the reality. Whatever bond existed could be easily broken. If either master moved, one partner went with him; a variety of circumstances could lead to a sale; the owner's death might bring the disposition of all blacks in the estate. And since the union rested on the consent of some white, the permission might at any time be removed. The case of a Charleston Negro illustrates much of the difficulty. He had been "married" for some time before his master sold him to one woman and his wife and children to another. "Though he was living in the same town with them," a traveler related, "he was never allowed to see them; he would be beaten within an ace of his life if he ventured to go to the corner of the street." [8]

The logistics, too, inhibited stability. "In cities, also," wrote a Northern sympathizer with slavery, "husbands and wives most commonly belong to different families. Laboring apart, and having their meals apart, the domestic bonds of domestic life are few and weak." Thus "a slave, his wife, and their children, around that charmed centre, a family table, with its influences of love, instruction, discipline, . . . are too seldom seen." And the explanation was fundamental. "To encourage and protect their homes generally would be in effect to put an end to slavery as it is." [9]

Even the best of circumstances and the most considerate masters could not give real permanence to a slave couple. When Nathan attempted to marry Letitia in Louisville in 1841, he had to do more than convince her it was a good idea; he also had to make sure she would be permitted to stay in the city. In April his employer, writing on behalf of Mrs. G. M. Bibb, his owner, asked Letitia's master's consent to the union. He added, however, that "Mrs. Bibb would be sorry to see them married and separated" and wanted assurances that Letitia's owner Orlando Brown expected to let her "remain here." [10] When no such guarantee was given, Nathan himself offered to "look out for a good master and prevail on some of his friends to buy his wife." But his employer, who thought Nathan a "most trustworthy and faithful servant," reminded his slave that there was "a very great risk" in arranging "a sale to anybody" because of the ever-present threat of a subsequent out-of-town sale.[11] The records do not disclose the outcome of the bargaining, but Nathan and Letitia must certainly have come to understand that the bonds of slavery were a good deal stronger than the bonds of matrimony.

Nor were other conditions of the "marriage" any more friendly to its success. The husband had no authority. His bondage deprived him of the status of breadwinner; he could neither provide nor protect. His children belonged to his wife's master. His first responsibility was not to his family but to his owner. "The annihilation by slavery, to a great extent, of the father in the domestic relations of the slaves," wrote Nehemiah Adams in 1854, "is inseparable from it, as it exists at present." [12] The woman's role was more important, though not more easily managed. The care of children, at least until grown or sold, was hers. To the extent that there was a family center, she was it. Her spouse came to visit her, shared her room, even took her name ("Mary's Alfred"). Except for the sexual relation, this union bore little resemblance to the marriage institution that whites understood.

Under these circumstances family ties were weak at best. Male and female slaves found their pleasure and love wherever they could, knowing that attachments could only be tem-

porary if not casual. Some contrived a more permanent arrangement, but their number was small. Generally relations were neither prolonged nor monogamous. Urban conditions provided many opportunities for such contacts and thus permitted the regular release of the elemental frustrations which afflicted many plantations. The very looseness of the mating, however, made a meaningful family unit even more difficult.

For the children of such a marriage, there could be no ordinary family life. "In effect the slave has no father," Adams noted sadly. Even the connection of the mother was bound to be tenuous since she knew full well that separation might come at any time. "Maternal attachments in slave mothers are singularly shortlived," the same observer wrote. Nor was it hard to explain "the cause of this limited parental affection. From the first moment of maternal solicitude, the idea of property on the part of the owner in the offspring ... becomes a neutralizing element" and "prevents the inviolable links of natural affection from reaching deep into the heart." [13]

The displacement of the family by the institution of slavery came home trenchantly to Adams when he visited a Sabbath school for colored children in Savannah. At the end, the superintendent told the children: " 'You must all try to be good children, wherever you are, remembering you are never out of God's sight. If you love and obey him, if you are good children at home, what a comfort you will be to your (*I* expected the words *fathers* and *mothers*) 'masters and mistresses.' " The "perfect naturalness with which other names came to fill the place of *father* and *mother*, brought to my heart the truth, the slaves generally have no homes." [14]

In addition, the constant shortage of young men in the cities increased this basic instability. In Charleston as early as 1820, female slaves between the ages of 14 and 25 outnumbered males by 2255 to 1609.[15] Twenty years later the disparity was still there. Between 10 and 24 years old, there were 2313 women and 1825 men; in the next category (from 24 to 36) the figures were 2312 and 1581.[16] In New Orleans female slaves of all ages exceeded males 4646 to 2709 in 1820, a proportion that did not decline in the next four decades and which was most marked in the "marriageable" age bracket.[17] Border cities showed the same trend, with the ratio in the younger set running almost two to one.[18] These statistics meant, of course, that, even if other factors had been more normal, many slave girls could not have found an eligible mate.

Richmond alone escaped this problem. There the widespread use of slaves in industrial enterprises put a premium on young males. Indeed, this preference created something of the same situation in reverse. In the First Ward, which embraced most of the manufacturing, the 1860 census listed 2880 men and only 1345 women. In the other two districts the sexes were evenly balanced.[19] This distortion had not always been present; in 1820 females outnumbered males by a narrow margin, and ten years later the proportion had shifted only slightly. It was the growing emphasis on tobacco and iron which produced the unique concentration of black youths in the town. What was crucial, however, was that no city developed a population distribution which might promote healthier and more stable relationships between the sexes.

III

If the colored population suffered a constant shortage of men in the cities, the white imbalance ran the other way. Among them the problem was not enough women. Every urban area in the South faced the same situation. In old established and less dynamic places like Charleston the deficit was modest; but in the more rapidly expanding towns like Mobile males outnumbered females more than two to one. The exact figures in 1840 were 5655 to 2607.[20] In the same year New Orleans had a surplus of over 10,000 men. The greatest gap moreover was always among young adults. Taking 1840 again, Louisville's census showed 2853 men and 1898 women in their twenties, and 1554 men and 1010 women in their thirties. Such disparities were always largest in the periods of swift urban growth; later the tendency was toward balance. By 1860 most cities approached a new equilibrium; yet for forty years the shortage of white women was considerable and continuous.[21]

For town slaves this imbalance had important consequences. The simplest arithmetic suggested that white men would find some compensation with colored women. In fact this happened on a large scale. Some intercourse between the races was to be expected; the extent in Southern cities, however, was dictated by these demographic facts. Defenders of slavery often admitted this, though inadvertently. South Carolina's Governor Hammond, for instance, while defending Dixie against the charge of racial mixing, declared that "its character and extent . . . are grossly and atrociously exaggerated," and that "irregularities" were "perpetrated for the most part, in the cities." "Very few mullattoes," he continued, "are reared on our plantations." Even his conclusion that "the number of the mixed breed . . . is infinitely small" had to carry a reservation about "the towns," where he blamed "natives of the North or foreigners." [22]

Relations between white men and colored women were common enough; so much so that local courts could seldom enforce effectively the general laws against such "amalgamation." [23] Southern writers avoided dwelling on something they considered unfortunate and admitted it only in the most circumscribed terms. Yet it could scarcely be concealed. Mulatto offspring could be seen everywhere, and especially, as Governor Hammond had observed, in the cities. "Any lady is ready to tell you who is the father of all the mulatto children in everybody's household but her own," wrote Mary Chesnut, adding, "My disgust is sometimes boiling over." [24] In Mobile and New Orleans vague allusions to early French and Spanish populations masked publicly what everyone knew privately. The practice pervaded "the entire society," as Olmsted was told, but the urban situation, with its denser populations, frequent contacts, and shortage of white women, increased the incidence of these unions. [25]

A young Cincinnatian, who visited Mobile in 1859 and concluded that slavery "is *not* morally or politically wrong," observed that "there are many more mulattoes and quadroons here than negroes" and that he knew of "few southern boys who would not sleep with Negresses." "These girls of mixed or African blood," he explained, "preserve the virtue of the white girls here, the same as women of loose character do in the North." [26] A Virginian in New Orleans found much the same thing, though he found it "somewhat revolting." "The fair skin and the Quadroon here," he wrote in his diary, "intermingle promiscuously." [27]

In New Orleans interracial relations became so common that a public tolerance if not acceptance grew up. "Individuals there are, of the first *respectability*," wrote a resident, "who take for their bed companions not only the Quadroon, but those of darker hue, and frequently those of the darkest shade, and live with them as wife; and by whom they have large families." [28] In the case of light-skinned women New Orleans even developed a kind of ritual. "Everything being satisfactorily arranged," Olmsted reported, "a tenement in a certain quarter of the town is usually hired, and the couple move into it and go to housekeeping—living as if they were married." [29] Later, of course, the man left for a white wife, and his mistress returned to colored society, or, when a slave, to another master.

Generally, however, such alliances were covert, casual, and

cursory. Free black women as well as slaves participated, some willingly, some resignedly, some resentfully. Whether the father took any responsibility for the offspring was quite haphazard. Some did; others did not. But in any case, it was the mother who had to shoulder the burden. In the longer run the consequences fell upon the children who took their status from their mother. The 1860 census listed 12 per cent of the colored people in Dixie as "mulattoes," a figure which underestimated the number of mixed bloods, since it was calculated wholly on appearance.[30] The proportion in the cities ran much higher. In places like St. Louis, Baltimore, and New Orleans it approached half. The prevalence of extra-marital relations which these statistics reflect further weakened family ties among urban slaves. Not only did the numerical imbalance between the sexes make normal mating difficult, but even when the match was made, the integrity of the bond was never free from outside incursion.

Nothing, then, in the city situation gave much encouragement to the establishment of stable families for slaves. Occasionally, maybe even oftener, it was possible for a Negro couple to discover each other, get the master's permission to "wed," "live out" in a rented house, have children, and create a life within the system that at many points approached that of the whites outside. Yet even this little contentment was necessarily precarious. "You may think you see bright spots," wrote a former slave, "but look at the surroundings of these spots, and you will see nothing but gloom and darkness. While toiling industriously, and living with a dear family in comparative comfort and happiness, the city slave (whose lot is thought to be so easy) suddenly finds himself on the auction block, knocked down to the highest bidder, and carried far and forever from those dearer than life, leaving behind a beloved wife and tender and helpless children" who are "all bereft, in a moment, of husband, father and protector." [31]

IV

If the city slave's lot was "thought to be easy," it was in part because his clothing was obviously so much superior to that of his rural counterpart. "I have seen large gangs coming in from the country, and these contrast much in their general appearance with the town negroes. The latter are dressed expensively, and frequently more elegantly than the whites." [32] The same thing struck James Stirling as he traveled across South Carolina's back country. "The negroes one sees at the stations of the railways have a very different look from the smart servants of Charleston. Yesterday was Sunday, and yet some of these poor creatures who we saw hanging about the stations were absolutely in rags; some, too, had marvellously foul linen." [33]

Slave clothing on plantations was, of course, drab and meager.[34] In some instances the pride of the owner resulted in something more than the essentials, perhaps an extra dress or two, a bright handkerchief for the head and some cheap jewelry for the women, and a felt hat, a cotton shirt and wool trousers for the men. More commonly, the rural slave lived in coarse "Negro cloth" and "Negro brogans," usually mended and remended, more often than not dirty and torn. While in Richmond, Olmsted saw many of these slaves just "in from the farms near the town," wearing "clothing of coarse gray 'negro cloth' that appeared as if made by contract, without regard to the size of the particular individual to whom it had been allotted, like penitentiary uniforms." But he did see "a few" who had "a better suit of coarse blue cloth, expressly made for them evidently, for 'Sunday clothes.' " [35]

Both the experience of travelers and the stereotype of the plantation slave produced the same image of country blacks. The physical appearance of urban Negroes invariably upset the normal expectation. "To see slaves with broadcloth suits, well-fitting and nice-ironed fine shirts, polished boots, gloves, umbrellas for sunshades, the best of hats, their young men with their blue coats and bright buttons, in the latest style, white Marseilles vests, white pantaloons, brooches in their shirt bosoms, gold chains, elegant sticks ... was more than I was prepared to see," wrote a Northern minister about Savannah.[36]

Olmsted saw the same thing in Richmond. "Some were dressed with laughably foppish extravagance," he wrote, "and a great many in clothing of the most expensive materials, and in the latest style of fashion." Walking down the main streets, he reported, "were many more well-dressed and highly-dressed colored people than white." Among the "dark gentry the finest French cloths, embroidered waistcoats, patent leather shoes, resplendent brooches, silk hats, kid gloves, and *eau de mille fleurs*, were quite as common as among the New York 'dry-goods clerks,' in their Sunday promenades, in Broadway." Nor were the women any less spectacular. "Many of the colored ladies were dressed not only expensively, but with good taste and effect, after the latest Parisian mode. Many of them were quite attractive in appearance, and some would have produced a decided sensation in any European drawing room."[37]

These two descriptions caught the town slave on Sunday when he no doubt was putting on a show. Yet on weekday evenings his dress was only slightly less subdued. "Rusticus," a country visitor to Charleston in 1822, was somewhat appalled by it all. "I saw as I conceived, the figure of an old acquaintance walking in front of me," he wrote; "his manner and dress were apparently the same, I therefore quickened my pace, came up, and slapt him on the shoulders, but, to my no small surprize (and equally so no doubt to the buck blacky) a sable Dandy stared me in the face." Somewhat chagrined, though "of course no apology was made for the mistake," he hurried on. "I had not, however, proceeded far . . . when I overtook a couple of well dressed ladies." They were clothed chiefly in "the modern large and costly *Leghorn,* trimmed off 'quite in style'—one in a black Canton crape, flounced with silk, black silk stockings (we country people are great observers when we come to town) and a fashionable pair of high heeled shoes to correspond, a fashionable half handkerchief trimmed with lace, adorned the neck, a parasol and bag (reicule) occupied the hands; her companion was no less fine, the only difference consisted in a white muslin frock in the same dashing style with corresponding 'accompaniment'—pretty faces must be under such bonnets, I thought, but lo! one was jet black and the other copper colored!" His conclusion drawn from this episode suggests how much the scene upset widely held images. "*How much* could either *of you do* in a Cotton or Rice field?" [38]

Regular work clothes of course did not maintain the gaudy standards of Sunday or evening wear; and for many, such standards were never met. Yet around the clock the urban slave was better dressed than his country brother. Since most of them were domestics this is not surprising. Whites did not want shabby servants around the house, and an ill-clad Negro reflected on the care and taste of the master. Slaves on heavier jobs usually had adequate clothing appropriate to their tasks. Indeed, the only constant references to poorly clad colored people in the towns involved either freedmen or those working in municipal street gangs.[39]

If the interests of the owner dictated good apparel, the bondsman was happy to co-operate. He not only readily accepted items specially bought for him, but he also took hand-me-downs from the master. In addition, when he saved a little money clothes were one of the few items he could buy with the ready consent of the owner. More importantly, though, a good suit somehow raised his status, or at least removed a part of the inherent indignity of his position. He now looked less a slave, more a man. Whites often mistook the improved bearing and self-respect of the well-dressed slave as pride in his master. Pride there may have been, but the significance of the clothes was that they carried the Negro, in a superficial but nonetheless important manner, away from the center of slavery toward the edge of freedom. The results often seemed ludicrous to observers, but to the bondsman it was no trivial matter.

Perhaps the last acts of two slave suicides in New Orleans in the 1850's convey the symbolism involved. In one, Sampson had saved up $1200 to buy his freedom in an arrangement with his owner. After succeeding "by long years of patient toil," he discovered that the man who was "banking" his money had in fact spent it all. "This turned the mind of the poor wretch," the *Bee* reported, "and caused him to commit the desperate deed." "Before killing himself," the story continued, "he had dressed himself in his best clothes and left a request written on a slate that he should be buried in them." [40] In the other case, an elderly woman hanged herself. But before "committing the fatal act," the *Daily Delta's* account ran, "the old woman had dressed herself in her best clothes, and was perfectly neat and clean, with the exception of the bottom of the stockings which were soiled while walking in the yard in quest of a cord." [41]

Whites as well as Negroes understood this deeper meaning of clothes. When apologists defended the system they often called attention to the appearance of town slaves; when they criticized the looseness of bondage in the cities, they emphasized the same thing. "The taste for dress and the extravagant gratification of it to which these people are so prone, have ... a very demoralizing effect," a Savannah editor contended. Observing that a turban or handkerchief for the head was good enough for peasants, he noted that "with our *city* coloured population the old fashioned turban seems fast disappearing. It is too humble—it is not up to the times. It may do for some veteran 'mommer' or contented drudge," but not for others. "This ambition of dress is absolutely a disease. The lady's maid treads upon the heels of her mistress in this regard, and *Dick* and *Jack* ... leave their more neglected masters far behind." [42]

The droll account of slave dress in Charleston by "Rusticus" in 1822 contained the same attitude. After his elaborate description of the blacks he asked, "how shall I distinguish our coloured Dandies and Dandresses from a Gentleman or Lady?" And referring to an alleged Negro plot led by Denmark Vesey which had been uncovered just a few months before, he added "I certainly do think that after our *late warning* we should not suffer this class to continue its encroachments." He wanted a "line of distinction in *every respect*" to be drawn, "and that so broad, that there shall be no encroachment upon it." For a fundamental solution, this South Carolinian urged the revival of the old state laws which prescribed the kind of dress that colored people could have. Meanwhile, he suggested that the city require them to wear "some distinguished badge, both before and behind, that we may distinguish their *false colours* 'front and rear.' " [43]

"Rusticus" realized that some might not grasp the significance of the clothes question. "No doubt to many, the subject may appear trifling, ridiculous, and unworthy of serious notice, (but they must not forget that often from trifling causes great *events* arise) but if it was not to prevent an evil, *present* or *future*, why did those who preceded us make *that law?*" And for those who doubted the question was real, he invited them to take a stroll, and "he will soon satisfy himself of the *appearance, impudence, and bold effrontery* of this class." [44] If the city council did not see the issue clearly, the Charleston grand jury did. The next month a section of its presentment read: "We recommend to the consideration of the legislature the regulation of the apparel of persons of colour—as we conceive the expensive dress worn by many of them highly destructive of their honesty and industry and subversive of that subordination which policy requires to be enforced." [45]

The memorialists put their remedy bluntly. Negroes should be permitted to dress "only in coarse stuffs, such as coarse woolens or worsted stuffs for winter—and coarse cotton stuffs for summer—felt hats, and coarse cotton handkerchiefs." The purpose was obvious. "Every distinction should be created between the whites and the negroes, calculated to make the latter feel the superiority of the former." Even the exception to this rule underlined the objective. "It is not the intention of your memorialists to embrace in these sumptuary regulations 'livery servants,' as liveries, however costly, are still badges of servitude." [46]

Some Northerners, too, perceived the larger importance of slave clothing. Perhaps the most celebrated commentary, *Uncle Tom's Cabin*, was also the most illustrative in this regard. At each stage of his journey Tom is dressed for the part. From Kentucky to New Orleans to Louisiana's cotton country, his status and life are expressed in his apparel. When first seen in his modest farm cabin, he owns a few "coarse but clean" shirts; in his New Orleans position he has "a well brushed broadcloth suit, smooth beaver, glossy boots, faultless waistbands and collar, . . . looking respectable enough to be a Bishop of Carthage"; when he arrives at the plantation he becomes one of the "men and women in soiled and tattered garments" who tend the crops in the field. [47]

The dramatic moment in this progress comes, significantly enough, after Tom has been sold from New Orleans to the cotton plantation. His new master, Simon Legree, defrocks him in front of the rest of the recently acquired slaves on the boat moving up the river.

Stopping opposite to Tom, who had been attired for sale in his best broadcloth suit, with well-starched linen and shining boots, he briefly addressed him as follows:

"Stand up."

Tom stood up.

"Take off that stock!" and, as Tom, encumbered by his fetters, proceeded to do it, he assisted him, by pulling it, with no gentle hand, from his neck, and putting it in his pocket.

Legree now turned to Tom's trunk, which, previous to this, he had been ransacking, and, taking from it a pair of old pantaloons and a dilapidated coat, which Tom had wont to put on about his stablework, he said, liberating Tom's hands from the handcuffs, and pointing to a recess in among the boxes,

"You go there, and put these on."

Tom obeyed, and in a few moments returned.

"Take off your boots," said Mr. Legree.

Tom did so.

"There," said the former, throwing him a pair of coarse, stout shoes, such as were common among the slaves, "put these on."

Legree then auctioned off the rest of Tom's wardrobe and personal things to members of the crew.

"Now, Tom, I've relieved you of any extra baggage, you see. Take mighty good care of them clothes. It'll be long 'fore you get more. I go in for making niggers careful; one suit has to do for one year, on my place." [48]

V

Urban blacks not only dressed much better than those in the countryside, they also ate better. Both the quantity and the quality were higher, and, just as importantly, the diet had greater variety. A Charleston slaveholder, comparing the cost of maintaining bondsmen in a city and on a plantation, put the differences neatly when he said that the town slaves were "in general clothed more expensively, and more daintily fed." [49] This could be expected since so many were domestics and ate out of their master's kitchen. But even those who "lived out" and "boarded out" probably fared better than country house servants and certainly far better than fields hands.

In part, this superiority rested on the low standards found in rural areas among both blacks and whites. Travelers and, later, historians differed on the adequacy of the nutriment A favorable view asserted that "the basic food allowance came to be somewhat standardized at a quart of corn meal and half a pound of salt pork per day for each adult and proportionately for children, commuted or supplemented with sweet potatoes, field peas, sirup, rice, fruit, and 'garden sass' as locality and season might suggest." [50] A less happy view declared that "a peck of corn meal and three or four pounds of salt pork or bacon comprised the basic weekly allowance of the great majority of adult slaves. These rations, to which were frequently added a few supplementary items, usually provided a diet of sufficient bulk but improper balance." [51]

The food of urban slaves differed both in amount and character. Since little was grown on town lots, it was not confined by what might be raised by the master. This meant that the range of edibles consumed would be much greater. Bondsmen usually ate whatever whites did, though not as much and not always openly. "They live with us—" explained a Charleston minister, "eating from the same store-houses, drinking from the same fountains." [52] The result was a varied fare, including not only meat, vegetables, fruit, bread, and milk, but also delicacies—cakes, pies, and candies. Moreover, the location of most cities on oceans and rivers provided seafood through most of the year.

The problem was quantity not variety. Regular meals tended to be spare, and were often made up largely of leftovers. Those living in the enclosures, however, dwelt near the kitchen; and the bulk of female domestics were at least part-time cooks as well. The result was, as the complaints of masters indicate, a good many between-meal snacks and evening raids on the ice box. In some households Negroes did at least part of the shopping, and it can be assumed that they sampled what they were sent to purchase. Owners expected this leakage and distinguished it from stealing. Punishment took place within the house rather than in court. Yet the storehouse was generally kept locked, with the master or mistress holding the key.

Owners with many slaves might do some buying especially for them. In this case economy would dictate simpler and cheaper foods. In addition, corporate owners, or those who had hired Negroes on the job, bought in bulk. The diet in these instances was probably plain; in fact, Charles Dickens became convinced that it was even worse when his hosts refused to allow him to enter the dining hall of a tobacco company in Richmond.[53] Blacks in municipal chain gangs working on streets and bridges were to receive by law "wholesome food, in sufficient quantity, such as bread, meat, rice, corn and vegetables," though it is difficult to know how fully this requirement was met.[54]

The town slave, however, was never wholly dependent on his master or employer for food. The city abounded with grocery stores, bake shops, and confectionaries; the market opened early and closed late; and hucksters plied their trade in all seasons. Legally, merchants could not sell to slaves who did not have a written order from their owner, but this was seldom enforced. Officials considered themselves successful if they kept some control over liquor sales; in fact they generally acted as if purchases of food were legal, if not made in large amounts. The defense of many a grocer before a municipal judge was that he had sold the black some fruit or raspberry juice not whisky. At any rate, few shopkeepers turned down slaves who could pay for the foodstuffs, whether they carried a "ticket" or not.

Shops also grew up that catered to Negroes. Sometimes these were run by free colored, sometimes by whites, and even occasionally by slaves. In Richmond, for example, "Jack, a negro, the property of William Lumpkin, and hired to T.C. Baptist," was charged before the mayor's bench in 1853 "with keeping a cook-shop on Cary street, contrary to law." More significantly, "the evidence showed Jack had been for years engaged at his unlawful business." [55] This case came to the court only a week after the mayor urged a crack-down on free Negroes who ran "cook shops and eating houses" largely frequented by slaves.[56] Every city had many such places, offering a congenial opportunity for eating and drinking and filling in any gaps in the diet offered by the master.

VI

Better housing, clothes, and food meant better health for urban slaves—not better, of course, than whites, but generally superior to slaves in the corn, cane, and rice country. The scarcity of reliable figures on sickness and death and the underdeveloped state of ante-bellum medicine make a more precise generalization hazardous. And the low level of care on plantations and farms reduces somewhat the significance of this comparison.[57] Yet enough evidence remains to suggest something of the health problems of urban blacks, their treatment, and probable results.

The most spectacular medical events in Southern cities were the epidemics which struck each place frequently, though irregularly. Yellow fever and cholera did the greatest damage, but others, like smallpox, were felt, too. These diseases were color blind, afflicting both whites and blacks. It was widely believed that Negroes had developed an immunity to yellow fever which accounted for smaller death rates. "In tropical cities they are classed with the exempts," a prominent Memphis physician noted, "and in New Orleans, Mobile, and other cities in the South, they are also considered as being liable to the disease only to a moderate extent, and in its mildest form." [58] When a medical report in Savannah indicated that a yellow fever epidemic had started with a slave, an editor uttered the folklore of the time: "These facts are remarkable, knowing as we do the comparative exemption of this race." [59] "It not only seldom attacks black persons, but [it] affects them less fatally than whites," the *Charleston Courier* reported in the midst of the 1839 crisis. [60]

Statistics tended to sustain the notion of immunity. In 1858, 619 whites died during the fever epidemic to only 15 "blacks and colored" in the Georgia port. [61] Dr. Bennett Dowler in New Orleans found the same discrepancy. Out of 1800 deaths in the epidemic of 1841 Negroes accounted for only 3, and in 1853 the figures were 14 out of a total of over 10,000. [62] His subsequent study of Charleston underlined the contrast. In seven major outbreaks between 1817 and 1858 whites' losses were 2689 while the Negro dead reached just 52. [63] In fact, however, the blacks enjoyed no genuine immunity. They simply had greater resistance to the toxin of the yellow fever virus, which led to milder cases and fewer fatalities.

Dr. Dowler's analysis also disclosed that, if Negroes avoided

the worst ravages of yellow fever, "they are the most liable
to suffer from *cholera*." [64] Mortality tables never displayed
differences of the same magnitude, but they did show a high
incidence among the blacks. The Richmond experience in
1832 was a grim illustration. Local officials made intensive
preparations to meet the plague as it moved slowly toward the
city. On September 18 they announced they were ready.
"Very little alarm exists among us," an editor assured the
residents.[65] But in the next days the bad news piled up. On
September 25, the Poor House reported that 54 Negroes and
9 whites had died five days earlier; 32 blacks, 13 whites followed in the next three days.[66] Shortly afterwards the *Enquirer* headed its statistical columns with a terse sentence:
"the Cholera has slain many victims in the City since our last
paper." Thirty-nine more colored, 13 more whites were
gone.[67] The epidemic lasted about six weeks; by the time it
subsided, 356 Negroes and 97 whites had perished.[68] Fatalities from this disease were usually more evenly distributed,
but some distortion almost always appeared.

Frequent scourges like this tended to obscure the more
routine health problems of Southern cities. Less dramatic ills
took a high annual toll, for sickness and death were the daily
companions of urban dwellers of both races. Medical practice
was still crude, diagnoses often faulty, and many suffered as
much from the cures as the diseases. General conditions in
the towns moreover scarcely encouraged good health. A
Charleston committee, trying to explain the yellow fever
epidemic of 1858, outlined the scope of the sanitary problems.
"Occupants of lots place the offal, garbage, and particularly
the filth of cowyards openly in the streets" instead of in
boxes, the report complained. "Another and greater evil"
resulted from "houses crowded, or rather packed, from basement to attic, with human beings, and the yards or lots of
small dimensions" cluttered with all kinds of things "and in

some instances hogs and dogs." The filth and refuse were then put outside "with the morning sun beating down on it and disengaging the foeted emanations from streets, alleyways and courts, the poisonous gases of putrifying animals and vegetable matter passing into the atmosphere to the injury of every section of the city, and all classes of society." [69]

Disposition of human waste further complicated the situation. The committee contended that "nearly eight hundred or more privies were reported by the Assistant Health Officer as nuisances or requiring attention of the proper officers." It also condemned the "filthy practice of emptying privies in pits on the same lot. It ought not be permitted in a Southern city." The result was that a large number of people lived "in the midst of so many thousands of sinks of pollution." Bad drains and sewers added hazards. [70] The report indicated that some people were aware of the connection between cleanliness and health, but systematic attacks on this problem were not yet customary.

Morbidity and mortality figures disclose that both races suffered badly from these conditions. The slave's health was, of course, the province of the owner or employer. When a bondsman fell ill, the family doctor attended. In the case of hired-out blacks, the responsibility shifted to the new master. Medical care was expensive, and owners were careful to pass it on to whomever used their slaves. And those seeking to hire Negroes gave assurances not only on food, clothing, and treatment but health as well.

When Sol Cohen's slave Diana fell ill in 1854, he called in Dr. Richard A. Arnold, Savannah's most prominent physician. The patient was lost in two weeks, but the physician's letter about the case suggests the normal conditions of such care in the quarters: "When she was first taken . . . the pestilence was at its height amongst us and neither love nor money could provide nursing." Her husband came and "did all he could," and Arnold prescribed some medicine. In the late stages "some of her Sisters in the Church began to drop in and gossip." The final days saw a confrontation of medicine and folk cures, with the women telling the husband that the doctor was not much good and was "killing her 'witt dat iron ting.'" [71]

This episode not only indicates that first-rate physicians did treat slaves, but also reveals the black's distrust of the care. Another Savannah slaveholder noted that bondsmen placed great faith in "the ability of some persons among the negroes to take the place of physicians in the cure of certain diseases common among them." For many ills, they believed that "some negro man had the ability to prescribe . . . concoctions of a certain nature surpassing medicine prescribed by the most skilled among white men of the medical profession." To illustrate this, he told of a slave child in his yard who had been seized with "infant lock-jaw." A family doctor declared it "to be beyond the help of medical treatment" and hence decided to prescribe turpentine "as an experiment." The mother preferred "tea made of boiled cockroaches." The child was given each and recovered quickly and completely. No doubt both treatments won converts by the infant's sturdy performance. But to slaves, the case bore out the efficacy of their own remedies. [72]

In case of serious sicknesses slaves were taken to hospitals. At first no special ones existed for them; instead they occupied separate sections or wards in city institutions. In Louisville, the Duke of Saxe-Weimar toured the city's most important facilities and found "roomy and well aired apartments for the white patients, and in the basement, those for the negroes and coloured persons." [73] New Orleans had two similar enterprises, Dr. Warren Stone's Maison de Santé and the Circus Street hospital. [74] But the tendency was always toward exclusive and separate treatment. Savannah had a Negro Infirmary with comfortable beds, airy wards, and spacious grounds for the sick and convalescent. Even Natchez supported a two-story Negro hospital, located just opposite the town's slave market.[75]

Occasionally, companies hiring large numbers of slaves established their own. Richmond was best equipped with industrial hospitals. The Tredegar Iron Works, for example, had one, as did the nearby Midlothian Coal Mining Company, which advertised that two physicians were in attendance at all times.[76] And the tobacco factories built infirmaries which were "fitted up in the most comfortable style." [77]

Most medical institutions, though, served a wider colored clientele. In 1855 two Charleston doctors, J.J. Chisholm and F. Peyre Porcher, set up a Negro hospital on the west end of Tradd Street. It accommodated those ill of "all diseases, but contagious ones, no small pox." The newspaper remarked that such an establishment "has been long wanted in our city," and that "the situation, also, is most salubrious." In announcing the opening, the physicians stated that "the usual medical and surgical fees will be charged. Board, with nursing, $2 per week." [78]

Most elaborate was the Slave Hospital in Richmond, opened in 1860. Situated on the river, it had "one of the finest localities in the city for such an institution, surrounded by tobacco factories, out of the bustle and din of business, where quiet, the ever welcome companion of the sick, seems to reign," the *Enquirer* declared. Rambling grounds included a "well for good water," and the building could accommodate 30 to 40 patients and had been "prepared and painted from basement to attic." Moreover, "the most rigid attention is paid to cleanliness—a *sine qua non* to health under any circumstances. On the first floor is the reception room, the laboratory on the second; each room furnished with the necessary beds and furniture." Three doctors under Phillip H. Hancock, resident director, looked after the patients. Rates were the customary $1 a day, or $5 for the week.[79]

Medical costs for slaves in hospitals were generally the same as for whites; in Mobile an ordinance made this arrangement mandatory.[80] Records of these institutions are scarce, and the few available yield only the sketchiest information. Mobile's annual reports gave only cumulative figures. But in 1842 they did list the slaves who had been patients during a seven-month period, the length of their stay, and the cost to the master. Sam was in for only five days, but Abraham spent 109 and Oswald 228. Ned died five days after admission. Each owner paid a dollar a day, a charge that covered "medical treatment and attendance." [81] Major illnesses were more expensive. A New Orleans owner's bill came to $47 for Joachin in 1856, covering $27 for the room and $20 for a "surgical operation." [82]

Whether the bondsman actually benefited from these facilities depended on the owner. Except in times of epidemic, no doctor answered the call of a slave; no hospital admitted a slave without the master's permission. Sanitary conditions in the house and yard, safety on the job, and to some extent food and clothing were beyond the control of the blacks. Hence the results were quite uneven. The proximity of Negro and white undoubtedly led to greater precautions and more immediate care, but neglect was common, too. Those who hired out and lived out often fended for themselves; slaves whose usefulness was impaired or at an end could hope for little. Josiah Nott, a prominent Mobile physician, explained this fact bluntly to insurance companies which considered entering the field of Negro insurance. "As long as the negro is sound, and worth more than the amount insured, self-interest will prompt the owner to preserve the life of the slave"; but "if the slave become unsound and there is little prospect of perfect recovery, the underwriters cannot expect fair play—the insurance money is worth more than the slave, and the latter is regarded in the light of a super-annuated horse." [83]

Free Negroes in the cities, however, fared much worse than slaves. Cut loose from those who had a stake in them, lacking the money required for medical care, even more ignorant than whites of the causes of sickness and death, they had the highest mortality rates of any urban group. Baltimore's colored community, the largest free one anywhere, suffered especially. As early as 1829 the consulting physician of the city observed: "We find upwards of three hundred deaths among free people of colour, this cannot but excite our commiseration for this class of society alike improvident and obnoxious to the diseases of our climate." [84] In 1851 the Board of Health reported a high incidence of smallpox fatalities among them, attributing it to their reluctance "to receive the proffered services of the vaccine physicians." [85]

"The chances for life . . . among the slaves in Baltimore appear to be considerably greater than that of the free blacks," wrote E.A. Andrews in a characteristic observation on this problem, "the deaths among the slaves being only about two thirds as great as among the free people of color." [86] Contemporaries explained this in a variety of ways, usually designed to argue that Negroes were better off in bondage. Even Niles supported this analysis in 1825: "This is well called 'evidence of improvidence'; and the fact certainly is, that the free blacks in Baltimore are not only less abundantly supplied with the necessaries and comforts of life than the slaves, but they are also much less moral and virtuous." To demonstrate his objectivity, Niles added, "No one can be a greater enemy of slavery than I am—but there is a *lesson* in the preceding statement." [87] Five years later, however, he added a new and important factor to his diagnosis. Part of the high mortality stemmed from "the unpleasant and oppressive fact—that the aged and infirm and *worn-out* negroes, from all parts of the state, are turned to Baltimore, to live as they can, or die, if they must." [88]

In his immediate environment, then, the urban slave enjoyed considerable advantages over his country counterparts. Living quarters were more comfortable, his food and clothing superior, and his general health better. Bishop Henry B. Whipple thought the distinction between rural and urban Negroes extended even to language. In contrast to the New Orleans black's love of high-flown words and his aping the manners of the whites, he declared, the "plantation nigger" is of an "entirely different species, coarser, poorer dressed and an entirely different dialect. He speaks a provincialism with as much of a brogue to it as cockney Yorkshiremen." [89]

Frederick Douglass, who had experienced both conditions, could write of his life in Baltimore: "Instead of the cold, damp floor of my master's kitchen, I found myself on carpets; for the corn bag in winter, I now had a good straw bed, well furnished with covers; for the coarse corn-meal in the morning, I now had good bread, and mush occasionally; for my poor tow-linen shirt, reaching to my knees, I had good clean clothes. I was really well off." Speaking less personally but from long observation, he added that the city slave "is much better fed and clothed, is less dejected in his appearance, and enjoys privileges altogether unknown to the whip-driven slaves on the plantation." [90] A Charleston minister made the same comparison, saying that Negroes living in towns have "greater facilities of rendering them more happy and contented. Most . . . are fed from the same table at which their masters dine, or are daily supplied with the greatest abundance of both animal and vegetable food—clothed in a superior manner—occupying rooms in out buildings, as good nearly as those in the family mansion itself." [91]

Chapter Six

———

BEYOND THE MASTER'S EYE

ONCE OUTSIDE the enclosure and beyond the master's eye, the slave entered a quite different world. The closely controlled environment of the compound suddenly gave way to the variety, diversity, and fluidity of the city. In place of the familiarity and intimacy of the owner's place, he found the novelty and anonymity of town living. While his color still betrayed his status, there were enough like him to blur a more precise identity. As he walked down the street, he was, to be sure, a slave, but he was no longer "Mr. Smith's boy, John," except to those who might recognize him. Law and etiquette governed his action and behavior, especially toward whites; yet, barring trouble, the bondsman could mix somewhat inconspicuously with other townspeople.

Slaves were not supposed to leave the enclosure simply to go out on the town. Indeed, legally they could never be out except for a specific purpose and then only with papers describing their errand. But only an emergency brought a rigid enforcement of these restrictions. If Negroes were off the street at night and at work or at least out of mischief during the day, interference with their casual affairs was sporadic. As a result, an informal life developed among urban slaves which was persistently at odds with state and local law and inconsistent with the institution of slavery. No memoir of either white or black ever chronicled this life, but the complaints against it afford more than an occasional glimpse of its existence and nature.

On any day in every city, slaves could be seen away from their master's supervision and still not at work. Presumably on an errand or hired out to an employer, they gathered at a friend's place, stopped in a nearby grog shop for a drink or conversation, chatted with other blacks on a corner or in the market. Some were chance meetings where the talk lasted only a few minutes; others became habitual, where the slave dropped in as often as he could and stayed as long as he dared. The line between free and slave, and sometimes between colored and white, broke down. Women joined the men, news and gossip passed by word of mouth, petty business was transacted, plans were made for seeing one another again. In short, in every part of town, slaves of different masters got acquainted, struck up friendships, mingled with free blacks, and came to know a fragment of the white community. These contacts were an inseparable part of urban life—for Negroes as well as whites, for bondsmen as well as freedmen.

Such meetings during the day usually assumed a clandestine flavor, since the time, for the slaves at least, was stolen from prescribed work. But at night, when the job was done and curfew had not yet sounded, this life took on a somewhat freer, less furtive air. After dinner some Negroes slipped out of their master's place, with or without papers, and headed for a customary rendezvous—a shop in the neighborhood, an out-of-the-way shed or lot, the house of a free black or another bondsman, the wharves, or even a remote street corner. Others soon joined, ordinarily just a few but sometimes many more. Things were more organized now. The cards might be brought out; the drinking was more serious; the conversation prolonged. Young couples often broke off in search of greater privacy, or perhaps a grudge would be settled in a rough-house. Nearly all owners disliked these gatherings and found them dangerous to good discipline. Yet, save for occasional crackdowns, this informal and irregular life was a normal part of the urban setting.

Sunday inevitably brought an increased tempo in this life. Religious services took slaves outside the enclosure with their master's sanction. The notion of the Sabbath as a day of rest gave many some time off and led to a relaxation on the demands of others. In addition, white families themselves often left home to visit friends and relatives, leaving a portion of their servants behind. Under these circumstances Negro life quickened. Those who shunned the more risky weekday loitering joined the gatherings. On festive occasions games and parades featuring colored participation were a regular part of civic celebrations. No matter what the particular cause, Sunday was always lively. "Passing along Baronne street, between Perdido and Poydras streets any Sunday afternoon, the white passer-by might easily suppose himself in Guinea, Caffraria, or any other thickly-populated region in the land of Ham," the *New Orleans Crescent* reported; "Where the darkies all come from, what they do there, or where they go to, constitute a problem somewhat beyond our algebra." [1]

The development of an extensive life outside the immediate surveillance of the owner was bitterly attacked by residents and officials of every Southern city. "This has gradually severed the ties which bind together the master and slave; removed restraints to vicious or criminal indulgence, broken the family pride of our servants, and to a great degree changed their whole character," [2] wrote a distressed Savannah editor. Police officers, judges, even vigilante committees, tried to stop it. If the restraints could be tightened and the law enforced, then discipline and control would be possible and slavery made secure.

But the perspective of the slave was quite different. What they sought was a semblance of organization within their limited independence; some ordering of their anomalous life beyond the enclosure. Formal association was, of course, impossible except in a dangerously underground way. Yet informal centers of Negro activity sprang up throughout the city —in houses, grog shops, grocery stores, and in the churches. Though free blacks and even occasionally whites made up a part of these shifting groups, the great majority in most cities were slaves.

II

The common—and simplest—nucleus of the slave's life outside his master's place was the house of another black. Sometimes this proprietor might be free, sometimes merely another slave who had contrived to "live out." In either case the modest spot became a magnet for others. Here the circle of acquaintances widened, friendships strengthened, and, for a brief period, these few could find a privacy which the institution of slavery otherwise inhibited. Such gatherings were generally quiet and, of course, covert. No doubt there were whites who knew how common they were. "In this city," a New Orleans critic contended, "hundreds of such places might be pointed out, in which the slave is the keeper of the house—a slave over whom the master pretends to exercise no control." To those who thought such places harmless, he warned that they become "the rendezvous of fellow slaves, who are still in their master's families—the resort of the depraved of both sexes, and the plague spots of a larger population." [3]

Every city was laced with these houses; everywhere their existence contravened at least a dozen ordinances; yet they persisted. No municipal official knew how to break the circle of which they were a part. Slaves could "live out" only if they were permitted to "hire out." No visitors could come without a pass. And certainly none could remain out without authorization from an owner. The only remedy would have been to make a jail of the enclosure, but then the master would have to be the jailer and exert a constant supervision over every black. Few owners would take that responsibility. Hence, while the restraints remained on the books, the slave's actual latitude expanded. The proliferation of small, scattered Negro refuges was a critical index of this process; by 1860 they had become a customary ingredient of urban slavery.

Less conspicuous than other aspects of black activity, generally involving only a handful of slaves at a single time, and conducted by those careful to avoid unnecessary attention, these gatherings seldom came to public notice. Within these confines, the normal run of human problems was doubtless discussed—a recent illness, a new romance, the children, clothes and food, the job, and the weather. Doubtless, too, talk would get around to the discipline of bondage—the behavior of whites, the different attitudes of various masters, news of runaways being secreted nearby, rumors of the impending sale of a friend or even a relative, an account of a public whipping. As the evening wore on, the conversation inevitably involved the habits of the night watch or a sly remark about the Mayor's Court's punishment for those caught without papers. Here the bitter and resentful emotion could be shared with others who could understand. Rebellion against the institution was probably seldom mentioned, at least not seriously, but day-to-day problems of slavery were surely a continuing part of the discussion.

The white community instinctively disliked this unsupervised Negro visiting, knowing full well the range of conversation included topics too delicate for general debate. Yet, except for occasional almost philosophical dissent, the only complaints and official action stemmed from sporadic breaches of the peace which could be traced to a Negro place. "Their little sheds and shanties soon become the rendezvous of the idle and dissipated of their own color," a Mobile editor argued, where "gambling, drinking, and debauchery of all kinds are practiced." [4] When a few slaves engaged in a little "ill-managed merriment" in the same city, they wound up before the judge.[5] And Anderson, "a fancy dressed negro," was arrested on his way home from a small party because he was "in company with 'a lady' without a pass." [6] In another characteristic case, "some ten or a dozen negroes, while indulging in music and dancing without leave or license, in a kitchen ... were broken in upon by the night watch ... and lodged in the Guardhouse. The mayor caused them to dance to the tune of ten lashes each." [7] But these events were simply the visible part of the iceberg; beneath, on almost any night in every city, slaves met, relaxed, chatted, and departed without incident and quite casually.

At few other points was the condition of urban and rural slavery so different. On the plantation Negroes gathered in the evening in their quarters where they amused themselves, talked, sang, and even bootlegged some additional food and a little liquor. But it was not the same social process. The overseer was seldom far away; everybody belonged to the same owner; all shared the same little world of events; no freedom mixed a new experience with theirs; gossip and small talk quickly became routine. Countryside distances managed to confine life in a way the urban enclosure never could. In towns, the opportunities ran the other way, for at least a portion of the day was spent away from the immediate oversight of either master or employer. Such independence was limited and precarious, to be sure, yet whenever it appeared the slave grasped it eagerly. Increasingly, in the cities he carved out a modest private existence which attenuated his slavery if it did not remove him from bondage.

III

A more apparent, though basically not more dangerous, portion of informal slave life centered on the cities' numerous grog and grocery shops. These were small stores for the most part catering to a neighborhood clientele and offering a broad range of goods in limited quantities. Run by a single proprietor, open Sundays and weekdays, and never closing before curfew, they attracted loungers as well as customers, the browser along with the buyer. Slaves dropped in often on an errand—some milk before breakfast, staples for the week, tobacco for the master, or some cloth for the mistress. This traffic became so common that slaves rarely needed papers to purchase anything. If the black had no cash, the amount would simply be placed on the books for future payment; if he had the money, the transaction was quickly settled. In Dixie's growing towns these small neighborhood stores handled a large part of ordinary commerce.

They also handled liquor, and it was this ingredient which gave them a peculiar character, transforming many modest grocery stores into "speakeasys" of sorts. Trading with slaves was always carefully restricted, but selling intoxicants to them carried the stiffest penalties. Yet, except for the most prosperous, local shopkeepers inexorably became enmeshed in the forbidden traffic. Even in Louisville, where the colored population was comparatively small, "A Taxpayer" could contend that "we all know that there are very few grocers in this city, who do not violate" these municipal regulations.[8] In fact, the illicit trade constituted in many cases such an important part of their annual income that proprietors formed associations to protect themselves against any serious interference with the business. Around these stores Negroes congregated, comprising a clientele at once profitable and illegal.

Less acceptable but more numerous were the grog and dram shops which sold liquor almost exclusively and dealt heavily with slaves. Some catered openly to them, others bootlegged in back rooms or nearby sheds. In every town the traffic thrived. When a Richmond judge gave six months to the owner of one, the *Enquirer* observed caustically that "hundreds of establishments similar to Keelings, where our own children and negroes are corrupted and made rogues, exist in the city." [9] In Mobile an editor found the same conditions: "There are little fruit and pop shops, as well as 'small fry' grocery shops, all over the city, with a half dozen bottles of pop on the counter, and a barrel of whisky in the back room, or a side of bacon and a broom at the front door, and a cask of rum under the bed." [10]

"Not a street nor corner can be passed," complained the *New Orleans Bee*, "without encountering these magazines of degradation. They spring up in all directions with inconceivable rapidity; within the last few years they have augmented in almost unparalleled ratio, and are fortified and sustained by thousands who flock to them." [11] And in Charleston a "large and reputable list" of prominent citizens asserted in a characteristic petition that there had been "a fearful increase of these establishments. They are multiplying in every street and at every corner; the temptation is brought to our very door." [12] Even very small towns felt oppressed by the problem. In Milledgeville, Georgia, it was soon discovered that despite the vigilance of the watch, "great numbers of negroes, without permits, and many of them runaways, are nightly infesting our streets, drinking and regaling themselves in tippling houses, in which they are encouraged to the great loss of their owners, and annoyance of the community." [13]

Few parts of any city were free of grog shops, and some neighborhoods were particularly cluttered. The Neck and the northern edge of Charleston were especially "infested with the lowest and vilest grog shops, poisoning and destroying our colored population." [14] New Orleans' Second District, just beyond Canal Street, became a notorious center of "cabarets and drinking dens" where slaves could "obtain liquor in any quantity, and at all times, day and night." By the 1850's, however, a strip of stores around the railroad depot presented some brisk competition.[15] Savannah's western and eastern edges spawned dozens of shops, while in Mobile "numerous shanties" catered to the Negro trade along the "famous thoroughfare" of St. Louis Street.[16] "From these recepticles of iniquity they came forth, surcharged with the fumes of whisky, and segars in their mouths, staggering on their way, bawling and rioting, totally regardless of decency and decorum." [17]

Officials waged almost continuous war on the groggeries, arresting proprietors, punishing Negroes, and revoking licenses. Yet they never succeeded in controlling their growth, much less in eradicating them. Even in periods of concerted crackdowns, when the police raided well-known haunts and forced others to shut down, new ones quickly opened. City councils found a disproportionate amount of time taken up with citizens' petitions, neighborhood complaints, and grand jury presentments which blamed the watch, the courts, or sometimes fellow residents. Ordinances were revised, tightened, and adjusted; state legislatures helped with new laws; occasionally vigilante committees arrogated police powers to themselves. Still, in the final years before the war the groceries and dram shops flourished—while the citizens fumed.

IV

Anyone who had responsibility for enforcing the laws against selling liquor to slaves soon discovered the complexities of the task. The mayor of Mobile in 1854 learned the hard way. With great publicity he launched a campaign to clean up the city. Soon he was observing ruefully that "the dens of iniquity are managed so adroitly as to almost defy detection and conviction." While the police were around, all looked legitimate, but as soon as they were "off the scent, slaves were invited to assemble, encouraged to gamble, steal and practice every species of vice." Moreover, "for the convenience of (black) guests side and back doors are provided, sufficiently numerous to assist a spiriting of the 'spirits' out of sight when *necessary*." [18] Though the council co-operated and the newspapers backed the drive, the number of prosecutions rose only slightly. Within three years another mayor, again responding to popular pressures, was pushing once more for a similar futile assault. [19]

Since buyer and seller both had a stake in the traffic, it was difficult to get court-proof evidence. Lookouts manned the windows and doors; at the slightest danger the blacks scattered and the retailer went about routine tasks. When caught, the grocer argued that he had sold only raspberry juice or a little pop. [20] Even carefully laid plans by officials came to nought. New Orleans police, for instance, staked out a notorious shop in the worst part of town. When they sprang the trap, they found "two slaves in the act of drinking at the bar after having seen them pay for what they ordered." The officers tasted the liquor and identified it as brandy and water. In court the next day, however, "the keeper of the cabaret and his employees ... swore positively that it was sasparilla and water." The judge dismissed the case. [21]

"The contrivances to escape the penalty ... are so ingenious," concluded one editor, "that the watchful supervision of masters and the utmost vigilance of the police" proved of no avail. In support of this contention he pointed to a place where "a number of blacks may almost always be found." The owner of the cabaret had built a connection to a neighboring barber shop so that "the liquor sold is not drunk on the premises, if paid for by slaves. It is sent by a private and secret communication" next door "and drunk there." [22] A South Carolina legislative committee looking into enforcement problems explained the difficulty by asserting that in "populous towns" it was "difficult to detect infractions of the law" because of "the combinations which are formed by the Army of Retailers for defeating and eluding the vigilance of the strictest police." [23] One judge, despairing of breaking up the trade, ruled that a license could be revoked and a fine levied even if the names, owners, and sex of the Negroes were not known. "Such assemblages usually disperse upon the least alarm," he said, "and few can tell the names or their owner's names. And as to their sex, it is easy to disguise it by a change of clothing" so that "the informer . . . could rarely prove the sex." [24]

The grocers, of course, were of no help. They argued that they ran legitimate businesses but were victimized by unscrupulous informers who received half the fine for peddling mere gossip. If new laws tightened up restrictions, they resisted enforcement and attacked the legislation. Though they were always involved in a kind of guerrilla warfare with the police, their real position came to the surface only occasionally. It was seldom stated more clearly than in Charleston in 1834 and 1835 when municipal officials tried to apply new restraints adopted by the state government. A great many people had high expectations because penalties for trafficking with slaves had been raised to $1000 with the possibility of imprisonment. "The scenes of beastly intemperance," "A Taxable Citizen" predicted optimistically, "which we have heretofore so often and so painfully witnessed in the streets, in the dram shops, and in our own yards among our servants, proceeding from that perpetual source, the licensed retail shops in our City, will soon, thank heaven, cease." The future would be blissful. "The thoughtless slave, no longer tempted, will return to habits of sobriety, honesty and fidelity, and instead of a curse, will be a blessing to their owners and to society." [25]

The proprietors had other ideas. They immediately challenged the law, for they claimed that cutting off the trade would drive "a hardy and hard-working class" out of business. They bore down also on the police and the city government. When some proprietors were arrested, a spokesman for the owners said that "the Docket of the present term" of the Court was swelled because of "the insatiate cravings" of officials who wanted "their victims brought to altar as a common sacrifice," and he hinted that political motives were somehow involved.[26] One grocer noted that the laws on the subject had been on the books "in substance" since 1796 but their "severity had hitherto deterred men from prosecuting or convicting." He also doubted that the whole campaign could succeed anyway, since "it is idle to suppose that a Jury can now be found to do what Juries have always hitherto set their faces against." No Charlestonian, he prophesied confidently, would "deprive the accused of his honest earnings, and blight his fair reputation." [27]

The sequel proved him correct. By 1837 the same laments about the trade could be heard. The law had prohibited the use of screens in the shops which had shielded backroom activity. Now "you will see barrels substituted, behind which, the negroes drink as much as they have money to purchase." [28] The traffic had returned to normal. A decade later, a group of residents petitioned against the practice again, saying "there is scarce a man among us, who is the owner of slaves, who has not *felt* the evil." [29] In 1859 the grand jury, after acknowledging that it knew "how difficult it is to arrest the evil," suggested "getting the owners of the shops on perjury since they have to sign a statement when they get the license" that they would not sell to bondsmen.[30] Thus, municipalities were always seeking some solution of this persistent problem.

V

The urge to control the grog shops was understandable, for they represented serious problems for the slaveholders. The most obvious was the inducement to steal. To buy liquor, slaves had to get some money and few could do so legally. The temptation was great, and the encouragement from the shopkeepers was constant. " 'Come, Jim, its *your* time to treat.' 'I swear *Joe*, I hav'nt a cent of money.' 'All fudge,' said Mr. S._____, a pewter faced looking man, from behind the *counter:* 'pawn your axe, and I'll let you have the liquor.' " In relating this episode, "A Taxpayer" of Louisville argued that similar events took place all over the city. "The proprietors of these groceries," he added, "appear to consider themselves no better than the negroes themselves, so that they sell their liquor &c. and will receive property . . . without any enquery." [31] "Every individual in this community sees and knows," "A Carolinian" wrote to a Charleston newspaper, that "the Slave will steal . . . to attain the means of paying for the intoxicating draught." [32]

Investigations in every city found the same thing. In 1836 a Savannah grand jury complained of "the great number of Retailers of Spiritous Liquors within the city, whose intercourse with slaves had a most injurious tendency, presenting an inducement to theft and intoxication and being recepticles of a large amount of stolen property." [33] A Charleston presentment had pointed to the way in which the shops "encourage negroes in pilfering, by enabling them easily to dispose of stolen articles, and avoid detection." [34] "What becomes of our missing plate and jewelry and money?" a citizens committee asked in the same town in 1848.[35] The *Rich-*

mond Enquirer noted that "it is a habit very extensively practiced" by the blacks who "steal to raise fancy funds." [36] In
point of fact, slaves seldom went after "plate," "jewelry,"
or "fancy funds," but the persistent petty pilfering substantiated the general criticism and supported many a grocer's
accusations.

Another problem was drunkenness. The dram shops built
up a regular Negro clientele, who undoubtedly drank too
much. Masters exaggerated the extent, perhaps because slaves
were not supposed to drink at all. The incidence of alcoholism
was probably in fact less than among whites who had uninhibited access to the supply. Still it was higher among blacks
in the cities than on plantations. Samuel Cartwright, the New
Orleans physician, went so far as to assert that Negroes generally drank very little and this only for medical purposes
or during holiday celebrations. While attributing this "fact"
to the "unwritten laws" of Southern states, he added that
restraints "do not so well protect negroes who reside in or
near towns and villages, and are not under proper discipline." [37] "We are in more danger from the intemperance of
slaves than other counties, where they are more equally diffused among the whites," "A Slaveholder" in Savannah suggested, while lamenting local conditions.[38] Exact figures on
this question were, of course, never kept, but the picture
of the drunken Negro stumbling through the streets or brawling with another black was a common part of the white
stereotype.

Beyond the problems of theft and intemperance, however,
were much graver ones. To lose property or put up with excessive drinking might be aggravating, yet such inconveniences
could always be counted among the costs of slaveholding. But
the peculiar conjunction of theft and liquor had a wider significance, for it brought together black and white, slave and
free, under circumstances of informality and familiarity. Cus-

tom and law were still too formidable to permit even approximate equality except at the margins of life. Still the broad demarcation between races that characterized slavery was attenuated; the distinction between free and enslaved blacks, always difficult to maintain, broke down, and, fleetingly, even the lesser differences melted away. Such meetings imperiled not only the system of slavery but even the historic sense of racial order as well. This explains the strident tones of the attacks on the grog shops, the persistent prodding of the police, and the anxiety of municipal officials.

"The mingling of blacks of different social conditions is bad enough," a New Orleans editor candidly stated, "without the additions and indulgences as are now found in the cabaret." [39] A Charleston jury spelled out the larger danger, asserting that "the unrestrained intercourse and indulgence of familiarities between the black and white, . . . are destructive of the respect and subserviency which our laws recognize as due from the one to the other and which form an essential feature in our institutions." [40] Five years later, another jury was even more explicit, arguing that the liquor traffic brought "the negro slave in such familiar contact with the white man, as to excite his contempt, or invite the assertion of equality, or draw from him exhibitions of presumption and insubordination." The central culprits in this indictment were not the police but the shopkeepers—that "swarm of men continually and perseveringly at work, undermining the character of our slaves, and so aiming an insidious but most effective blow at the system itself." [41]

If the slaves did not become insubordinate, at the very least their character degenerated. They "spend their nights drinking, carousing, gambling, and contracting the worst of habits, which not only make them *useless to their owners*, but dangerous pests to society." [42] The *Mobile Register and Journal* explained that, after some time in the groggeries "the morale of the slaves, nine cases out of ten, are completely ruined; industrious habits soon give place to laziness; good temper and honesty to doggedness and dishonesty." [43] "The negro daily indulges more and more freely in intoxication," the *Louisiana Gazette* said tersely, "and in a few years becomes worthless and dies." [44] And summing up the popular view, "A Friend of Good Order" wrote to a Charleston paper that the trade "will destroy the bodily health of the Slave, corrupt his morals, lessen his value to me, and ultimately make him a nuisance and burthen on the community." [45]

The most disturbing and nagging fear of the white community, however, was the conviction that Negro gatherings would inevitably produce insurrections. Free blacks and slaves, low whites and perhaps abolitionists, drinking and talking together would soon get around to scheming the overthrow of the institution of slavery. A New Orleans journalist stated the view very simply: the shops were "places of temptation to the lower classes, where intoxication can be cheaply purchased, where mobs and caucuses of our Slaves nightly assemble at their orgies, to inflame the brains with copious libations, and preach rebellions against their white masters." [46] "Should a servile outbreak ever occur in the City of New Orleans—of which event the probabilities are at present not very great—," another editor pointed out, "we shall have to thank the keepers of these negro cabarets and club houses for it, within the precincts of whose damned halls, at the dead hour of midnight, heaven knows what plots are hatched against our peace." [47] Everywhere the attack on the backroom speakeasy reflected the fear that such spots formed the perfect setting for those who sought to destroy the entire system of bondage.

The perspective of the slave, however, was quite different. What was a problem of discipline for whites was harmless tippling to the blacks; what looked like an ominous assemblage to the police was conviviality to the bondsmen; what seemed a dangerous indulgence to the master was simple release to the servant. No doubt the slave sometimes became "imprudent" after a glass or two. Bolstered with whisky, he said things among friends he never dared say elsewhere when sober. He might even boast of what he would do, or fabricate an episode when he had turned a trick on his mistress. If he had too much, he might swagger on the way home, talk too boisterously with a friend on the street, perhaps tempt the watch by a little bravado. When the liquor was too potent, he might wake up on the floor, in a backroom—or in the guardhouse.

But drinking and night reveling were incidental; it was what the white community could see of this irregular Negro life. The bizarre episode, however, merely masked the more important reality. To many slaves, the shabby shop on the corner, or the little liquor store in the neighborhood, or the shed on the edge of town was an important institution. The physical surroundings, to be sure, were not inviting. Space in the back was small, crowded with boxes, barrels, and odd things. The back door was both entrance and exit. But a makeshift table could easily be contrived; for a few pennies there would be some liquor and a little food. Most of the clientele were familiar; the conversation revolved around people and events all understood; and the slave here became an individual and personality apart from his owner and status. Even the white proprietor became a part of the loose circle, with at least a stake in the security of its privacy if not always a friend. Time spent in these clubs was always prized, for it was never certain when next the slave could get away from the enclosure or the job.

Occasionally these places became a little more elaborate, finding a more refined location and feigning a greater gentility. In the rear of Richmond's Exchange Hotel, for instance, a group of slaves dropped in "day and night ... to get julips, some port-wine sangarees, some whiskey punches, some lemon-pops, &c. for which they paid from 3 cents to a fip a drink." Customers found here "marble tables, . . . cards, dominoes, dice, et cetera" and on special evenings "ladies (of a certain class) rustling in silks and odoriferous as pinks or honeysuckles." Negroes called it "Taylor's Hotel" after the "fine moustached mulatto" who rented the rooms from the white owners.[48] But most patronized the modest, out-of-the-way spots which were presumably safer if considerably less elegant.

VI

If the homes of some blacks and the grog shops and groceries furnished scattered but persistent centers for the slave's informal life, the churches increasingly provided still another focus. Generally, this activity met with white approval, for it was widely believed that religion sustained rather than threatened slavery. "The Gospel is our mightiest safeguard," a Charleston minister explained; "for it governs in secret as well as in public; it cultivates the conscience, and thus establishes a more vigilant watch over individual conduct than Foucher himself ever accomplished by his unrivalled police." His conclusion was both pointed and typical: "If any community on earth is bound by considerations of personal interest, to encourage the diffusion of sound religious principles among the lower orders, we are that community." [49] Nor was this mere theory. "The best servants I know, are those who have the most religious intelligence and piety," another asserted. "Those among them who are most intimately acquainted with the Bible, understand best the relation between themselves and their masters, and are best contented with it. The communities where the most prudent and energetic measures for the improvement of the colored population have been adopted, have the least trouble in controlling that population." [50]

Religious leaders also thought the opportunities for work among the blacks in the city seemed much brighter than in rural areas. "We know," wrote one of them, "that to negroes in the country, there are insuperable impediments to the full use of the ordinary provision for worship and instruction in parishes and neighborhoods." The reasons for this were not hard to see: "The distance of many plantations from the churches; the insufficiency of the accommodation, were it practical to attend them; the inability of the negroes generally to be reached by ordinary pastoral care— . . . make the fact indisputable, that arrangements for these purposes . . . must be provided *at home*. The Gospel must be carried to them." "In our cities and villages," however, "opportunities of religious improvement are freely enjoyed by negroes." [51]

This judgment, though accurate in its description of rural problems, was optimistic in its assessment of the urban scene. In fact, in no city did white leadership succeed in meeting either the hopes of slaves or the official responsibilities of their own churches in ministering to the colored population. In part, the failure can be explained by the sheer numbers involved; in the larger towns the scale of the job overwhelmed already overburdened organizations. In Charleston, where the effort was greatest, the Reverend Paul Trapier put the question in cold statistical terms. "There are, as it appeared in the census of 1840, about 20,000 slaves in our city and its suburbs [the Neck]." He calculated that a thousand were "connected with our six Episcopal Churches," while in all other denominations "it is estimated that more than 5000 can be accommodated. This leaves an appalling residue of about 14,000." He asked plaintively, "Where are they? What is becoming of them?" [52]

A greater problem than numbers, however, was the difficulty of finding a system of worship and instruction appropriate to the "peculiar institution." "All concur in the confirmation of the improvement effected by religion in the moral condition, docility, and submission to authority, of those slaves to whom it has been communicated," an Episcopal newspaper pointed out. "On the mode of religious teaching only, does a diversity of opinion exist." [53] Should bondsmen attend the same services as the master as part of the family, in the way Catholics did? Others advocated separate worship under white clergymen and tutelage as practiced by some Methodist and Baptist churches. Still others sought a mixture of the two procedures. In any case, the objective was to bring some religious instruction to the blacks without encouraging independent organization among them.

Few doubted the receptivity of the Negroes; indeed it was their enthusiastic response to any overture that continually forced the issue. "Our own security is best consulted not by violent resistance to any original impulse of the heart —not by attempting to extirpate or destroy it—" wrote the Reverend Thornwell in the midst of Charleston's debate on the question, "but by giving it a wise direction and turning it into safe and salutary channels." He even thought it was impossible to prevent slaves from organizing their own churches: "Separate congregations, therefore, they *will* have. If our laws and public sentiment of the community tolerate them, they will be open, public, responsible. If our laws prohibit them, they will be secret, fanatical, dangerous." A prudent policy would save the bondsmen "from secret convocations which the white man cannot witness—we save him from appeals which madden rather than instruct—from a religion which puffs up but does not edify." [54]

While whites debated the proper methods, the Negroes went ahead organizing their religious life as best they could. And the need was deep, for slavery had stripped them of any meaningful pattern of life beyond that of the master and their bondage. The family could furnish none. No tradition could provide roots into a history without servitude. Neither today nor tomorrow offered any expectation of a life without the present stigma. Deprived of nostalgia for the past and unable to discover any real meaning in the present, the blacks sought relief and consolation in a distant time. In the church, with their own kind, amid songs of redemption and the promises of Paradise, a life-line could be thrown into the future.

"And here rises a poor slave, unlettered, and in the darkest ignorance, so far as human knowledge is concerned," wrote a visitor to a church in New Orleans, "and yet rich in his Christian faith, and as he unfolds a Saviour's love, he sways the hearts of his auditors as no other conceivable theme could move them." It was an unforgettable experience. "My eyes were dim with tears, as in broken language, he spoke of patience under life's cares, and depicted the glory of that world where there shall be no night, and where all tears shall be wiped from every eye." The congregation responded with "an extempore wail, without articulate words, such as I have never heard before from earthly voices." [55]

But other whites who dropped in occasionally to watch the services found them unusual and even shocking. Some believed the worship "a mockery of religion" or, more soberly with Olmsted, "a delusive clothing of Christian forms and phrases" added to "the original vague superstition of the African savage." [56] But these observations missed the significance of religious life for the Negroes. What seemed a burlesque was in fact a reverent, emotional experience. The clapping, chanting, shouting, and sometimes dancing, the fervent response to the minister's preaching, all expressed a longing that had no other sanctioned outlet.

This coming together was of itself important. It was the

only colored meeting which needed no special permission; indeed, it had found some approbation among whites. The occasion called for the best clothes, the most proper behavior, the fullest participation. Once there, one was not only a spectator but part of a congregation. The words, the prayers, the exhortations, even while they admonished the sinner, held out the promise of eternal happiness. Put aside for the moment were the burdens of bondage, the daily, fruitless toil, the sense of inferiority. It was no wonder the church was filled at dawn and candlelight on Sunday, and parishioners were active on weekday evenings.

The character of the services reflected these considerations. Many observers described the worship in great detail, but Olmsted's account of a New Orleans meeting was among the most careful and included the familiar elements and sequences. While walking through a "rather mean neighborhood," he was attracted by "a loud chorus" singing in a "chapel or small church." He found there only three whites, one of whom "looked like a ship's officer" and was "probably a member of the police force in undress—what we call spy when we detect it in Europe." The congregation was wholly colored, and the preacher was "nearly black, with close woolly hair. His figure was slight, he seemed to be about thirty years of age, and the expression on his face indicated a refined and delicately sensitive nature. His eye was very fine, bright, deep and clear; his voice and manner generally quiet and impressive."

No sooner had Olmsted been seated than he noticed an old Negro, whom "I supposed for some time to be suffering under some nervous complaint; he trembled, his teeth chattered, and his face, at intervals, was convulsed." He then began to respond to the preacher: " 'Oh, yes!' 'That's it, that's it!' 'Yes, yes—glory—yes!' " Others joined him whenever the speaker's voice was "unusually solemn, or his language eloquent or excited." Sometimes the frenzy included "shouts, and groans, terrific shrieks, and indescribable expressions of ecstasy—of pleasure or agony—and even stamping, jumping, and clapping of hands." Olmsted himself found "my own muscles all stretched, as if ready for a struggle—my face glowing, and my feet stamping."

The second preacher was even more extraordinary. "He was a tall full-blooded negro, very black, and with a disgusting expression of sensuality, cunning and variety in his countenance, and a pompous and patronizing manner—a striking contrast . . . to the prepossessing quiet and modest young preacher who had preceded him." Dressed gaudily, he spoke in "a low, deep, hoarse, indistinct and confidential tone." But soon "he struck a higher key, drawling his sentences like a street salesman, occasionally breaking out into a yell with the strength of extraordinarily powerful lungs, at the same time taking a striking attitude and gesturing in an extraordinary manner. . . . This would create a frightful excitement in the people," and they responded with the "loudest and most terrific shouts." Olmsted confessed that he could "compare them to nothing else human I ever heard."

The meeting then returned to the hymns. "The congregation sang; I think everyone joined, even the children, and the collective sound was wonderful." The women "rose above the rest, and one of these soon began to introduce variations, which consisted mainly of shouts of oh! oh! at a piercing height." Many of the others "kept time with their feet, balancing themselves on each alternately, and swinging their bodies accordingly." The preacher now "raised his own voice above all, turned around, clapped his hands and commenced to dance," laughing aloud and "leaping, with increasing agility, from one side of the pulpit to the other." Before he was finished he had thrust aside the other ministers, hurled the Bible into the children's pew, and fallen prostrate across the floor. Shortly thereafter the meeting was closed, and "the congregation slowly passed out, chatting and saluting one another politely, as they went, and bearing not the slightest mark of the previous excitement." [57]

The tumult of the services was simply the most conspicuous aspect of the colored religious life in the cities. More significant was the fact that increasingly Negroes took over basic responsibility for most of the activity of their churches. Of course, formally the law vested supervision and control in white leaders, but the fundamental tasks—recruiting members, finding and supporting ministers, paying rents, and staffing the Sunday schools—fell to the blacks themselves. If this activity had been left to regular denominations, the churches would have scarcely survived, much less flourished. Behind their success lay the enthusiasm of Negroes—slave and free. And throughout urban Dixie colored religious activity burgeoned.

In Richmond the growth is easily traced. In 1823 a number of slaves and free blacks petitioned the legislature for the right to establish a church. The address observed that there had been a "rapid increase of population in the city, especially among slaves and free persons of color." Yet "it has been the misfortune of your petitioners to be excluded from the churches, Meeting Houses and other places of public devotion which are used by white persons." The Negroes had turned to private places "where they are much crowded and where a portion of the Brethren are unable to hear or partake in the worship going on." The congregation consisted of 700 whose names had been submitted to the "Head of Police," who found "no objection . . . to their moral character." The petitioners wanted to build "a House of Public Worship which may be called the Baptist African Church." Realizing they could not expect this "privilege" without "such restrictions and restraints as are consistent" with "the peace and good order of society," they agreed to submit "most chearfully to all regulations." They wanted, however, to choose their own teachers, subject to the mayor's approval.[58]

Many years later, Lyell found the situation greatly improved. The Episcopal church had recently designated a side gallery for the blacks in the hope that masters and slaves "might unite in the worship of the same God, as they hoped to enter hereafter together into His everlasting kingdom." The Negroes preferred other services and few responded, but Lyell was assured that if "I went to the Baptist or Methodist churches, I should find the galleries quite full." [59] By 1856 the Virginia capital had four "African Churches," one of which a Sabbath School convention declared to be "the largest in the world," with a choir "not equalled in America." To these were added several classes for religious instruction carefully supervised so as "not to change the civil status of the negro, or alter relations of masters and servants, or teach them to read." The Governor moreover supported the program on the ground that it took from "Northern fanaticism its sharpest weapon." [60]

Every city witnessed the spread of formal Negro organization where slaves and free mingled in religious exercises. Baltimore headed the list with thirteen churches.[61] By 1843 Louisville had four, three Methodist and one Baptist. The latter had a colored pastor and catered to free blacks, though slaves attended too; the others were "under the care" of either the Fourth Street or Brook Street congregations.[62] The City Council officially tolerated if it did not encourage this development by passing a resolution in 1835 which permitted Negroes "to worship their God without molestation from any of the city officers, provided they are orderly, and under the supervision of some respectable white man." [63]

Even New Orleans, where the Catholic population was large and itinerant churches many, advertised three "colored congregations" in 1857 with "public services every Sabbath morning upon the oral system with Reverand H.N. McTyre as superintendant." [64] In addition, the African Methodist Episcopal Church owned three chapels scattered across the town with buildings assessed at $15,000, $4000 and $2000. The council was less happy about this growth than Louisville's had been and in 1857 passed an ordinance which closed even the authorized separate churches. Three years later, the edict was extended to "all churches where colored persons free or bond, assemble." [65] Yet the four pre-war decades had seen an acceleration of Negro religious life both within and outside white organizations in the city.

The Charleston story was the most interesting of any, for it was widely believed that Negro churches had nursed the abortive Vesey plot of 1822. The city's official account of the affair contended that "among the conspirators a *majority* of them belong to the *African Church*." This congregation, "comprised wholly of persons of color and almost entirely of blacks," had been established in the preceding December. Among other activities it had set up class meetings conducted by a "colored minister or leader as they were termed" for religious instruction and worship. Though the Methodists selected these men, no whites attended the gatherings.[66] The creation of this organization with a separate building just before the Vesey affair led many to associate the two events. And it accounted for a "morbidness" on this topic which could be found "in no other city of the Southern States." [67]

Despite this sensitivity, Charleston's Negroes managed slowly to widen their religious latitude. By 1845 the lowest estimate of church membership was about 6000, while the highest ran over 8200.[68] In slavery's last years there were at least 6000 colored Methodists alone, a figure nearly five times the number of the whites of that denomination. In Trinity Church, out of a total of 2123 there were only 299 whites, and these, of course, discharged supervisory duties. In 1859 the Presbyterians, finding their own building overcrowded, erected one for the blacks at a cost of $25,000. Immediately it became a thriving center where every Sunday afternoon over 1000 slaves and free colored people attended.[69]

The range of the churches' concern was not limited to worship. It extended to Sunday schooling for the young, to Bible classes for adults, and to prayers for the sick. Funerals and burial services further involved the churches. Indeed, in death the religious connection took on special meaning. Without it the slave would have been interred without ceremony and with little care in some out-of-the-way cemetery for colored people. The master or the city might provide the plot, and perhaps a wooden slab would mark the spot. But as a member of the congregation the passing was attended with due solemnity. The minister—sometimes white—presided, prayers were offered, and a procession of friends carried the body to be placed in the church burial grounds among other parishioners. Thus the church, for a moment at least, became a surrogate family for the bondsmen. It was little wonder that a leading guide book for white ministers could observe simply: "Funeral services are much esteemed by the Negroes." [70]

"There was a decent hearse, of the usual style, drawn by two horses; six hacking coaches followed it, and six well dressed men, mounted on handsome saddle horses, and riding them well, rode in the rear of them," ran Olmsted's account of a Richmond funeral. "Twenty or thirty men and women were also walking together with the procession, on the sidewalk. Among them all was not a white person." [71] In Charleston he witnessed a humbler, similar affair. "The exercises were simple and decorous, ... and were conducted by a well-dressed and dignified elderly negro. ... The grave was filled by the negroes, before the crowd, which was quite large, dispersed. Besides myself, only one white man, probably a policeman, was in attendance." [72]

The ceremonies were often held at night to accommodate those who could not get away from work during the day. In such cases the crowds increased and whites, at least, thought a carnival spirit replaced solemn mourning. A Charleston critic contended that "sometimes every evening in the week" Negro funerals, attended by "three or four hundred negroes and a tumultuous crowd of other slaves," made such a racket that they disturbed the neighborhood of the Pitt Street cemetery. "It appears to be a jubilee for every slave in the city," he observed, while concluding ominously that "let it be remembered too that the officiating priests are black men." [73]

On special occasions the gatherings were immense. When a deacon of the Third Colored Baptist Church in Savannah died, a visitor recorded the scene: "In the procession were four uniformed fire companies. The Porters' Association, of which he was a member, turned out, and wore black scarfs, with white rosettes. ... A spectator counted fifty-two carriages, well filled, besides a number on horseback, following the hearse. It is estimated that between two thousand and two thousand five hundred colored persons were in the procession." [74] For most, however, the ceremony was plain and the witnesses few. Yet the religious sanction, the words of the ministry, and the prayers of friends were crucial.

It did not matter so much that the cemeteries were poorly kept. "A few trees, trailing with long moss rise above hundreds of nameless graves, overgrown with weeds," William Cullen Bryant wrote sadly after visiting one in Savannah, "but here and there are scattered memorials of the dead, some of a very humble kind, with a few of marble, and a half dozen spacious brick tombs like those in the cemetery of the whites." [75] What was important was that, when life was finished, the body would not be disposed of like that of a dead animal but the book be closed with some dignity and solemnity.

Colored churches increasingly performed these rites, even though many whites thought it a dangerous extension of their activity. When a Virginia law in 1832 prohibited slaves and free blacks from officiating at funerals, a long petition by Richmond Negroes asked for repeal: "Many colored human beings are inter'd like brutes, their relatives and friends being unable to procure white ministers to perform the usual ceremony in the burial of the dead." Eleven clergymen joined in the memorial, explaining that "pressing engagements of white ministers left no time for this function." [76]

Helping in this activity were various church groups. Most important were small societies called "bands." They cared for the sick and handled the burial of the dead. Though religious in impulse, they usually existed outside of church supervision. White ministers knew they existed and worried about their influence. "They exist among those who are members of every Church in the City, though without the cognizance or recognition of the constituted authorities," one observed. Though he appreciated their usefulness because "there is nothing so dear to a negro than a decent funeral," he feared "they have been perverted and abused." [77]

The capacity of the blacks to organize their religious life surprised both visitors and white ministers alike. "To see a body of African origin, who had joined one of the denominations of Christians and built a church for themselves," Lyell wrote with some awe about Savannah, and "who had elected a pastor of their own race and secured him an annual salary, from whom they were listening to a good sermon, scarcely, if at all, below the average of the compositions of white ministers—to hear the whole service respectably, and the singing admirably performed, surely marks an astonishing step in civilization." [78] In Richmond, Mrs. Finch was impressed to find the African Baptist Church "entirely supported and attended by coloured people" and run by "several intelligent black elders, and deacons." [79]

Local residents sometimes showed great pride in these churches when visitors inquired about the condition of slaves. But their real response was more skeptical. It was not only that neighbors complained of the noise that often accompanied services and classes. More fundamentally, they feared the independence which separate churches implied. Never certain of what went on inside, they became convinced that abolitionist literature was circulated clandestinely and that insurrection was nightly plotted. The churches were, as one Charlestonian put it, "nurseries of self government" and hence dangerous. The slaves get "excited by the privileges they enjoy, as a separate and to some extent independent society," warned another.[80]

The fear of white townspeople was in part justified, for in these churches the Negroes did in fact get some experience in managing their own affairs. Those most active achieved moreover a special position in both colored and white communities. Black religious leadership carried a broad status that was not confined to spiritual matters. Though not ministers in the conventional sense, the preachers and class leaders were something more than mere slaves. And the formal connection with white ministers and lay boards gave them some prestige, at least among the congregation. In the life of these churches the first signs of traditional Negro leadership were visible in the cities even before the abolition of slavery. Already the church had become the cardinal point of colored affairs.

VII

Part of the objection to Negro religious activity stemmed from the widespread adoption of Bible classes as part of church programs. Instruction in the Scriptures raised the question of literacy among blacks, a tendency which whites feared at least as much as separate services. To be sure, the law forbade the teaching of reading or writing; yet a clumsy oral system was devised, as the inducement was always there. If the Bible contained God's word, would not everyone—black and white, bond and free—profit from reading it? The fact that Negroes, including slaves, conducted the classes indicated clearly that some were already literate, and the knowledge of reading and writing would no doubt spread.

Even without religious instruction this would have happened. The opportunities were numerous. Newspapers abounded; signs lined streets and shops; books and pamphlets circulated freely. Urban slaves managed moreover to get enough time away from their masters or employers to pick up the rudiments of literacy. As early as 1822 Thomas Pinckney saw that there was no way to stop town blacks from acquiring "the dangerous instrument of learning, which many of them have already attained." "It is probable," he concluded after examining the problem in Charleston, "that, in spite of all endeavors to the contrary, the evil will increase rather than diminish." [81]

Pinckney's prediction proved accurate. The increase of literacy among slaves, always higher in the cities than in the countryside, continued throughout the ante-bellum decades. Occasionally a master or mistress provided the instruction, but usually the blacks picked it up by themselves. Free Negroes sometimes had schools which slaves attended; one slave taught another; and the more ingenious managed alone. No matter how it happened, the knowledge spread; reading and writing were no mystery to large numbers of urban blacks. "No barrier, legal or social, can effectually shut out from them the subtle influence of intelligence and virtue," wrote one observer, ". . . in the towns of the Slave States they have made great progress. Many slaves have learned to read in spite of all prohibitions." Indeed, "the very prohibition has stimulated exertion." [82]

Travelers were often struck by this fact. Stirling asserted, perhaps with the exaggeration which comes from discovery, that "in Richmond . . . almost every slave child is learning to read" and that "even in Columbia, the capital of South Carolina, hundreds of slaves can read, and twenty or thirty negroes regularly teach in the evenings to their fellow slaves, receiving a fee of a dollar a month." [83] "It is not unusual," wrote another from Augusta, "to see slaves reading newspapers, and familiar with the current news of the day." [84] In Charleston, Lyell found the laws had been "rigorously enforced and made more stringent" in the years just before his second visit. "Nevertheless, the negroes are often taught to read, and they learn much in Sunday schools, and for the most part are desirous of instruction." [85]

The narratives of former slaves stress the same compelling theme. "When I came among the colored people of Baltimore, I found, to my surprise, that they were advanced in education, quite beyond what I had conceived of," wrote Noah Davis, a back-country Virginian who had bought his freedom and became a Baptist minister. "Of course, as I never had such advantages, I was far behind the people." [86] "I used to carry, almost constantly, a copy of Webster's spelling book in my pocket," Frederick Douglass remembered, "and when sent of errands, or when playtime was allowed me, I would step, with my young friends, aside, and take a lesson in spelling." By the time he was thirteen he knew how to read.

Taken out of the city for a while, he welcomed the return to the Maryland port, where he was "once more in a favorable condition to increase my little stock of education, which had been at a dead stand since my removal from Baltimore." [87]

Henry Morehead went to classes in Louisville, even though "my owners used to object...saying that I could learn rascality enough without it—that 'niggers' going to school would only teach them rascality." He continued his bootleg education until his master found out again and "set policemen to break the school up. This put an end to my schooling— that was the only schooling I ever had." [88] William Wells Brown, who thought "no part of our slave-holding country is more noted for the barbarity of its inhabitants, than St. Louis," learned to read and write in a print shop there. And Peter Randolph, who contended that "the slaves in the cities do not fare so hard as on plantations," found that "many" could read and write in Richmond, Petersburg, and Norfolk.[89]

What visitors and Negroes knew, white residents also knew only too well. Though others might consider the spread of literacy as evidence of black improvement under slavery, municipal officials fought the tendency in every way they could. In the ante-bellum decades, Southerners often argued that the restrictions on teaching slaves to read and write were a response to abolitionist activity.[90] Yet from the outset most whites considered literacy incompatible with slavery. As early as 1800 Charleston's City Council declared that "the law heretofore enacted for the government of slaves, free negroes, mulattoes, and mestizoes, have been found insufficient for keeping them in due subordination," and it gave authority to the police to "break doors, gates, or windows" in dispersing any gatherings "for the purpose of mental instruction" of the blacks.[91]

Despite the law the diffusion of knowledge could not be

contained. Twenty years later, 147 Charlestonians, petitioning the state legislature on the same matter, accused officials of "suffering school or assemblages of negro slaves to be taught reading and writing, organized and conducted not only by negroes and colored people and in some instances by white persons of the State." They further argued that South Carolina law forbade "Negroes being taught to write, but the act is silent as to their being taught to read, which is easier attained, equally mischievous and impolitick and at variance with slavery." [92]

The next few years, however, brought no improvement. In 1826 a memorial from the Charleston City Council put the question to the legislature again—this time in even stronger terms. The schools were still open, and the grand jury had called them "injurious to the community." The city concurred: "To be able to read and write is certainly not necessary to the performance of those duties which are required of our slaves, and on the contrary is incompatible with public safety." Nor was it hard to see why: "The facility with which this knowledge of the art of writing will enable persons of this class to carry on illicit traffic, to communicate privately among themselves and to evade those regulations that are intended to prevent confederation among them, renders it important" that the laws be enforced. Already "some evil minded persons" had circulated "inflammatory writings" among them which "seriously affect the peace and good order of our Society." [93]

After 1830 the campaign against Negro literacy quickened, but no new element was added to the argument, nor was there any measure of success. Every piece of evidence indicates that an elementary knowledge of reading and writing continued to spread in the cities. Though whites preferred to think of blacks as ignorant and totally untutored, at moments of crisis they recognized things as they really were. During the excitement following Nat Turner's rebellion, "Publicola" wrote plainly: "Many free negroes and slaves too, can and do read newspapers." Would it not be a "far wiser course," he asked, to use the papers to warn bondsmen of "the utter madness of insurrection?" [94]

The urban setting, then, provided opportunities to slaves to acquire the rudiments of learning which their status presumably denied them. Literacy, though known among country blacks, was rare. In the city, however, in a hundred places and in numberless ways, the precious knowledge seeped into the colored population, carrying with it the mysteries of religion, opening up the world of newspapers and even books, affording a glimpse into things outside their immediate experience, and providing a lifeline to the world beyond slavery.

VIII

Occasionally the informal life of the urban slaves, with its irregular foci around private homes, shops, churches, and Sabbath schools, found expression in a more glittering event. A fancy ball, an extravagant dinner, or a formal tea sometimes broke the otherwise fugitive and underground social routine. These affairs had the blessings of the master and even the permission of local officials. Sponsoring whites looked upon the proceedings with mock-seriousness, usually congratulating themselves for the tolerance they permitted within the institution of slavery. Yet to slaves and free blacks, despite the awkward emulation and necessary deference involved, these gatherings represented a momentary entrance into the world of forbidden gentility.

The incongruity of these special events was seldom missed by the newspapers. "The immense dining-hall was filled with repletion by representatives of the 'peculiar institution,'" the

Louisville Daily Democrat wrote of a New Year's Eve ball in 1856 given by slaves owned or hired by the Falls City Hotel. The reporter counted "four hundred colored persons present, and they deported themselves generally in the most unexceptional manner." Bedecked with "jewelry, crinoline, *moire antique*, furs, and such like," they did "the gentilities of the dance, the promenade, and supper table in many instances with commendable ease and grace." The paper calculated that "each individual member of the Terpsichorean assemblage" was worth "the reasonable rate of $500," but the "profuse array" of clothes and adornment "greatly enhanced their value." Stephens, the proprietor of the hotel, and J. R. Valleau, "his gentlemanly assistant," the account concluded facetiously, "exerted themselves to render their colored guests comfortable and their entertainment agreeable." [95]

In New Orleans the formal dance was a common occurrence. "We omitted to mention a fancy dress ball given by a select body of colored men on the 4th of March at 137 Poydras street," ran a story in the *Daily Delta* in 1859. "It was handsomely gotten up, and surpassed in style and arrangements many of the 'white folks' balls given this season." It was arranged "with the full sanction of the Mayor, who has his officers placed there to maintain order." [96] A few days later the social column announced another. The editor received "invitation tickets, which were gotten up in a style eclipsing anything seen before." The hosts, two free blacks, intended to make the affair "remembered by the colored young ladies of the 'upper ten' and 'lower twenty.' " [97] "We like to see our slaves enjoying themselves occasionally," the paper observed patronizingly. "Such a ball and such happy looking dancers never was heard of north of Mason and Dixon." [98]

In every city the same kind of activity occasionally brightened up the bondsmen's social landscape. In Washington ten slaves threw an elaborate dinner party for fellow church members. Held in the house of one master, the occasion had all the trappings of high society. "The two parlors below [on the first floor] were filled with ladies of color, of various ages, matrons and maidens, dressed in satins, thules, bareges, flowers, muslins, with bouquets, fans, and embroidered handkerchiefs." At the door guests were met by their hosts "who wore large white satin rosettes, and who were indefatigable in their attentions to all." One room, open the entire evening, served "hot chocolate, cakes, oysters, lemonade and punch." Because of the religious sponsorship there was no dancing or music. "Now, what a country this is, this land of slavery," *De Bow's* crowed, "where such enjoyments for the colored race are sanctioned by the whites." [99]

The glitter and gayety of a formal event was not, however, a routine part of the slave's life. Only a few of them ever attended such festivities. Nevertheless their very occurrence is revealing. The character of urban life had so broken the traditional disciplines of slavery that patterns of behavior drastically altered. Without lifting the legal restrictions, indeed in the face of more stringent local ordinances, slaves carved out an area of independence without analogue on farm or plantation. In the privacy of a modest dwelling, in the recesses of the grog shop's backrooms, in the church or makeshift Sunday school, or, under special circumstances, in the ballroom of a hotel or mansion, the city slave found a latitude unknown elsewhere. Yet, even when beyond the master's eye, the reminders of his servitude were everywhere evident. The policeman on the beat, the public whipping post, the jail and workhouse, the auction block, the habitual deference of his own race, and the expressed superiority of whites drained even this measure of freedom of all but occasional enjoyment.

Chapter Seven

THE LASH AND THE LAW

"It has long seemed to us," ran a characteristic comment of one of the South's urban leaders, "that there is a spirit of insubordination among the colored gentry that requires checking. There is a carelessness, a disrespect, and *'devil may care'* sort of independence, and absence of wholesome restraint, a neglect of common propriety and courtesy of manner, which is becoming almost intolerable." Of course, this observer omitted " 'de fuss color'd circle' " in his remarks, since they were "justly noted for real politeness and obligingness" of manners. "But take off the respectable upper crust, and you shall find enough material, which would be seriously improved by the application of a few good, sound affectionate floggings." The correction, however, should not be vengeful. "We mean floggings on principle, not in passion, and such administration of the birch as any idle, disobedient, churlish, good for nothing child deserves at the hands of its parents. Something is wanting to 'rectify the alignment of these sables,' and the sooner it is one the better." [1]

If whites believed that discipline in the cities was dangerously loose, the Negroes thought it tight enough. The symbols of servitude surrounded bondsmen almost everywhere they went. It was not only that they were slaves owned by another person, but their color carried a general stigma. "*Color* raises the presumption of slavery," a Missouri judge had asserted flatly in enunciating the familiar equation.[2] Hence even when outside the immediate supervision of the master or employer, the blacks were made aware of their status.

Every contact between the races, casual as well as formal, reminded Negroes of their inferiority. In ordinary conversation they were expected to show deference to all whites. Even the tone of voice and use of words could be offensive. Being "out of place"—a phrase which covered the whole range of etiquette—might bring a quick reprisal on the spot or a trip to the Mayor's Court and a "correction" in the municipal jail. "In the city," a runaway remembered, "a black man must get off the side-walk if he meets a white man, or stop on the curb-stone and raise his hat: if he meets a lady and gentleman he must step clean off the walk and raise his hat."[3]

Years of the system conditioned both blacks and whites to acceptance of this sense of social distance. Northern Negroes, who had their own reasons to know discrimination, found the extent of racial deference in Dixie vexing. G.E. Stephens, a sailor whose ship stopped over in Charleston, fumed on hearing bondsmen refer to the children of their owners as "Master and Mistress." When he reprimanded one of them, she was "astonished" and said "those children were entitled to this distinction." The visitor ruefully concluded that, "the Blacks here invariably believe that white men are superior not only mentally, but physically."[4]

The subtle inhibitions were just as revealing as the more obvious ones. Blacks, for example, could not smoke in public. The rationale was often baldly stated. "The negroes, habitually careless, care not where they throw their cigars; whether on the ground, in a pile of shavings, or under a bale of cotton," the *New Orleans Bee* asserted, adding that this objection did not take into account "the offensiveness to some, of coming into contact with a negro's cigar puff."[5] A Savannah editor found the habit of "Puffing cigar smoke into the faces of passers-by" an "offense against good manners." [6] Alexander, " a brawny-shouldered black negro," came before a Richmond judge after having been picked up while "strutting along a public street with a lighted cigar in his mouth" and was lectured on racial propriety and proper subservience.[7]

Many blacks became inured to this relationship, and no doubt believed it natural. Yet others never could. The records of the courts are replete with punishment for "being out of place." "John, a mulatto," ran a typical sentence, "was disorderly and saucy in the market, showed a large amount of independence" and got "20 heavy stripes for his impudence." [8] A drayman, Ben, received 39 lashes, another account noted, "for not remembering the courtesy due a white man, both in word and deed." [9] In another case "a negro girl was sentenced to twenty-five lashes for using insulting language to a white lady and otherwise acting disorderly." [10] Occasionally a bondsman would reject the whole business. A Mobile slave, for example, found himself in great trouble for saying that "negroes are equal to whites," though the judge went "lightly" on him because he admitted to being "three sheets to the wind" at the time.[11]

This etiquette was, of course, common to both city and country. But it took on special importance in town because there the races mingled most frequently, black and white dealt with each other constantly, and the social distance had to be maintained in the face of physical proximity. Ordinances might provide a legal blueprint for these numberless encounters and the courts punish any transgressions; yet the functioning of daily affairs rested on the broader subjugation of Negro to white, and observances in the smallest matters seemed almost as crucial as acceptance of slavery itself. Hence the slave—indeed, the free colored person too—was never allowed to forget his servitude whenever a white man was near.

II

When smaller, informal restraints broke down, the slave was confronted with the organized power of the white community. A lenient owner might permit a wider freedom, but in so doing he invited the intervention of local authorities. "If the masters of families do not check ... [the] impudence and abandon in their dependents," a Savannah observer advised, "it is time for the City Marshal and constables to take the matter in hand." [12] And "in hand" usually meant a more rigid enforcement.

Municipal interference occasionally protected the slaves from the worst excesses of a brutal owner. In one case, after a particularly grisly episode, a judge explained the rationale: "It is admitted on all hands that the treatment of slaves is a delicate subject, and our laws in their wisdom have left the subject to the discretion of the master; but when masters degenerate into relentless and bloody tyrants ... then indeed does the self defense of the community" require that measures be taken against the white. Not only did the "dictates of humanity" suggest such a course, but, more practically, it would "induce the blacks to rely upon the justice of free inhabitants to remove any causeless severity which may be exercised toward them." [13]

Still the usual thrust of the official machinery was against the slave. The constables by day and the watch by night made the supervision of Negroes a special concern. Slaves found their ubiquitous presence a constant danger. At any time one might stop a black, ask for his papers, and frisk his clothing. A small matter or a slight infraction could end in a trip to jail. Resistance was foolish, an attempt to run away was worse. The prudent slave acquiesced in any encounter with the man on the beat and hoped nothing would happen.

After curfew, it was particularly important not to be discovered away from the premises without proper authorization. The public might complain that the patrols were inefficient and ineffective, still, they arrested often enough to keep the colored community alert, if not always in awe.

The fear of being picked up was considerable, in part because the next step was the jail. Prisons for either race were hardly attractive; and for Negroes conditions were especially bad. To be sure, a visitor might find one "neat and clean," yet this was never characteristic.[14] A grand jury in New Orleans in 1837 brought in a report that could have been filed in almost any city in any year. While one of the town's three jails was adequate, the other two were worse than "dreadful" accounts had indicated. In the Second Municipality, Negroes were kept in five "dens" which measured ten feet square with a small door fifteen inches wide providing the only outlet. The temperature outside was between 90 and 95 degrees, while the rooms were much hotter and filled with "filth and abominable odors." The second cell contained three slaves; the third had seven "light women" either slaves or free persons of color and "one *white* (comment on such indiscriminate imprisonment is not thought necessary *in this state*)"; the fourth apartment held six men. This last, "the largest and lightest, and best ventilated," housed fourteen slaves, "most of them naked by choice." Because it faced Lafayette Square, the presentment found the prison absolutely intolerable.[15]

Conditions were not much better elsewhere. In the same city a few years later, a committee of the First Municipality issued a sharp rebuke to its jailor when it found the walls without whitewash, great overcrowding, sick slaves mingling with the healthy, and others idling about when they should have been on public work gangs.[16] A Louisville grand jury made a similar indictment in 1834, describing the cells as "most filthy, offensive and disgusting." In one they found "twenty four persons crowded into one room twenty-two feet square." [17] Those who claimed that bondsmen would just as soon go to jail as work had obviously never been in one.

Patrolmen and jails were only the beginning of woe for the slave entangled with the law. No explanation of his arrest need be given him, and conditions in prison would almost certainly be shoddy. However, he would not languish there long. Masters insisted that their property not be detained needlessly.[18] Hence in the morning the bondsman faced the judge. Of course, no trial in a meaningful sense followed. The slave had no right to plead, none to call a witness, indeed, no right to speak unless the presiding officer asked a question. Curiously, however, his bondage might be some protection. His owner could insist on proof, or at least a statement of why his chattel was in court. On a rare occasion a master would carry a case to a higher tribunal.

But the routine presumed guilt, and the owner often did not bother to appear. The only question to be decided was the sentence. At this point the magistrate often questioned the black, especially to find out if any circumstances should be considered in fixing the punishment. Sometimes, the slave protested innocence but seldom with any success. "However jealously a negro seeks to affect innocence, the eye always betrays guilt and a great evil capacity," the Richmond *Whig* explained. "Bill, the slave of Mrs. Elizabeth Johnson, who stole the coat and five dollars from Richard, slave of T. Cauthorn, who works on board the canal boat Glazebrook, was ordered thirty by the Mayor on yesterday, in disregard of the most solemn protestations of innocence on the part of Bill. There was an amount of villainy reflected in his eyes that could well contradict all the protestations he could utter for a month." [19]

The anxiety of the slaves in municipal courts sprang from hard experience. Occasionally, the punishment could be simply demeaning rather than bruising. Bishop Whipple once came upon a slave in a pillory, his head "mounted with a fool's cap, a paper pinned to his breast—'Stolen $5.00.' " Others he saw working as scavengers in the street, chained to each other as "punishment for some offence."[20] But the workhouse, irons, and even branding could be ingredients of the sentence. Above all there was whipping. "Negroes will be negroes in cunning, stupidity or stubbornness," a Richmond court reporter mused after listening to Mayor Mayo dispose of the "ordinary run of misbehavior by colordom, . . . so it is impossible to think of changing their nature, unless by the lash, which is a great institution for stretching negroes' skin and making them grow good."[21]

No other penalty carried the same meaning or so embodied the social relations of the "peculiar institution." The lash in the white hand on the black back was a symbol of bondage recognized by both races. "No man should ever use a cowhide on a white man," the *Richmond Enquirer* contended. "It is a cutting insult never forgiven by the cowhided party, because white human nature revolts at such a degrading chastisement."[22] A Charleston grand jury embedded its objection in a still broader context. Noting that blacks looked on intently whenever whites were whipped, it explained that they were "activated" by two sympathies: one was "of sorrow for the suffering of the criminal without reference to the justice of his punishment," and, secondly, "self gratulation in the degradation of the white by the same punishment to their own level."[23]

Whipping, then, was more than an ordinary punishment; it was meant to express a particular relationship as well. It served the system of bondage by permitting stiff penalties without depriving the master of his chattel's labor for any extended period. And, just as important, it came to be a social gesture embodying discipline, deterrence, and degradation. These purposes were clearly stated, and magistrates developed methods to give emphasis to one or another function. "A flogging in the Market is always given as a mark of disgrace, in contradistinction to a flogging in the Work House which is characterized by its *severity*," a Charleston constable explained. "In the former instance, the exposure is more considered than the Laceration of the criminal's body." Moreover, the blacks understood this. "It is a well known fact," the same authority added, "that every negro in this community regards a whipping in the Market as the greatest disgrace which can befall them." [24]

The distinction was more significant for the masters than slaves. They found whipping in either setting a dreadful thing. James Watkins, a Baltimore bondsman picked up for being out after hours, described the ordinary punishment from the victim's end. His friend, arrested at the same time, was called first. Watkins heard "a dreadful scream" and became very uneasy "knowing that my turn came next." After being called, he stated, "I was told to strip off my clothes, and was then placed on a wooden frame, my head down, and the other part of my body up." The jailor then "got a long paddle which was perforated with a number of holes, about a quarter of inch in diameter, and laid it on the fleshy part of my body with great violence." Lumps formed and broke with successive strokes. "These blows were repeated six times, and the torture was such I never experienced either before or since." [25]

Watkin's stripes might have been severe, but the number was fewer than the usual sentence. Judges generally prescribed much nearer the upper limit even in minor cases. The minutes of Richmond's Hustings Court for 1825, for instance, recite typical penalties for theft: for stealing three dollars, twenty lashes; three blankets, fifteen; four dollars, twenty-five; a calico dress, fifteen; a pair of boots, thirty-nine; one featherbed, ten.[26] In Mobile the Mayor's Court thirty years later encompassed still another customary range of punishments: ten lashes for "keeping Christmas by getting drunk"; fifteen for "impudence"; twenty-five for "insolent language"; twenty for imbibing the "expressed juice of corn"; twenty-five for being "out of place"; thirty-nine for a "charge too indelicate to be published." [27]

In other instances the penalty ran well beyond the legal limit, though it would be executed at different times. In such a case a Charleston girl, for example, was accused of making "several attempts to fire" a building; her sentence: "to receive twenty lashes on the first three Fridays of three successive months, and to remain two hours in the stocks each time; then to remain five years in solitary confinement." If the owner thought this excessive, he could take her out of the state after the first year.[28] In other decisions the magistrate indicated a higher severity by directing that the lashes be "laid on hard." [29]

In some places, too, at least for a period, burning on the hand was added to the stripes. A Richmond magistrate ordered a slave to be "burnt" and receive fifteen stripes on his bare back at the public whipping post for "stealing thirty dollars." In the same year of 1825, more than a dozen other sentences involved this same punishment.[30] Finally, a decade later, the court ordered the practice abolished, since it was "cruel and unsuited to the age" and "the effect upon that class of people on whom it is inflicted for the correction of crimes is at least doubtful." [31] Like whipping, burning was designed to combine severity with servitude, and the resultant scar was to be a constant reminder to the Negro of his "place."

In short, the character of the punishment was as important as its harshness. In the countryside, master or overseer wielded the lash on their own slaves with much less regard to social ritual. Only when a bondsman was sent to a nearby

plantation or court house for correction did outside considerations enter. In the towns, on the other hand, the patrol,
the courts, and the custom of using the municipal jailor became widespread. In such a situation, a large part of ordinary
discipline devolved upon the whipping post and workhouse.
What was private on plantations became public. Hence, punishment often became an event charged with a broader significance than the mere chastisement of a single black.

An episode in Charleston in 1837 neatly caught the social
overtones. Two slaves had been adjudged guilty of theft,
Sarah for stealing thirteen yards of linen and a "negro fellow"
for a "similar offense." Her sentence was two whippings of
twenty stripes and two weeks solitary confinement in the
workhouse; his was "a like number of lashes." But the administration of the penalties differed. "*Sarah* walked free and un-
shackled in advance of the crowd" which had gathered for
the affair. She carried a piece of watermelon, "looking much
more like a favored slave, rewarded for good conduct with
dainties for her stomach, than a thief returning from public
punishment, to be incarcerated in a solitary cell." The man
"was severely chastised, tied and carried (as he deserved)
among the hisses of the mob like a felon, to the workhouse." [32]

Some whites criticized the constable for his handling of the
proceedings, and in the discussion that followed the rationale
for public discipline was laid bare. "Civis," who claimed that
this was the first "public execution" he had ever seen, contended that the jailor applied the punishment on Sarah so
delicately that he virtually extinguished the sentence. "The
ceremony occupied about 90 seconds, a small whip being
lightly dropped upon the shoulders of this favored brunette,
...I have seen a gauze-wing fly who would have kept his
hold upon the neck of my horse in defiance of such an ad-
monition." Moreover, other Negroes gathered around whose
sympathy "was poured forth without measure." Sarah thus

won the "glories of martyrdom" and "paraded through the crowd, conscious and proud of the punishment, not inflicted on her by the law, but the law by her." [33]

"Civis" had a direct remedy. "If the negroes are to be whipped," he proposed, "they ought to be carried to the workhouse, not suffered to be marched through the streets and highways in open defiance of decency and law—and for a moment at least, they should be separated from the caresses and comfortings of their accomplices in vice." [34] Another Charlestonian joined in this view, though not on the score of harshness, for he "did not consider the good effect to be derived from corporal punishment dependent as much upon its severity as upon its publicity." But "Justice" did think "she should have been tied and carried through the streets, as an example and warning to others of her color, who are too prone to follow in her footsteps." [35]

Constable John Myer responded with the official view. Answering the charge that Sarah's lashes had been light, he observed that he had used cowhide and had no doubt that "Civis" would have "quailed under the severity of their infliction." But more significantly he argued that public punishment was more effective than tougher treatment. Slaves would "cheerfully submit (notwithstanding the severity) to a punishment of twice the number of stripes in the Workhouse," he contended, "rather than be tied to the public post, exposed to the gaze of every bystander, and liable, forever afterwards, to have the finger of scorn pointed at them as one who had been flogged in the Market." [36] Negroes, not a party to this debate, might well have found it without real meaning, yet the nature of the discussion suggested what whites intended to express with the lash and the whipping post.

The whip itself conveyed enough terror to the slave, but the public whipping posts served to institutionalize the cruelty. They were, in the bitter words of a former slave, "the monuments of the religion and greatness of Southern cities." [37] The installation itself was an elaborate contraption which reminded many of a medieval rack. There were variations, of course, but Mobile's contained most of the usual elements. "It was constructed like a sash frame," wrote a traveler: "The lower board on which the feet of the unfortunate being were to stand, could be pushed up or down, to accommodate the height of the individual. Upon it is a block, through which the legs are passed. The neck and arms passed through another." Designed for both personal punishment and public disgrace, usually located at the market in the heart of town, it was for the black the grotesque embodiment of the slave regime.[38]

III

The lash and the whipping post were the pivots of the system of discipline in Dixie's cities, but beyond, and always at hand, were other instruments of control. The workhouse, usually equipped with solitary cells and occasionally a treadmill, provided an alternative to the judge who delivered an extended sentence. Available too were irons, the historic emblem of bondage. And, of course, in the last extremity the hangman stood ready to dispatch the dangerous and intractable. Since none of these punishments was confined to blacks, they were seldom identified with the system of slavery. Yet the Negro community had every reason to see them in the context of that institution.

Indeed, the argument for the treadmill was usually put in terms of discipline. In the midst of the Vesey crisis in 1822, "City Rustic" suggested that Charleston adopt the device "*as a punishment amongst our domestics.*" Addressing himself to "every owner of town Negroes," he said it would be especially important "to the female owners of slaves, whose humanity but too often stands between the Negro and the well merited visits to the Workhouse." The "good effects to be derived from this excellent invention," he predicted, "would be incalculable. No lady even, would hesitate to send a lazy insolent waiting man, or a sulky seamstress, to the refreshing exercise of a week's walk in the Stepping-Mill." Moreover, "our male and female dandies, *and even some ladies who are not dandies*, could find their silk stockings and corsets considerably more lasting through its influence." [39]

Its establishment later in the decade met some of these requirements. The Duke of Saxe-Weimar found that whippings had been reduced, since the device made it possible to punish twenty-four people simultaneously, and women could be included with the men. In addition, he was told, "the negroes entertain a strong fear of the treadmills, and regard flogging as the lighter evil! Of about one hundred and sixty, who, since the erection of the treadmills, have been employed on them, only six have been sent back a second time." [40] Basil Hall was less impressed with this "sort of Bridewell," and thought it would never replace the lash as "an essential part of the system of slavery." [41] At any rate, not enough cities adopted the practice to permit it to become a competing symbol to the whipping post.

Irons, too, played a role in the system of discipline. There was nothing unique in their use in the cities since they appeared wherever the institution went. In fact, this punishment was probably employed more sparingly in the towns than elsewhere. Whites often criticized the practice, sometimes bitterly. A St. Louisan, for example, complained of the "shocking spectacle" of seeing "an unfortunate Female Slave crawling about the house in the ordinary business of the kitchen and compelled to drag along the grating manacles." He then asked why "the humane citizens" of the town should be "compelled to witness a scene at which barbarians should blush." [42] Still the books of the blacksmith employed by the municipal government in the same town carried such entries: "putting on three pair of hand irons, $2; . . . Ironing Negro hand and foot, $1; . . . putting irons on negro, $.50." [43] In addition, the authorities shackled runaways, jailors used the device when so instructed by judges or masters and whenever they found a prisoner difficult to manage. Certainly for the slave, the relationship between irons and servitude was uncomfortably clear.

Behind all these measures stood the gallows, the ultimate exercise of power. The hangman, of course, handled whites as well as blacks and probably he saw no connection between his craft and slavery. The noose could be swung over a limb in the countryside as well as dropped from an elaborate frame at the edge of town. Yet the subtleties in both instances counted. The level of tolerance for crimes was much lower for colored people and especially slaves, and an execution in the city was always more of a public event than in remoter areas. Hence capital punishment occupied a crucial position in the disciplinary system. This display of final authority, even though used only occasionally, was the ultimate and swift response to any who sought too boldly to move across the broad line dividing the races.

To be really effective, the act, or at least its result, had to be very public. It would serve no deterrent purpose if a slave was whisked away and disposed of quietly. Hence the jailyard usually formed the setting for the grim proceedings. On special occasions when the whites considered either the slave or the offense particularly threatening, the execution was conducted in a way to strike fear into the whole colored community. In 1822, for example, those presumably implicated in the Vesey plot went to the gallows in full view of the city. In another instance in Richmond a "promiscuous assemblage of persons, variously estimated from five to ten thousand,"

watched Giles put to death. The *Enquirer* noted that at the
end the prisoner warned "his fellow servants to shun his
course of wickedness," thus vindicating the publicity that attended the spectacle.[44]

The list of crimes for which a magistrate might prescribe
death for a slave was long, and it included many small offenses. Yet the courts hesitated to invoke it for trivial matters
since owners would protest the loss of property. Even when
bondsmen were sent to the gallows for insurrection, the master might sue for damages. In addition, in some cases where
the judge prescribed hanging, the owner was given the privilege of "transporting" his chattel, which meant selling the
slave elsewhere. Nevertheless, custom and law lodged in the
court this weapon to be used not only to satisfy some accepted
sense of justice, but as a tool of racial discipline as well. And
in every city the hangman was employed often enough to
remind the blacks of this residual authority.

IV

The Negro's response to this system of discipline is difficult
to discover. Few municipal court records or police blotters
remain; newspaper accounts are spotty, irregular, and not always reliable; memoirs of both whites and colored on this
question are scarce and often misleading. Even at moments
of great tension, as in Charleston during the Vesey affair or
in St. Louis after the burning of McIntosh, a free black, little
was revealed, because city officials drew a veil over the events
and secured a news blackout from local editors. And, of
course, what went on behind the enclosures was known outside only in cases such as that of Madame Lalurie in New
Orleans which involved extraordinary brutality.

Yet something of the slaves' response to these methods can
be pieced together. One fact is especially important. Few

adults could expect to escape corporal punishment altogether. Getting into trouble was just too easy; a brush with the law was almost certain. To be out after curfew, to loiter in conversation or on an errand, to be without papers when the patrol asked for them, to break one of the elaborate regulations surrounding the sale of goods or hiring time was so simple that few avoided an occasional mistake. In addition there was always the chance that the capricious action of some white would place the Negro before the magistrate on completely trumped-up charges. Like the modern motorist, no matter how careful the slave might be, he was certain to get ticketed from time to time.

For those who might possibly keep clear of the patrol, the judge, and jailor, there was always the master and his family who could wield the whip for much lesser offenses, indeed for none at all. "Good character" provided a shield against persistent punishment, but it was no guarantee. Nicholas in Charleston, for example, was known to be of "excellent character," to be civil and industrious, of "good temper and submissive of authority," yet he "needed chastisement" several times.[45] When Frederick Douglass compared slavery in the towns favorably with its rural counterpart, he did so on the ground that floggings were fewer, not eliminated, and that severity, while not unknown, was less common.[46] The sting of the lash, the humiliation of corporal punishment, was something every slave came to know sooner or later.

This central fact gave substance to discipline in all its aspects. If the whip had been so rarely used as to be the exception, if some had no personal experience with this punishment at all, and if there had been a clearer relationship between bad conduct and chastisement, the element of fear would have been greatly reduced. The uncertainty, the capriciousness, the universality of flogging connected the lash with bondage and struck terror in the slave. The knowledge that the whip was always there and that none was immune threw a pall over nearly every aspect of his existence.

Those who were fortunate for the moment had only to behold the back of a friend or listen to the conversations among other Negroes to be reminded of their position. To have your papers when asked merely made you remember what would have happened if you had not had them. The bells of the church or the rolling of drums sounding a curfew at night brought to mind the predicament of those who could not make it back to the enclosure in time. Casual talk in the master's household or bits of gossip by whites on the street concerned "correcting" blacks often enough to make one's servitude impossible to forget. The fact was ever-present; the fear pervasive. This atmosphere facilitated the task of maintaining discipline.

No one slave's narrative completely captures the feelings of those living under the shadow of the system. Yet the prosaic diary of a Charleston white indicates something of its nature. Jacob G. Schirmer, a prominent townsman who served on freeholders' courts from time to time, noted in his journal the disposition of cases which he heard, many of which involved Negroes. The newspapers did not report the court's findings, but the word moved quickly in the black community. The entries for 1831 were typical: July 8, "tried a Negro for stealing a Uniform coat / found him guilty and sentenced him to 1 week solitary confinement in Jail and two whippings at work house"; August 5, "served to try four negroes of Mr. Lagare for beating a free person / found 3 guilty and sentenced them to 10x20x30 lashes"; September 24, "a Negro was tried for attempting to stab Mr. Roche the tailor with a pr. of shears, was found guilty and sentenced to be hung on 26th. He was accordingly executed in the jail yard"; October 17, "a Negro belonging to Mr. McLane was tried for attempting to poison his master, was found guilty and sentenced to be hung on the 21st. He was accordingly executed in the Jail Yard." [47] The matter-of-factness of these notations represent the white perspective; the reaction of Charleston's slaves can only be imagined.

V

One of the most compelling symbols of servitude did not rank as a conscious part of the apparatus of discipline—the auction block. To slaveholders the block served an essential business function, permitting a somewhat orderly and continuous re-distribution of labor and establishing prices in a fluctuating market. For the slave the block represented the very heart of the whole system; it signified the transformation of the man into property. So long as it existed, no normal life was really possible. Even those who had managed the best accommodation to bondage were deprived of any security. No family relations could have permanence; no employment, though faithfully pursued, was fixed; no comfort allowed by an indulgent master could be considered lasting. In short, the possibility of sale added decisively to the already precarious position of the bondsman.

Nor was such an event unlikely. A slave could expect to be sold at least once in his lifetime, and for urban blacks the chances were much higher. The increasing instability of the institution in the cities meant wide-scale trading, especially of young men into the cane and cotton country. Women domestics were less apt to be sent into the fields, yet the possibility of their staying with a single master was never strong. The source of the Negro's fear of changing owners was understandable—though he might do better, he could also do worse. No doubt those afflicted with particularly cruel masters would have gambled on a trade, but most found the prospect frightening.

Yet the slave trade was very much a part of the regime of slavery in every town. Blacks were brought in from the surrounding countryside, housed in depots, then sold either privately or at auction. In the early decades these exchanges involved a large number of urban Negroes; later the plantation traffic dominated. At either time, however, the city's major role was not to provide the slaves but the facilities for marketing them. Even in the face of dwindling slave populations, Dixie's metropolises served as the centers of an extensive trade which constantly re-adjusted the supply of colored hands to meet the demands of the institution.

The depots were the familiar sites of the traffic. Here the purchaser could find available blacks, size them up, and strike a deal with the agent. Every city had many. They were licensed by municipal governments; they advertised their stock in newspapers; their locations were known to all. In the busy seasons the slave pens were filled; in slack periods they might contain few or none at all. From time to time, the proprietor left the place to scour the surrounding area for slaves who might be ready for the market. Occasionally the trade or the mongers came under attack by residents, yet both occupied a significant place in the economy of urban communities.

New Orleans was the special focus, "The Mistress of the Trade," in Frederic Bancroft's phrase.[48] Located at the water gateway of the growing Southwest, it funneled Negroes from the older sections into the new country. The Atlantic and border cities largely accumulated slaves from the hinterlands and sent them into other areas. New Orleans did this, too, but it also became a major distribution center for the traffic flowing from Eastern ports to the emerging cotton lands in the Mississippi Valley and beyond. To this dual function was added a third, at least until the 'forties. The city itself took on additional blacks, many coming from seaboard towns as well as the rural hinterland.[49] For these reasons the annual volume exceeded that of Charleston and Richmond both in transactions and in dollar value.[50]

To care for this thriving enterprise, slave depots sprang up all over the city. By the 1850's they dotted the area around the St. Charles Hotel and had become familiar sights in other neighborhoods as well. Gravier and Baronne Streets, especially, attracted the trade. A "Census of Merchants" in 1854 listed no less than seven "slave dealers" in a single block on Gravier, and eleven in one square.[51] Some distance away, Moreau Street housed a row of pens, including some of the largest anywhere.[52] Others were scattered around the edge of the business district. In addition, auctioneers, brokers, commission merchants, and even editors sold blacks, though only as a fraction of their regular activities and then without the elaborate apparatus of pens and depots.

The volume usually proved great enough to keep all these dealers busy. Conveyance records show over 4400 sales in 1830, and, though the figures fluctuated annually, over 3000 transactions took place in the last ante-bellum year.[53] Daily newspapers carried advertisements which reveal something of the extent and flavor of the trade. William F. Tallbott, for instance, announced on October 27, 1848, that there was "just arrived, and for sale" at his pen on 7 Moreau Street "a large and likely lot of negroes, consisting of field hands, house servants, and mechanics." For those not ready to purchase at the moment, he would be "receiving new lots, regularly during the season, from Virginia." On the same day J. B. Phillips offered "a number of negroes" at Bank's Arcade, while Joseph A. Beard invited buyers to an auction of 26 bondsmen.[54]

Two years later, Tallbott still kept the usual stock of slaves and advertising superlatives, and he was offering for sale "the largest and most likely lot of negroes ever imported by subscriber."[55] Not far away, Carmen & Ricardo sought both supplies of blacks as well as purchasers. They proclaimed that the firm had "one of the best show grounds in the city, and large and comfortable quarters, where every attention will be paid to the comfort" of the slaves. On hand, too, "at all times" were "Mechanics, Labourers, field hands, cooks, washers and ironers, house servants, seamstresses, and hair dressers, either on time or cash." [56] Some of the inventories were substantial. Thomas Foster brought to "the attention of merchants, planters, and purchasers" that he had 250 Negroes, a "stock" that he pronounced "the largest and equal, if not superior, to any in the city." [57] On Esplanade Street, buyers could find a "choice lot" of over 100 "Virginia and Maryland Negroes, field hands, house servants, coachmen, cooks, washers, ironers, seamstresses, and mechanics." [58]

While the dealers advertised, the blacks were cooped up in the depots being readied for sale. "It was an awful gloomy place," a former slave remembered from his experience in a New Orleans pen. Located across the street from the St. Charles Hotel, it consisted of "a block of houses forming a square, and covering perhaps an acre of ground." Three tiers of rooms housed the inmates. "The windows in front, which overlooked the street, were heavily barred, as were those which overlooked the yard." The jail's foreman was a mulatto who wielded immense power and had the task of fattening and "brightening up" his wards.[59] Most depots were less commodious, but the urge to sell blacks at good prices resulted in some comfort, if not always kind treatment.

Sales took place both at depots and auction centers. The purchasers could drop by the premises, examine the stock, and bargain on the spot. On entering he would run across a scene very much like the one Charles MacKay witnessed in a New Orleans pen: "On one side of the room the male slaves, with clean linen, and shining new hats and boots, were arranged, and on the other the females were disposed in their best attire, most of them exceedingly neat, but some bedizined with ribbons of colors more flaring and tawdry than elegant or appropriate." [60] For those just looking, the exhibition would be more modest. "The blacks passed in review before us," wrote another traveler, "the men and boys in smart blue attire and clean shoes, the women and girls in gaudy calico dresses—all tidily combed and curled." [61] If negotiations were serious, the examination would be thorough. The buyer quizzed the slave as to age, experience, and capacity; he stripped the blacks, male, or female, looking for imperfections or diseases; then, if satisfied, he began haggling over price.

Even more celebrated than this semi-private trade was the auction sale. Held at a public place and governed by customary rules, it became for the enemies of slavery the symbol of the whole regime. The most publicized sales took place in Washington before 1850, but more important and more extensive sales were in New Orleans. The most famous of these spectacles took place in the lavish surroundings of the St. Charles Hotel or the equally extravagant St. Louis. At the latter, the French Exchange took place in the grand rotunda, eighty feet around with marble floors and a towering dome. The surrounding walls were covered with "works in *chiaroscuro*, representing various successful actions gained during the struggle for independence." Here the fashionable, the curious, and the morbid watched the blacks "knocked down" by the auctioneer. One could hear French and English mixed charmingly, as buyers and sellers shouted prices and the crowd chatted casually. A specialty of this exchange were the "fancy girls," often beautiful and intelligent with colors ranging from the darkest to the lightest hue. In these sales ribaldry and indecencies mingled with the earthiness and matter-of-fact vulgarity which was an inescapable part of the traffic in human beings.[62]

Though none could match the extent or variety of New Orleans's pens, depots, or exchanges, every city had numerous slave dealers as well as merchants and auctioneers who did some business in chattels. In Richmond, Bancroft listed fifteen who advertised as "Negro Traders," fifteen who came under the heading of "Agents, General and Collecting," and twenty "Auctioneers." All, he calculated, trafficked to some degree in slaves just prior to the war.[63] At the same time at least forty-three were so engaged in Charleston, while Savannah and Mobile, having to share the trade with neighboring places, had fewer, but still enough to keep the market lively.[64]

The market also existed in the border cities. Though their own slave population declined sharply in the later ante-bellum decades, they continued a brisk commerce in blacks. Baltimore had about twenty resident traders in the 'fifties, Louisville had nearly half that number, and St. Louis, with more than thirty, was "one of the five or six cities that sent the most negroes to the insatiable 'Southern Market.' " In addition, smaller places like Montgomery, Memphis, and Natchez played a significant role.[65] Everywhere, then, the peculiar function of the city, even when its own colored community dwindled, was to provide the facilities—a central place, the congregation of buyers and sellers, the pens and depots, and the exchanges and auction blocks—for the trade.

There was no sacrifice involved, for the traffic contributed importantly to the economies of these towns. Exact figures are difficult to find, and both historians and contemporaries disagreed in their assessment of volume and prices. Yet even the lower figures indicate that slave-mongering was a sizable business. Bancroft calculated that at the height of the "negro fever" in 1859-60 the annual value may have run as high as $150,000,000.[66] Of course, not all the sales took place in cities, and prices had never before been so high. Still, in 1856 the transactions of a single firm in Richmond "reached the enormous sum of *two millions*" and the sales of "other houses of a similar kind" raised the amount to "over four millions—and still the business is increasing." [67] A year later, an editor in the same town placed the receipts from auctions and private jails at $3,500,000; the three largest operators employed 19 people and had depots assessed at over $25,000.[68] The municipal government's own revenue for licensing and taxes amounted to over $10,000 annually.[69]

Profits and losses for those engaged in producing this volume are even more difficult to reckon than total figures. But it is certain that commissions were good enough to permit many dealers to live very well. Louis D. DeSaussure made nearly $11,000 in 1860, and over a dozen fellow Charlestonians had incomes of $2000 or more from the trade.[70] Large operators in New Orleans grossed anywhere between $100,000 and $450,000, the take fluctuating with their luck on the market and the character of the sales.[71] State laws often restricted the commission that merchants could charge, but in a speculative venture, where the monger bought and sold the blacks, there was no ceiling on profits.

The account book of John R. White, a St. Louis dealer, provides a closer look at the normal operation of the business. In 1846 he listed the 172 slaves bought and 166 sold, six having died in his pen. The investment ran to over $82,220 with receipts of $100,896.25. His most expensive purchase cost $775 and brought in $1000. Ten years later he handled 117 blacks, and though all the figures are not legible, the range of exchange can be seen. Average prices to him ran around $700 and to buyers about $1100, leaving a handsome profit, since he had no losses or deaths. In 1859, his final year, his speculations netted about $50,000, as he marketed 186 slaves with total sales reaching $248,018.[72] White was only one of many dealers in St. Louis and by no means the largest, but his records convey something of the magnitude of the trade and the extensive earnings that might be expected even in a border town.

Urban economies might welcome the contribution made by these enterprises, but town dwellers were not always happy about it. The auction block was open to many objections. Visitors gawked at the scene and then often wrote unflattering accounts of the whole process. As the issue of slavery itself became more pressing, the trade in blacks became the aspect most difficult to explain. Even some supporters of the "peculiar institution" found the merchandising of people obnoxious, however necessary. In addition, few residents wanted a slave depot in their own neighborhood, with the coming and going of blacks and the constant fear that some might break out of the pens. Hence municipal governments established control over the whole business by restricting the areas where slave jails could be located and regulating the activities of auctioneers.

There was little discussion of the jurisdiction of the city. Some authority resided in the issuance of licenses; some in the control over the market; and still more in broad, if undefined, police power. Indeed, Louisiana placed on New Orleans a "duty" to prevent "slaves that might be brought or introduced into the city for sale or hire" from being seen in "the public and most frequented places," and to make regulations "in regard their exposure, and the parts of the city where said slaves shall be lodged, kept and sold." [73] In 1829 the council passed the first comprehensive ordinance banning the trade from the center of town ("within Canal, Rampart, Esplanade and Levee Streets").[74] Subsequent legislation usually extended the quarantine, ultimately to include even "the suburb St. Mary." [75] Depots had to be "built of bricks and not less than two stories high" and "kept constantly clean and properly ventilated." [76] Later enactments required close supervision of the blacks, and forbade them "to dance, run, or go through any exercise inconsistent with decency or public peace" or even to "stand on or walk" on the sidewalks.[77]

The laws, however, did not always stop the practice. Dealers sometimes petitioned successfully for variances which permitted pens inside the prohibited area. Occasionally councils rescinded parts of restrictive ordinances. But neighborhood hostility was easily aroused. After three Negro traders sought changes in the Second Municipality of New Orleans in 1845 a resolution replied flatly that "the keeping and sale of slaves within the densely populated portions of the limits of the municipality is in opposition to the wishes of a majority of the citizens." And "partial permissions" were so "productive of complaints" that the council re-instated the old, broader exclusion.[78]

Sporadic attempts to strangle the traffic by regulations brought the debate down to its essentials. The business must, one mayor observed, be considered "perfectly legal"; in fact, the slave regime could not exist without it. In addition, the trade "necessarily increases the revenues of the municipality" through the sale of licenses (which in his city ultimately rose to $500) and a fee on each transaction.[79] There was thus no way to avoid making some provision for depots, pens, exchanges and the other facilities that slavemongering required. Yet persistent neighborhood opposition managed to keep most of the operations out of residential districts.

Though the problem was most acute in New Orleans, every urban community took steps to control the unsavory aspects of the business. In Louisville an ordinance to "prevent persons who deal in slaves from conducting them through the streets of the City, chained," lost by a single vote in the council, but the usual restrictions passed easily.[80] Mobile excluded depots from downtown and established an elaborate registration system that kept tabs on everyone engaged in the traffic.[81] Richmond put the dealers under the regulations governing "houses of entertainment," which involved expensive licenses and more exacting health standards.[82]

Charleston's effort at control was the most ambitious. In 1839 the council memorialized the state legislature for power to establish a single mart where all transactions would be held. The reason for the request was plain: "the daily sale of slaves at auction which take place about the exchange in the midst of the greatest thoroughfare of business in the city . . . are a source of annoyance." A separate spot "was very much desired by public opinion and the interests of planters and others having large bodies of slaves" for disposal. Admitting the expense to be "considerable," the petition said nonetheless it was necessary to "carry out an important measure of public policy and to accommodate the public." [83]

In November an ordinance designated an enclosed lot next to the workhouse to be the "exclusive place within the city, for the sale, at public auction, or outcry, of all sales other than at Sheriff's sale." The master of the workhouse was given jurisdiction over the facilities. Those using any other building "as a house or place for the reception or accommodation of the slaves of other parties, for entertainment, safekeeping, correction or sale" faced a fine of $500.[84] By this piece of legislation the town took over entire control of the traffic. Within a few months, however, the dealers began a drive to regain their old privileges. By May 1841, it was again possible to sell blacks privately, so long as it took place on the owner's premises.[85] By the next year the experiment had collapsed. The public monopoly was rescinded, and Charleston went back to the looser system customary elsewhere.[86]

VI

If whites found many aspects of the trade distasteful, colored residents found them even more so. Slaves on the block could scarcely conceal their anxiety. "The quivering lip, the convulsive twitching of the face, the suppressed tear, the heavy sigh, & the broken reply to different interrogators" conveyed to Bishop Whipple the inner torment of the awful moment.[87] The fact that they could be sold at all, of course, constituted the overwhelming indignity. Some blacks no doubt became accustomed to the possibility, but they could scarcely be expected to like it. In the cities this was especially true, because slaves saw and knew many free blacks. Every part of the traffic brought home to the slave the precariousness of his own condition. Whether he watched a coffle clanging through town toward a depot, glanced at a flag hanging over a local pen announcing impending sales, saw a newspaper notice of a leading dealer's new stock, or, most baldly, strolled past the auction block itself, the Negro understood well that chance alone separated him from those about to be traded.

Fear of the auction block was, of course, not unique to urban Negroes. For every slave the prospect of sale brought the same anxieties, the same pangs of separation, the same uncertainties about the future, the same affront. From youth, blacks found sale a part of their probable destiny. An English visitor, while looking for a slave jail in Richmond, ran across a group of colored children playing in the street. "An intensely black little negro of four or five years of age, was standing on the bench, or block, as it is called, with an equally black girl, about a year younger, by his side, whom he was pretending to sell by bids to another black child, who was rolling about the floor."[88] To adults it was no playful matter. As Peter Randolph, a former slave, dolefully observed, at any time the bondsman could suddenly find himself on the block "knocked down to the highest bidder and carried afar."[89]

The urban slave, however, was placed in a more tenuous position than country blacks. His fears were heightened because he had more to lose than others. His greater opportunity, greater comfort, and better life were always jeopardized by the auction block. In case he was sold, he would not only get a new master but perhaps be sent into a strange location and saddled with harsher tasks and unfamiliar routines. Cotton and sugar-cane work had everywhere a fierce reputation; this held particularly true of Negroes who had tasted town life.

Indeed, any kind of farming was difficult for the city slave. "As I had been some time out of the field," testified William Wells Brown, who had suddenly been sold to a rural master, "and unaccustomed to working in the burning sun, it was very hard." Nonetheless he was "compelled to keep up with the best of hands." He longed to get back to his old job on the river, since he found "a great difference between work in a steamboat cabin and that in a corn field." Later, after several more years in St. Louis, when his owner wanted to sell him, he allowed Brown to find another local master. "As I had been used to living in the city, he thought it probable that I would prefer it to country life." [90]

Not many were given the choice. And even the option for the metropolis carried few illusions. Town life might mitigate the harshness of slavery, but it did not eradicate the institution. The repressiveness was still there; the indignities continued; the chances of freedom remained hopelessly remote. If the city harbored some escape from the overbearing scrutiny of masters, it also presented the slave with an awesome array of power ready to maintain the "peculiar institution" against subversion or rebellion.

Chapter Eight

———

RUNAWAYS AND REBELS

THE ELABORATE machinery for controlling slaves in the cities was more the measure of a felt need than a gauge of success. Despite constant surveillance, a complex system of restraints and punishments, and the presence of overwhelming force, many Negroes refused to become accustomed to their bondage. Unlike those isolated on plantations, "where no visions visit him to remind him of his servitude," [1] they saw all around them every day the possibilities of what they considered a better life. The free blacks in their midst, for all their hardships, enjoyed greater independence; colored sailors might have trouble in Southern ports, but beyond the sea in Northern and foreign cities things were different; newspapers and tracts, the gossip around town, even the conversation in the master's house, indicated that many Americans believed slavery to be evil, or at least unjust. This perception resulted in constant unrest among a significant number of urban slaves, an unrest that manifested itself not only in persistent pressure to widen the latitude within slavery but also in sporadic attempts to get outside it by escape or mutiny. "The cities," a Southerner told a visitor, "is no place for niggers! They get strange notions into their heads and grow discontented. They ought, everyone of them, be sent back onto the plantations." [2]

Whites felt this restlessness, and municipal officials recognized its existence. Yet it could never be generally admitted, for Dixie's official position was that blacks were contented in bondage. The image of the happy slave filled the writing of its advocates; any difficulties could be explained by outside tampering. From the standpoint of the cities, however, the usual picture of the blacks, surrounded by cotton, warmed by the sun, gaily singing while they picked, seemed inappropriate. It even suggested that the soil and agricultural pursuits were the natural environment of colored chattels. Hence town spokesmen developed a series of portraits which depicted the slave at his urban tasks, living in comfort, without care, fashionably dressed, and devoted to a kind master.

"If the negroes on our *plantations* live in the manner we have shown," a Charlestonian explained, "those immediately around our persons have still greater facilities of rendering themselves more happy and contented. Most of the latter are fed from the same table at which their masters dine, or are daily supplied with the greatest abundance of both animal and vegetable food—clothed in a superior manner—occupying rooms in the outbuildings, as nearly as good as those in the family mansion itself—and in every respect treated more like children than servants." It was nearly perfect. "They have no wants that are not immediately supplied." Even their spiritual needs were fulfilled, since "they are allowed privileges of moral and religious instruction, and every church has a portion of its galleries set apart for their accommodations. Here they may resort and listen to the word of God, and partake, with their masters and mistresses, and under the same benedictions, of the Holy Sacrament." [3]

"If the colored people of Savannah, Columbia, and Richmond are not, as a whole, a happy people, I have never seen any," another defender asserted. The idyll was now given an urban setting. "The city of Savannah abounds in parks, as they are called—squares fenced in, with trees," Nehemiah Adams wrote with satisfaction. "Young children and infants were there, with very respectable colored nurses—young women with bandanna and plaid cambric turbans, and superior in genteel appearance to any similar class, as a whole, in any of our [northern] cities. They could not be slaves. Are they slaves? 'Certainly,' says the friend at your side: 'they belong to some master or mistress.'" Though the author had not yet visited a plantation, he could say "a load was lifted from my mind.... A better-looking, happier, more courteous set of people, I had never seen, than those colored men, women and children whom I met the first few days of my stay in Savannah." [4]

Sometimes the slave was seen contentedly working at his particular tasks. Asserting that "there is no office, which the negro or mulatto covets more than that of being a body servant to a real gentleman," Samuel Cartwright found them delighted "to be at the elbow, behind the table, in hotels and steamboats, ever ready, brush in hand, to brush the coat or black the shoes, or to perform any menial service which may be required, and to hold out the open palm for a dime." This "innate love to act as a body-servant or lacquey, is too strongly developed in the negro race to be concealed," he concluded. [5]

The *New Orleans Daily Picayune* came to the same belief after watching the waiters in Hewlett's restaurant. Before customers arrived, they gathered opposite the entrance where "they frisk, and play, and sport like young colts in a meadow," completely oblivious of the troubles in the world. "They care not the 'first red cent' whether Van Buren be re-elected or not.... They feel indifferent about the state of the cotton crops ... or the settlement of the boundary question." Occasionally they "shake the glass roof of the Arcade over their heads with laughter, and whistle the Stars Spangled Banner and Yankee Doodle just as currently, note for note, variations and all, as Carey plays them on his fife." In short, they formed "a little commonwealth ... and the youngest as well as the oldest appear to enjoy the same immunities and privileges, and to speak, to sit, and to laugh just as he had 'a mind to.'" "Happier mortals," the editor wrote confidently, "do not exist on this earth of ours." [6]

Such sketches of happy city slaves were not necessarily vague. Indeed, they often detailed the physical and psychic attributes of slavery: "Bob was accustomed to live like a gentleman, in his own room, well furnished,—to smoke his own cigars, to take his own meals from the same dishes which were prepared for his master, to take his stroll of afternoons through Lafayette Square,—now and then attending a soiree, and illuminating the upper circles of opera, with his shining molars," ran one description. "Of work, Bob did just enough to keep his mind and body active, and prevent his faculties from rusting," and his master demanded only "fidelity and promptitude, politeness and cleanliness, and Bob was happy as a prince." But, unlike the prince, he had "no notes to pay, no debtors to look after,—no cares or troubles for the future." It was true, of course, that this "body servant" was "sometimes troubled to get a catfish for Sunday's chowder, and his cabanas sometimes ran short—but as to the main comforts, necessaries and luxuries of life, Bob was relieved of all care and anxiety." [7]

A Charleston visitor to Savannah could enthusiastically report the annual parade of colored firemen on the Fourth of July: "Never have I seen a finer body of well dressed and happy looking human beings, proud of their office, and zealous in its execution." The broader significance of the event was clear. "It was a spectacle to confound the evil spirit of abolitionism—the negro and colored population of Savannah organized to extinguish, not to kindle conflagration—the arm of safety in the hour of peril!" [8]

And the young were as happy as the old. "For hours, every morning," a New Orleans reporter noted, "we hear this 'little nig' whistling and whistling away the time, the perfect picture of contentment." As he made his daily errands, his serenity was almost contagious. "He must enjoy the full measure of happiness," the account continued enviously, "or he could never pour out such a flood of unalloyed contentment with no other gamut than cheerfulness, no other law for his guide than the fact of his being debarred all cares, no other to take up than those he makes as he goes along . . . if you want to see real happiness, look at our whistling negro while he is making all the streets, lanes, alleys, backyards, etc., etc., within two squares of 72 Camp Street." The inevitable query followed: "Wonder what his master asks for him?" [9]

Even if freed and allowed to go North, the slave would want to return to Dixie and his master's care. John Jones, for example, who left Charleston in 1832, petitioned the South Carolina legislature from Philadelphia for the right to come back "to mingle with and embrace the friends and associates of my youth" and bring his wife with him, since "she cannot adopt the manners and habbets of the North." The request was granted in the expectation that the Joneses would be living symbols of the contented slave theme and "the dissemination of their opinion and experience, among the colored population, . . . would be salutary, and calculated to do much good." [10] A St. Louis black, presumably whisked away by abolitionists, returned so frightened by his sojourn in freedom that when the boat brought him home "he could not be induced to go on shore until his master came for him; his dread of falling into the hands of another set of abolitionists was so great, that he would not trust himself unprotected even in a slave state." [11]

The stereotype of the smiling slave thus acquired an urban twist. Unlike his rural brother, he was not confined to picking and planting, his leisure time to lolling in a sun-drenched field, or his amusements to group singing at nightfall. He emerged as a full-blown city slicker, appearing in a wide range of employments, dressing in snappy fashion, taking in cultural events, and enjoying the varied delights of the metropolis. This image not only described the actual condition of slaves to some Southerners, but seemed to preclude a servile uprising. "There is greater necessity of many of the masters rising against their slaves, who have been corrupted and degraded by the indulgencies allowed them," one editor suggested. "They are allowed more liberty, indeed license, than any other class of our population. Their work is light; they are well fed—cared for in sickness . . . —and do pretty much as they like." What more could they want? "They must, indeed, indulge in views, as wild as those as Plato and Sir Thomas More, if they desire any more freedom than they now enjoy." [12]

II

The facts of urban slavery, however, every day belied this comforting portrait. Far from shunning freedom, Buckingham observed, "the slaves constantly take their liberty without it being offered them, by running away from their masters." [13] Though this problem was a plague everywhere, cities found it particularly vexing. In seaports, almost daily traffic with the outside world afforded a constant inducement to the discontented; in the interior, the river presented a similar opportunity; in border towns, the proximity of free soil offered even greater allure. The urban environment moreover permitted many runaways to find a sanctuary within municipal boundaries, either by hiding out in some obscure place or with the connivance of other blacks. They came in "great numbers," a New Orleans mayor lamented in 1834, "crowd in the city, hide, and make of our City a den." [14]

Towns always attracted more fugitives than they lost. Rural runaways headed for the nearest cities and quickly lost themselves in the congestion, protected as much by the anonymity of urban life as the collusion of other Negroes. Despite the extent of this movement, it never received the same attention as the attempt to close the escape valves which permitted bondsmen to slip out of Dixie altogether. A Charleston group, for example, warned that the port afforded "the greatest facilities" for hostile elements to "inveigle away our slaves," and the introduction of packets from Boston and New York magnified the evil.[15] A grand jury in Savannah, worried about the leakage there, urged the establishment of a "Marine Police" which would remedy the "want of proper vigilance on the part of the officers of ships in the harbor" and break up the "connivance of the crews" which had resulted in the flight of slaves to the North or Europe.[16]

Inland cities did not furnish slaves with a convenient ocean exit, but there were other means. In Richmond they used hackney coaches and the railroads; in the river towns steamboats provided handy escapes; and everywhere bondsmen, feigning errands, took wagons and drays as getaway vehicles.[17] Officials found that even more prosaic means needed watching. In New Orleans slaves "professing to be fishermen" went into the bayous and Lake Pontchartrain in "pirogues and other craft" and were "thenceforth lost to their owners." [18] At Louisville and St. Louis skiffs, rafts, and canoes got the blacks to the other side of the river; a good pair of legs and a little time did the rest.

Still other runaways left their masters without actually skipping town. They either fled the enclosure or simply did not come back at night. Finding lodging with friends or sleeping in sheds, lofts, or outbuildings, these slaves cut their connection with their owner, avoided him on the streets, and tried to put together a tolerable existence outside the law. The line between a black who was at large without papers and one opting for independence was never clear. The courts and police decided quite capriciously in individual cases, and no doubt the slave himself was often not certain what he intended, like Fortune, "an old limpy Negro ... who for two months has been looking out for a lost turkey." [19] Yet their number was always sizable, and attempts to halt this internal leakage was a continuing concern of local authorities.

"John has absconded from my service," ran a typical advertisement of a Louisville master, "he is lurking somewhere in the city." John had been seen by "several in the streets on Sunday last, and very probably is in the employment of some one during the working days of the week." [20] Nor was this situation unusual. A few weeks before in the same city, Priscilla, who was more conspicuous because she "expects shortly to be confined," disappeared. She had taken all her clothes with her, but her owner suspected that "she has concealed herself in some free negro's house in this city." [21] In New Orleans, Sam, a twenty-five-year-old laborer, who had worked in stores along the main streets, stopped coming home nights or bringing his wages back; "it is supposed," his master conjectured, "that he keeps himself in the lower and back parts of the city." [22] Nancy, too, left her enclosure. Soon she was seen "frequently ... in the company of Harrison, a slave, who works at bricklaying and plastering." [23]

A Charleston slave who was "so well known that further description" was "unnecessary" kept himself employed on the wharves for a long time while his owner desperately advertised for his capture. And while he looked for that one, another "took advantage of a badge" and also disappeared into the congestion of town life.[24] Even Stephen, also "well known about the city," who had worked as a storeman for sixteen years, slipped away from his master's place and lived with a free Negro woman for at least two years without detection.[25] An owner in the same town once illustrated, no doubt unknowingly, the irony of the familiar slave everyone knew and saw but no one could quite locate. Advertising for his bondsman, he observed that "he is pretty extremely acquainted in Charleston, particularly with the Ostlers, at the several Livery Stables, and the servants at the Hotels, and with many free persons of colour, and has been seen about the Planters Hotel and Frances' Stables, during the races." Despite this visibility neither master nor police could find him.[26]

The case of Scipio, a slave of Captain William Simms of Charleston, suggests something of the difficulty of detecting runaways. He had been sold out of the state "to atone for" his connection with the Vesey "insurrection." He soon reappeared in the city. Despite his notoriety, Scipio was hard to find. He escaped a net thrown by the patrol at one time and was only captured after the mayor, sheriff, "several of the ward constables, many public spirited citizens," and a "detachment of the city guard" surrounded an outbuilding and closed in on him.[27] Less famous runaways usually fared better.

Bolder fugitives, rather than hiding out, tried to pass as free. For instance, J. D. Digg's young coachman in New Orleans changed his name, forged some papers, and then claimed he had never been a slave. Though caught once, he succeeded for some time on the next try.[28] Similarly, Cato, a Richmond black who could both read and write, left his owner; the newspaper notice observed that he would "attempt to pass as a free man and possibly may have fabricated a certificate to that effect." [29] A Charleston runaway, described by his master as "very intelligent" and a "tailor by trade," used bogus papers for many years.[30]

Not all were so lucky, for the Mayor's Courts continually imposed penalties on those picked up trying to pass as free or for harboring runaways. Indeed, the frequency of the cases indicated how widespread the practice became. "Rosa Gozat, sporting as a free woman of color, but having no evidence of her freedom," ran a common notice, "was arrested on Liberty street, yesterday morning and committed till she can prove that she is not a runaway." [31] The same reporter had watched "Marie Claire, Jane and Rosine, free women of color, . . . sent to prison on a charge of concealing and harboring for the last four months, the slave Brosine, belonging to S.F. Hezeam." [32] Jacob, a Richmond bondsman, met the same fate for "harboring a runaway female slave, the property of Mr. Henry Johnson." Found guilty, he got punished "with stripes." [33] "A couple of slaves," the *Enquirer* related from another routine meeting at the Mayor's Court, "were treated to a whipping for infringing on our city laws with wrong papers." [34]

The cities, then, offered some slaves an uneasy sanctuary from the master, as well as a springboard to freedom beyond. For rural slaves these inducements were even more alluring. Once off the plantation, they headed for town, where other blacks could conceal them while they sought means for further flight. At any moment probably most runaways in every city came from this source. A portion were former residents who had been sold into the country and returned at the first opportunity; a larger part were fresh refugees who felt vaguely that they could find some safety in the nearby metropolis. No doubt, most fugitives expected to stay only briefly; yet to many the new town became as fixed a home as they would ever know.

In any case they comprised a significant fraction of the colored population of every urban center. Of course, no exact figures are available at any time, and even estimates would be misleading. But whenever statistics do appear the numbers are strikingly high. For instance, police records in New Orleans for fifteen months in 1858-59 list 913 arrests of "runaway slaves." [35] Since no special crackdown had been ordered and newspapers noticed no increase in the problem, it is reasonable to assume that this was a routine catch. Indeed, in the following month officials picked up 69 more, and this figure did not include blacks who claimed free status but could not prove it.[36]

Even border cities with many fewer Negroes brought in some each week. A jailer's account for 1837 in Baltimore revealed that 149 blacks had been arrested as runaways and 148 more for not having papers; some of the latter were subsequently declared fugitives.[37] Two decades later, despite a precipitous drop in the number of slaves there, 62 were charged with escaping and 421 "without proper security." [38] Those living illegally in the city must have been several times as numerous as those who were discovered.

Certainly contemporaries viewed the towns as infested with refugees who mingled easily with local slaves and free blacks. And when bondsmen disappeared it was usually assumed that they had sought concealment in the closest city. A Georgia master who purchased four Charleston Negroes soon found them missing; he immediately advertised in the metropolitan newspapers on the grounds that they had "certainly gone back where they were brought from." [39] Amos, owned by an upcountry planter, presumably headed there, too, because, as his owner declared, "he has a number of free acquaintances in Charleston." [40] And Caesar, "country born" and hitherto always faithful, fled a South Carolina plantation and was sought as a matter of course in the port town.[41] When John escaped in the Marlborough District, "he was pursued for two days, on his route to Charleston, where he probably now is," another notice reported.[42]

In the same way, Louisiana runaways headed for New Orleans. "He is also a Sugar maker at Vacuum Pan process, and a full Field hand," one owner advertised, expecting his slave to be in the city, where he would be "found at negro meetings" because he fancied himself a "Singer and Preacher." [43] Another said his bondsman, "having many acquaintances in New Orleans," would "probably go there, as he has done when he ran away before." [44] An Arkansas planter got only one day's work from four blacks fresh from the city's auction block; he presumed their instincts would take them back to their familiar haunts. [45] Solomon, too, sold into the country was presumed "to make his way to New Orleans, as he lived there several years," while a cotton master asserted that Henry, "an old runaway" at the age of twenty-five, "will make his way to New Orleans if possible. . . ." [46] In short, owners and officials assumed this to be the pattern of flight by fugitives.

This urban undertow was so strong that in border areas runaways left outwardly free soil for towns within the slave regime. Thus St. Louis not only attracted bondsmen escaping Missouri masters but refugees from across the Mississippi as well. Legally, the "peculiar institution" did not exist in Illinois, but a thinly disguised system of indenture imposed many of the same restraints on blacks. In 1828 the Illinois governor wrote to Mayor William Carr Lane complaining of "the encouragement our negroes have received to run to St. Louis." One of his own had recently found safety there, and, though he might retrieve her, he considered it too "troublesome . . . as she would doubtless run back again." Still, he contended, if "our negroes are to find refuge in your state," some systematic way ought to be devised for their capture and return." [47] Louisville had the same experience, with the objections filed from Jeffersonville and New Albany in Indiana. [48]

III

The runaway problem mounted despite every attempt of municipal officers to solve it. The slaveholders' fear of fugitives was understandable. For one thing, the traffic usually involved many of the best bondsmen—those with the highest skills, the most literate, the most energetic. Some were also the most obstreperous and ungovernable. Yet an examination of contemporary notices discloses that owners were usually losing valuable property. "Brought up a weaver; he is also a good brick moulder," Nice's master wrote to a local newspaper. "I am unable to describe his clothing; and think it more than likely that he will frequently change his dress, as he is very well off for clothing; he is, in every respect, a very sensible, cunning shrewd negro." [49] When a hack driver made off with Nice's wife and two daughters, all slaves, another owner noted that "the whole of them [are] well dressed, and all of them [are] unusually smart and intelligent." [50]

"As he is very intelligent," a Charleston master reported about his runaway, "he may attempt to pass by forged papers as free." [51] Another began his advertisement for Lucy by noting that she was "sensible, smart and active in the house at any kind of business," adding that she "probably has altered her name . . . for she is very artful." [52] Mobile notices emphasized the same thing; the refugee was skilled in some trade or service, knew reading and writing, "speaks quick and with much confidence," assumes "a degree of boldness," or "is a smooth tongue fellow." [53] Whether a fugitive from the countryside or one who jumped bondage in the city, the description, carefully drawn by an owner anxious to recover his property, usually conveyed the notion that it was no ordinary Negro at large.

New Orleans, always a little more sophisticated than other

cities, had a superior brand of runaway. Jim, who left the
Louisiana Bakery, spoke "both French and English" and was
"very intelligent." [54] Another claimed "a knowledge of Italian,
Spanish and Latin languages," could read and write, and
was "very vain of his accomplishments." [55] Almira's creden-
tials matched these, since he managed German along with
three other languages.[56] Another, besides being literate, boasted
"some knowledge of the carpenter's trade, printers, white
washers, &c," while Harry was more versatile, "a carpenter by
trade, and . . . a very good fiddler." [57] The conclusion was inescapable: some of the best slaves opted for freedom.

The damage to owners could not be calculated only by the
disappearance of valuable chattels, however, for successful
runaways left a deposit for discontent among former associates. Whenever a slave escaped, the word got around
quickly, often emboldening others who had dreamed vaguely
of making a break. A rash of flights invariably led to demands
for tighter patrolling and immediate steps to halt the seepage.
"Do you not see its mischief," an alarmed Richmond master
asked, "not only in the loss of property, but in the effects
it perceptibly has on those who remain behind?" [58] The fact
that some had managed to shed their bondage increased the
restlessness of those still enslaved.

The persistence of this problem created a singular difficulty
for the contented-slave thesis. Some, like Samuel Cartwright,
argued that the urge to run away was a peculiar Negro disease
which could be early diagnosed and usually cured. When the
slave appeared dissatisfied, the master ought to find out why.
If the cause was not apparent or justified, then "whipping the
devil out of them" was the proper remedy.[59] Yet most fugitives concealed their intentions before leaving; indeed, many
masters were surprised to find among the missing the most
coddled, pampered, and spoiled, who had always seemed
happy enough.

Hence Southerners increasingly found an explanation of the sizable number of runaways in the enemies of slavery—abolitionists from the North or emancipated Negroes in Dixie. These were the serpents who had crept into the garden and subverted paradise. Insinuating themselves into the slaves' affairs, they created the discontents, stirred up the disaffected, and intrigued in their escape. They used every weapon, corrupted every church, stooped to every ruse to carry on their warfare against slavery. Nor was it a spontaneous, unorganized campaign, for the abolitionist power had established an intricate and widespread network of agents and agitators who busily plotted the overthrow of the regime.

Any increase in the number of fugitives brought this suspicion to the surface. Thus a Richmond editor concluded an examination of the problem in 1855 on a characteristic note: "There is little doubt that there are agents in this city who are in communication with the North and have every facility for running off slaves." The slave was "doubtless the instrument in the hands of designing white men, who have been carrying on the business so extensively in this City of late." [60] This complaint, of course, was not new. Two decades earlier, in a single weekend, more than a score of blacks disappeared; Virginians found the explanation easy: "there is a regular system for removing them. Depend on it, some infamous whites are concerned in it." [61]

A grand jury in Savannah, investigating "several instances" when blacks got away, leveled the blame on "the seductive misrepresentations of secret enemies" as well as the "facilities offered by the connivance of the crew" in the harbor. [62] Nor were the "enemies" hard to identify. A New Orleans resident traveling in New York claimed in 1854 to have discovered there "the source of the heavy losses which are usually sustained in this city by the escape of slaves." The culprits were "some of our Northern BRETHREN and SISTERS" who

"think it very cute to come here in the winter, drive a prosperous trade, and when summer approaches, lend their names
and countenances to some negro, to enable him to obtain passage on some ship or steamboat." [63] Chicago, too, "that negro-
worshipping city," was leagued in "a scheme for running off
slaves from this city" and part of "an organization existing
in New Orleans, of which but a few persons are aware." [64]

By the mid-'thirties Dixie's spokesmen placed the main responsibility for runaways on the abolitionist movement. This
interpretation permitted a definition of the fugitive problem
without upsetting the conception of the happy slave enjoying
his work and status. It also provided a concrete explanation
lacking in the vaguer assertions, since abolitionists, or presumed ones, actually appeared in Southern cities. Arrests of
these agents always set off great excitement and occasionally
mob action. When two itinerant preachers addressed street
crowds in New Orleans with "doctrines . . . not precisely of
the character calculated to advance the well-being of the colored population," Corporal Delarue "at once" took them in.
A room search turned up writings asserting "the equality of
races—a theme by no means suited to this latitude, and which
of itself must produce discontent amongst the colored population." The editor of the *Bee* applauded this swift action, because "it requires but the very feintest penetration to discover
that these itinerant and psalm singing chaps are Abolitionists in disguise, and of the most dangerous kind." Slaves, it
contended, always come home from these churches "discontented with their position, happier by far though it is than that
of the labouring classes of other countries." [65]

Border towns confronted this question more directly,
for across the river lay at least nominally free territory from
which abolitionists could operate without surveillance. By
1835 a prominent St. Louis resident could warn against "the
foolish, reckless and wicked interference of the Abolition-

ists" who "have been among our slaves and have infected them with a spirit of insubordination." [66] A few months later, in the midst of the city's turbulent racial crisis, a judge found the greatest mischief in "those incendiary publications" which "deeply injured the slave population" by encouraging its restless spirit.[67] And in Louisville, the constant trickle of fugitives across the Ohio brought a similar reaction. In sum, Negro discontent was early equated with outside agitation in Dixie.

Northern anti-slavery forces bore no exclusive blame; for free Negroes in the South were also considered an unsettling factor. As residents of the city, exempt from many of the restrictions slavery imposed on other blacks, the freedmen excited envy among the slaves and contributed to their disquiet. "Abolitionists and free negroes," wrote a Louisville editor, "are among the greatest curses of the land. The first are fanatical, devilish, unprincipled; the latter are ignorant, lazy and thriftless ... they both act as promoters of discontent among the slaves." Without them, he concluded, bondsmen would be "as well satisfied, as happy, as well provided for, as their conditions would admit of." [68] "They are a plague and a pest in the community," the *New Orleans Daily Picayune* asserted plainly, "besides containing the elements of mischief to the slave population." [69]

IV

This explanation of runaways was more comforting than accurate. No doubt both abolitionist activity and the presence of free blacks transformed some unhappy slaves into fugitives; perhaps, too, by suggesting an alternative life, they changed an accommodating slave into an unadjusted one. Yet the causes of unrest lay deeper and would not have been removed by the expulsion of both abrasive elements. In fact, the Negroes expressed their resistance to the compulsions of slavery in a variety of ways. Occasional sabotage, self-maiming, and inadequate workmanship were common enough to bring complaints from owners and employers. More frequent still was the slow-down. Masters could never be certain how much of this was a vote against the system itself and how much simply reflected the low incentives that characterized slavery. In any case there were "so many aches and pains, so much imaginary suffering of the keenest kind to be assuaged by pills and plasters and cataplasms and embrocations—so much rheumatism and pleurisy, so many 'delicate situations,' and all-overish feelings" that masters could detect a lack of enthusiasm that bordered on passive resistance.[70]

In some cases, the alienation ran so deep that they sought a more radical remedy than flight. They hoped to shed their chains and rid the whole country of the "peculiar institution" by armed rebellion. To be sure, such action was only occasional, usually unco-ordinated, and always unsuccessful. But that it appeared at all is significant. And the white community's constant fear of racial violence represents an important commentary on the nature of slavery whether in town or country.

In point of fact, no actual significant uprising took place in any Southern city. The Gabriel mutiny in 1803 and the Turner rebellion in 1831 started on the Virginia countryside, though they may have hoped to use Richmond as a base. Denmark Vesey's conspiracy in 1822 never reached the climactic stage, if indeed it actually existed in the first place. Sporadic jail breaks, some of which inflicted casualties on whites, never possessed any broad anti-slavery intent. Despite the record, however, white anxieties never really diminished. "We should always act," a group of leading Charleston residents asserted, "as if we had an enemy in the very bosom of the State, prepared to rise upon and surprise the whites, whenever an opportunity be afforded." [71] The papers continued to demand increased police vigilance; municipal officials sought wider powers and additional arms from state governments; vigilante committees stood ready to quash the colored rebels. Yet no insurrection occurred. The blood bath feared by so many was never drawn.

"Christmas is passed and we are not yet annihilated," the *New Orleans Daily Crescent* noted with relief in 1856. "Whether there was any preconcerted plan or not among our servile population, we do not know, but so far, although the strictest watch has been kept over them, nothing has occurred to cause suspicion to the most timid." [72] In 1835 Mobile bubbled with rumors of a rebellion, some believing that the police had "detected a conspiracy"; others heard that a white man or free Negro had been hanged for complicity, still others believed that the blacks were ready to strike. "We feel assured," one editor wrote after consulting local officials; he added that no one should be "unnecessarily excited by the thousand tales ... which are now a days afloat." Most reassuring, however, was the revelation that "the well regulated system of espionage w₋ have now established" precluded any serious difficulty. [73]

Times of particular stress stirred latent uneasiness in every city. Nat Turner's uprising in 1831 left a trail of fear and anxiety through urban communities everywhere. In this instance Baltimore's mayor received news of a gigantic plot to culminate in an invasion of the city. A secret document, somewhat mysteriously intercepted, spun out the details "for our violent deed and act ... which will end in the overthrow of the whites and our freedom." The instructions told the accomplices to "distribute yourselfs about the houses where our female people of color live" and wait. "As soon as you hear the signal which is known to all our colur," the confederates were "to rise and murder our masters." A footnote added that "Brother John told me that there was eight hundred people in town that are going to help murder the damnd white people." [74] To increase the mayor's apprehension, an anonymous letter claimed that "a number of Blacks have been in the habit... of assembling in military uniform toward the west of Saratoga street" around midnight for "military exercises." [75] The alarm, of course, was false and was not unusual, except perhaps for its precision. In other places, patrols were strengthened, while civic leaders counseled against undue panic.

A discussion of slave unrest in the cities invariably turns to the Denmark Vesey plot of 1822. Like a sharp knife, its memory cut into the conscience of Dixie's town dwellers. More than Nat Turner's rebellion, more than any rumor of a country uprising, it embodied the fullest range of terror, raised the most awesome possibilities, and disturbed even the most complacent residents. What happened in those sultry summer months in Charleston was never very clear, but it was generally believed at the time that the blacks had hatched a plot on the grandest scale to overthrow white rule by force, butcher masters and mistresses, sack the city, and then escape into the Caribbean. The numbers involved presumably ran into thousands, and only a last minute betrayal scotched its successful execution.

The real facts are still obscure. Charleston newspapers imposed a nearly perfect blackout on the details and confined themselves to a simple reporting of sentences and executions. Months later, the city printed an official version of the plot with testimonies and confessions which claimed to be as "originally taken, without even changing the phraseology, which was generally in the very words and by the witnesses." The court, in ordering publication of the record, instructed the editors "*not to suppress any part of it.*" [76] Out of such spare materials contemporaries and historians pieced together a design of hair-raising proportions.

It all began on May 25, 1822, with the casual meeting of two slaves on the fish wharf in Charleston harbor. They had been chatting idly about the ships that lay at anchor before them when William Paul asked Devany Prioleau if he knew that "something serious is about to take place." Then, more precisely, he said that "many of us are determined to right ourselves" and "shake off our bondage." Devany had not heard of the plot. "Astonished and horror struck," he quickly broke off the conversation and hurried away.[77] After a few agitated days he confided the news to a free Negro, George Pencil, and asked what to do. His friend told him to tell his owner. On May 30 at three o'clock Devany gave the fateful information to Mrs. Prioleau.[78]

Two hours later, the mayor called the city council into extraordinary session. The police picked up both Devany and William; officials began an intensive inquiry. They kept William in solitary confinement in the "black hole of the Work-House" for a week and interrogated him every day.[79] Finally he gave them the names of Mingo Harth and Peter Poyas. Yet these men disclosed nothing. In fact, they "behaved with so much composure and coolness, and treated the charges . . . with so much levity" that the wardens were "completely deceived" and released them both.[80] Later William implicated others, but they too claimed no knowledge. The authorities were further baffled when Ned Bennett, a slave of the governor of South Carolina, came in voluntarily to clear himself of suspicion.[81]

Having turned up nothing—but suspicious of everything—the mayor strengthened his patrols, armed his men for extensive action, and waited. On June 14 the break came. Another slave corroborated William Paul's testimony by disclosing that the strike originally set for July 2 was now moved forward to June 16. For the first time the public knew something was up. A strong guard surrounded the city; the police appeared in force. Still nothing happened. Two days later, ten slaves were arrested; on the 21st they brought in Denmark Vesey. But even before this, on the 18th, a hastily assembled court of freeholders began hearing secret testimony. On July 2 the bodies of six Negroes swung from the gallows at the edge of town.

The uprising now seemed quashed. But as word of its scope spread, public shock turned into hysteria. No master could be sure his slaves were not involved; whites who owned no slaves had little more assurance. Every Negro became a possible enemy, indeed assassin; every action by a black could be construed as a prelude to violence. Since the slaves lived in the same yard, it was not even possible to lock out the intruder.

As the terror spread, so too did the presumed magnitude of the conspiracy. "Their plans were simply these," wrote a daughter of a respected judge and a niece of the governor, during the trial: "They were to set fire to the town and while the whites were endeavoring to put it out they were to commence their horrid depredations." Then in more detail: "It seems that the Governor, Intendant [Mayor], and my poor father were to have been the first victims—the men and Black women were to have been indiscriminately murdered—& we poor devils were to have been removed to fill their—Harams— horrible—I have a very beautiful cousin who was set apart for the wife or more properly, the 'light of the Haram' of one of their chiefs." [82]

Panic gripped the colored community too. As more and more blacks disappeared into prison, as rumors widened, and as the newspapers announced arrests and executions, the alarm deepened. Was someone putting the finger on his neighbor? Had the police picked up so many that some had to be housed in a nearby county? Were white irregulars about to take things in their own hands because the court was too slow? In the awful uncertainty the Negroes found an uneasy unity. Most of those questioned by municipal officials professed no knowledge of any plot; others wore armbands of crepe in mourning for the dead, until officials forbade demonstrations of sympathy.[83]

Outwardly, the normal deference to whites increased. "There was a wonderful degree of politeness shown to us," a white recalled, "bows and politeness, and—give way for the gentlemen and ladies, met you at every turn and corner." [84] In a few weeks the crisis waned. The handful of executions seemed to have ripped the heart out of the rebellion. "We thought it was ended," a Charlestonian wrote to her friend, "the court had been dismissed and the town was again sinking into its wonted security when information was given that another attempt would be made." The tip came from a Negro who later became a key witness. The council quickly set up a new court; the patrol returned to its stations. "There are now between 50 and 60 of the leaders in our jail," Ana Hayes Johnson wrote on July 18.[85]

A new excitement swept the city. "In all probability the executed will not end under 100," Miss Johnson estimated, and others asserted that "even should there be 500 executed there would still be enough" conspirators to pull off the scheme. "How far the mischief has extended heaven only knows," she lamented fearfully.[86] Her next letter contained the morbid mathematics: "22 unfortunate wretches were at one fatal moment sent to render their account 29 had been sentenced but 7 had their sentences commuted to perpetual banishment—but on Tuesday 6 more are to be executed . . . gracious heavens to what will all this lead . . . and I am told that there are an awful number yet to be tried." Miss Johnson had more knowledge than most, but she could observe on the street that "there is a look of horror in every countenance." "I wish

I could act for myself," she added, "I would not stay in this city another day . . . my feelings have been so lacerated of late that I can hardly speak or act." [87]

From the beginning municipal authorities were no less frightened but they also had to act. On June 18 the council appointed the first court of five freeholders, chosen because they possessed "in an eminent degree the confidence of the community." The tribunal quickly drew up the rules: no slave could be tried without the presence of his owner or the owner's counsel; "the testimony of one witness unsupported by additional evidence, or by circumstances, should lead to no conviction of a *capital* nature"; witnesses would confront the accused except "where testimony was given under a solemn pledge that the name . . . would not be divulged" because the judges feared the informant might be "murdered by the blacks"; a master or free Negro could have counsel if asked, and "the statements of defenses of the accused should be heard, in every case, and they be permitted themselves to examine any witness they thought proper." [88] The freeholders worked in complete secrecy because of the "peculiar nature of the investigations" and because "it was also morally certain that no coloured witness would have ventured to incur the resentment of his comrades, by voluntarily disclosing his testimony in a public court." [89]

The court divided the conspirators into two groups. The first comprised those "who exhibited energy and activity"; they were executed. The other included those "who did little (if any more) than yield their acquiescence to the proposal to enter the plot"; they were deported. The judges later confided to the governor that the distinction did not wholly meet the facts, but "the terror of example we thought would be sufficiently operative by the number of criminals sentenced to death" that "without any injury to the community . . . a measure might be adopted ... which would save the necessity of more numerous executions than policy required." [90]

The court found it difficult to get hard evidence. Vesey and the first five went to the gallows without confessing—indeed asserting their innocence. In the second group, however, three men under the sentence of death with the promise of leniency implicated scores of other blacks in the plot. In asking the governor to pardon Monday Gell, Charles Drayton, and Harry Haig, the judges described the conditions of their testimony: "Under the impression that they could ultimately have their lives spared they made ... disclosures not only important in the detection of the general plan of the conspiracy but enabling the court to convict a number of principle offenders." Like "the terror of example," the officials wanted deportation in place of the hangman so that "negroes should know that even their principle advisers and ring-leaders cannot be confided in and that under the temptations of exemption from capital punishment they will betray the common cause." [91]

Despite the problems of establishing evidence, the court moved energetically and decisively. Of the 131 picked up, 35 were executed, 31 transported, 27 tried and acquitted, and 38 questioned but discharged.[92] Throughout July the gallows was kept busy. On "the Line" which separated the city from the Neck, the neighborhood numbly watched the public display.

Most of the condemned died without admitting any guilt, and some with almost defiant contempt. Bacchus Hammett, who had "confessed," "went to the gallows *laughing and bidding his acquaintances in the streets* 'good bye,' on being hung, owing to some mismanagement in the fall of the trap, he was not thrown off, but the board canted, he slipped; yet he was so hardened that he *threw himself forward, and as he swung back he lifted his feet, so that he might not touch the Board.*" [93] Others were dispatched more expertly, and the bodies left to dangle for hours to make certain that no colored resident could mistake the point of the punishment.

Constable Belknap, the executioner, later complained that the frequency of the hangings had caused him great "personal inconvenience" and had "deranged" his "private business." At the height of the crisis he had spent "all his time and services" in the "call of the public, both by night and by day, in assisting at the preparation of the Gallows, the digging of the graves and various other offices connected with the execution." [94] The city's budget too felt the strain. In December the council asked the state to reimburse it for the unusual expenses surrounding the plot and trial. The bill came to $2,284.84¼, including costs of confinement, a payment of $200 to "Col. Prioleau's man Peter for secret services rendered," the price of "erecting a Gallows," and for "carts to carry the criminals to the place of execution." [95]

As the court wound up its grim business, the city tried to recover something of its old composure. The *Courier* closed the books on the episode: "The legal investigations of crime have ceased. The melancholy requisitions of Justice, as painful to those who afflicted, as to those who suffered them, have been complied with; and an awful but necessary, and, it is hoped, an effectual example has been afforded to deter from further occasions to offense and punishment." [96] The editor then called on the council for a day of thanksgiving to God for "his preserving care" and because "He has watched and guarded the tranquility of our City" and "endowed our magistrates with firmness and wisdom, rendered necessary by an alarming crisis." [97]

Not all, however, considered the matter finished. Some demanded new safeguards against a future rebellion. Writing under the pseudonym of "Experience," one argued for a drastic "revision of our present code of police and the formation of new regulations for the government of our servants." This meant not only state and municipal laws but also the "regulations of private families" whose laxity had emboldened the slaves. He warned further that if no action were taken immediately apathy would again smother the chance of reform. "The moral material is now hot, and may be moulded to good shapes and ends: let us strike before it is suffered to cool." [98]

The city council went even further. In a memorial to the South Carolina Senate it argued that "by some wise enactment" the number of male slaves "be greatly diminished" within "your metropolis." The thinning process should be uniform "comprehending . . . the Domestics, handicraft persons and all those who hire themselves out or are hired by their owners." In addition, to protect the town against "another sudden attack," a "citadel ought to be constructed within the Lines for securing the arms, and capable of continuing a competent force for its defence." On a permanent basis this fort should be supplemented by "a military force of not less than two hundred men under Martial Law . . . organized and commanded by experienced officers." And more immediately those blacks who had disclosed the plot be "liberally remunerated" and this reward be given "the most distinguished notoriety." [99]

In an extended analysis a leading citizen, Thomas Pinckney, supported the policy of reducing the town's black population. He had no criticism of the handling of the Vesey revolt. Indeed, he liked the "vigor and decision which marked the conduct of the City Authorities" and "the patient investigation, sagacious conduct, and inflexible justice of the Court," because "the example made of those infatuated miscreants who have rendered themselves obnoxious to the severity of the law, will, probably, for sometime, preclude the danger of similar conspiracies." Furthermore, he was confident that state and local governments would "adopt such measures as their wisdom and patriotism can devise, to prevent forever the recurrence of such enormities." [100] Yet the urgent need was to "reduce the proportion of blacks in the city so that our families shall be safe from the horrors" and "may retire to our repose at night, with the certain knowledge of our immunity from the dagger of the treacherous internal assassin." [101]

Though this remedy was not adopted and even more modest proposals won only partial success, Charlestonians could not easily forget the terror of those summer days of 1822. Indeed, if anything, the event became more vivid and bloody in the retelling than it had been in fact. "From what I could glean of that fearful drama," wrote a visitor many years later, "the slaves in the surrounding districts, on a concerted signal from their confederates in Charleston, made a descent upon the city, . . . proceeded to fire it and massacre the inhabitants." Finally, "the tocsin was sounded," and the whites rallied "and after much hard fighting, the rebellion was crushed, and large numbers of the insurgents were slain or arrested." [102]

Other accounts stopped short of street fighting, but all spun out an extensive plot which was providentially uncovered. "In 1822 a project of insurrection was discovered in South Carolina," another traveler remembered from a planter's version, "according to which 10,000 negroes were to have risen, sacked Charleston, murdered all the whites, and sailed to Santo Domingo." After the trial, "twenty-four of the ring leaders were hanged, and such precautions are now taken as to render an outbreak improbable." [103] Stuart, hearing it from a source hostile to bondage, referred to the episode as "the most horrible butchery of slaves which has ever taken place in America," 35 executed "on account of an alleged conspiracy against their masters." [104]

Even Negro commentators assumed the existence and ripeness of the plot. "A Colored American," writing nearly three decades after the event but presumably on the testimony of a witness, placed the blame on the whites for passing "uncivilized laws" prohibiting manumission which "cut off entirely all hopes" for liberation. "Justly incensed," the blacks "conspired to free themselves from the yoke of the most unholy bondage ever invented by man" and "to become owners of their own sacred persons over the bodies of their masters." When "a traitor to their supposed righteous cause" leaked the information, the city was "saved from a bloody servile contest." The "mock and summary trial of these brave men" was "upon the plan of Judge Lynch." It resulted in "sending thirty six brave men to a premature, but honorable grave." In this perspective a justifiable plot failed because of the treachery of a single black and the "unchristian ferocity" of slaveholders.[105]

Contemporaries and historians alike thus assumed the broad validity of this narrative. Yet there is persuasive evidence that no conspiracy in fact existed, or at most that it was a vague and unformulated plan in the minds or on the tongues of a few colored townsmen. No elaborate network had been established on the countryside; no cache of arms lay hidden about the city; no date for an uprising had been set; no underground apparatus, carefully organized and secretly maintained, awaited a signal to fire Charleston and murder the whites. What did exist were strong grievances on one side and deep fears on the other. When combined with a conjunction of somewhat unrelated circumstances it was possible for many people, both white and Negro, to believe in the existence of a widespread scheme to overturn the institution of slavery.

In the years before the "plot," several developments had worsened what were always uneasy relations between the races. The census figures conveniently summed up white fears. Officially Negroes outnumbered whites 14,127 to 10,-653.[106] During the summer, when many families left the city to escape the heat, there was an even greater proportion of colored people. Thomas Pinckney, in an extended post-mortem on the grim event, expressed the consequent anxiety. He called the imbalance "the principal encouragement to the late attempt, for without it, mad and wild as they appear to have been, they would not have dared to venture on a contest of force." In a word, numerical superiority was the "*sine qua non* of insurrection." [107]

Numbers alone, however, would not have produced panic. Some rural areas had a higher percentage of slaves than the city without the same alarm. It was the kind of colored population, not its mere predominance, that frightened white leaders. Charleston's Negroes, like urban blacks elsewhere, were quite different from their country brothers. They were more advanced, engaged in higher tasks, more literate, more independent, and less servile than those on plantations. Even the domestics who comprised the bulk of urban slaves afforded slight comfort, though they were popularly believed to be loyally attached to their owner's family.[108] In fact, Pinckney thought them "certainly the most dangerous," because they had an "intimate acquaintance with all circumstances relating to the interior of the dwellings," because of "the confidence reposed in them," and because of "information they unavoidably obtain, from hearing the conversation, and observing the habitual transactions of their owners." Having "the amplest means for treacherous bloodshed and devastation," this group would comprise the core of the conspiracy. Yet these slaves, he complained, had been "so pampered" by "indulgencies," even "being taught to read and write," that the "considerable control" embodied in ordinances and state laws had been frustrated by the "weakness of many proprietors." [109]

Nearly all those believed to be ringleaders by the court came from these areas of Negro life. Denmark Vesey, the only free black in the group, was a successful carpenter who enjoyed widespread confidence in the white community. Obviously intelligent, an avid reader of the Bible, facile in languages, he fit no stereotype of the happy, ignorant Negro.

His presumed associates were no less impressive. Peter Poyas was a "first-rate ship carpenter" of excellent reputation and had his master's implicit confidence. Monday Gell not only hired his own time but kept a shop on Meeting Street where he made harness; his owner entrusted arms as well as money to him. He read and wrote "with great and equal facility," the court observed, "and obviously seems to have been the individual who held the pen, at all the meetings." [110] Two others belonged to the governor of the state, one of whom tended the family's business when his owner was at the capital. Only Gullah Jack, who claimed to be a sorcerer with mysterious powers, seemed irregular.

White fears fixed on this urban elite, on those who managed to "succeed" a little in bondage. To the whites the character of the Negro population made an uprising seem possible, indeed reasonable. The extent of literacy brought the "powerful operation of the Press" on "their uninformed and easily deluded minds," and, more precisely, made them privy to events outside the city and the South. The example of Santo Domingo, where the blacks had risen successfully against the whites, and the debate over the Missouri Compromise were thought to have "directly or indirectly" heightened the unrest and encouraged insurrectionary activity. [111] At any rate, both the quality and the quantity of Charleston slaves rendered the whites uneasy.

The Negroes, too, were edgy, for things had not gone well for them in the preceding months. New state legislation had made manumission more difficult, nearly closing the door on those who hoped to get their freedom either by purchase or the generosity of their masters. [112] "The uncivilized laws" were "a great and intolerable hindrance" to the slaves' "peace and happiness," "A Colored American" recalled, since some had already made arrangements to buy their liberty. [113]

In addition, a protracted controversy had arisen over the

establishment of an independent Methodist church for colored people. When it was closed down in 1821, the Negro community became embittered. Bible-class leaders, especially, felt aggrieved because it deprived them of one of the few positions of modest status open to slaves. The resentment of this articulate group was scarcely a secret. In fact, the city later charged that almost all the ringleaders were connected with this church.

The atmosphere, then, was charged with fears and grievances. No doubt conversations among whites turned often, if hesitantly, to the topic; and certainly in the grog shops, in Negro houses, and on the job, the slaves talked about their difficulties. But the gap between the races was great, calculatedly so. The void between was quickly occupied by gossip and rumor. Blacks heard the whites were going to "thin out" the colored population; that a false alarm would bring out the militia and volunteers to butcher the slaves on the spot; that new restraints were under consideration in city hall and the state legislature. Circulating among the whites were equally harrowing notions: a servile uprising, the seizure of the city, the carrying off of women after all males had been exterminated.

Under these circumstances, anything specific—names, places, target dates, etc.—seemed to give substance to a rumor, suggesting a plot not only existed but was ripe. Prudence dictated preventive action and a withering show of force by the city. Not only the ringleaders but even the remotely connected had to be swiftly seized, tried, and punished. Hence, the chance encounter of Devany Prioleau with William Paul on the wharf on May 25, 1822, with its garbled but ominous portent set off a chain of events which did not end until 35 had been executed, still more deported, and a town frozen in terror for almost a summer.

Thus Charleston stumbled into tragedy. The "plot" was

probably never more than loose talk by aggrieved and embittered men. Curiously, its reputation as a full-scale revolt has endured because both sides of the slavery controversy believed insurrections to be essential to their broader argument. Apologists for the "peculiar institution" contended that the stringent laws against Negroes in the South were needed to protect whites from violence; opponents asserted that the urge for freedom was so embedded in human nature that none would passively remain enchained. In either case the Denmark Vesey uprising became a convenient illustration of a larger view of slavery. No closer examination seemed necessary.

V

What happened in Charleston nonetheless illuminates significant aspects of urban slavery. For a concerted revolt against slavery was actually less likely in a city than in the countryside. The chances for success anywhere, of course, were never very good, but ordinary circumstances favored a Nat Turner over a Denmark Vesey. And the reasons for this were clear. Nowhere, not even in Charleston, did the blacks have the great numerical superiority that was present on many plantations. Police forces in the towns, large and well-organized, moreover constituted a more powerful deterrent than the irregular vigilante-patrol system characteristic of places with scattered populations. And ironically, the urban environment proved inhospitable to conspiracies because it provided a wider latitude to the slave, a measure of independence within bondage, and some relief from the constant surveillance of the master. Hiring out, living out, church activities—whether authorized or makeshift—grog and tippling shops, wharves and stables, in a word, the innumerable crevices in the city environment, offered enough latitude to frustrate, absorb, or deflect any serious insurrectionary movement.

Successful rebellion would also have required a greater stability than the institution ever achieved in urban areas. The personnel changed too often; numbers fluctuated; no permanent leadership could be assured among slaves. The shortage of men, characteristic of nearly every city, further deprived any ambitious group of the necessary muscle. "The greater portion are women and children," wrote the *New Orleans Daily Crescent* in 1853, after rumors of a slave uprising had excited the townsfolk, "they are not strong enough to make any movement that could not be crushed by our police alone, without calling on the military." [114] These conditions made a massive assault on slavery very unlikely, and, if attempted, doomed to quick failure.

These facts, however, never removed the fear. Rumors of plots and imminent uprising marked the ordinary routine of every city. If whites learned to live with this anxiety, they could not long forget it. Just as the patrols, whipping posts, and auction blocks reminded Negroes of their servitude, so these symbols made the townspeople aware of their own insecurity. The incidence of slave insurrections was actually low in the cities, but even the possibility was enough to make the metropolis uneasy.

Chapter Nine

THE TRANSFORMATION OF SLAVERY
IN THE CITIES

By 1860 the institution of slavery was in great disarray in every Southern city. The number of Negroes had declined precipitously. Discipline over those remaining proved difficult to sustain. The network of restraint so essential to bondage no longer seemed to control the blacks nor wholly govern the whites. The distance between the races as well as separation of free colored from slave could not be maintained in the kinetic world of the city. In the most dynamic towns the whites overwhelmed the Negro population; even places with a larger proportion of slaves and less impressive growth tended to slough off at least their male blacks. In any case an institution which had been an integral part of urban life in Dixie in 1820 was languishing everywhere in 1860.

The census figures outlined the story. Though the number of slaves rose throughout the South, the proportion living in cities declined. In addition, the Negroes lost their earlier share of the urban population. In 1820, 37 per cent of all town dwellers were blacks; by 1860 that portion had dropped below 17 per cent. Urban slaves fell from 22 per cent to 10. The most dramatic shifts came, of course, in the border area, but everywhere the same pattern appeared. The New Orleans statistics demonstrated the tendency most clearly. In 1820 one out of two residents was Negro; in 1860 only one in seven.

To be sure, the black populations of smaller and newer cities, like Montgomery or the Texas towns, showed some vitality, but there is no reason to believe they would not have shared the same attrition as they expanded.

This decline did not stem from any economic reasons. There was plenty of work which whites had traditionally considered appropriate to blacks and particularly suited to slaves. Industrial employment, moreover, had proved feasible in a variety of enterprises. Hiring rates continued to rise throughout the last ante-bellum decades. And, perhaps most conclusively, the price of urban slaves on the market more than matched the general increase. In short, the usual indices suggested the continuing profitability of slavery as an economic institution. "In all departments of mechanical labor, the slaves of the South are profitably employed," the *Richmond Enquirer* asserted confidently in 1853. "As carpenters, as blacksmiths, as shoe-makers, as factory hands, they are far more valuable than field-laborers—indeed, intellectual expertness and manual dexterity are much more important elements in the price of a slave, than mere physical strength and power of endurance." [1] Or, as a visitor put it, "those whom good treatment has rendered most fit for freedom, are the most desired as slaves." [2]

Slavery's compelling problem in the city was not finding work for bondsmen, but controlling them when they were off the job. While busy, in the house or around the yard, on the docks or driving a dray, toiling in a factory or cotton press, they caused little trouble. When the task was finished or the supervision lifted, however, when the slaves became idle or contrived some free time, when dusk fell and the demand for service slackened, then the system weakened. And when the Negroes gathered by themselves, beyond the eye of masters and police, in homes, churches, or grog shops, the "peculiar institution" itself was jeopardized.

It was the total environment rather than industrial or commercial employment which eroded slavery in the cities. The problem was not what happened in the factory or shop but what happened in the back street, the church, the grocery store, the rented room, and the out-of-the-way house. It was not contact with machines or an industrial process which broke the discipline, it was contact with people of all kinds in numerous ways which generated the corrosive acids.

"The city, with its intelligence and enterprise, is a dangerous place for the slave," wrote a shrewd analyst. "He acquires knowledge of human rights, by working with others who receive wages when he receives none; who can come and go at their pleasure, when he from the cradle to the grave must obey a master's imperious will. . . . It is found expedient, almost necessary, to remove the slave from these influences, and send him back to the intellectual stagnation and gloom of the plantation." [3] Bondage "does not thrive with master or slave when transplanted to cities," a Louisiana planter observed, adding that in such surroundings "the slaves become dissipated, acquire the worst habits," and were generally "corrupted." [4]

An editor commenting on the Louisville scene contended that the "negroes scarcely realize the fact that they are slaves" in the city. They became "insolent, intractable, and in many instances wholly worthless. They make free negroes their associates, and imbibe feelings and imitate their conduct, and are active in prompting others to neglect their duty and to commit crime." [5] "The evil lies," a Charleston committee contended, "in the breaking down the relation between master and slave—the removal of the slave from the master's discipline and control, and the assumption of freedom and independence on the part of the slave, the idleness, disorders, and crime which are consequential." [6] Even more directly, a Southerner told a visitor that "the city is no place for niggers. They get strange notions in their heads, and grow discontented. They ought, everyone of them, be sent back on to the plantations." [7]

Slaves, on the other hand, found urban life to their liking. "The negroes are the most social of all human beings," De Bow asserted, "and after having hired in town, refuse to live again in the country." [8] Slavery's most famous refugee to attack the institution in all its aspects made the same point with elequent simplicity: "Life in Baltimore, when most oppressive, was a paradise" compared to "plantation existence," Frederick Douglass wrote. [9] When masters were forced to sell, their bondsmen pleaded to be kept in the city because—in the words of some Richmond blacks—"they had acquired town habits." [10] And often those sent into the country headed back at the first opportunity to run away. In short, how could you keep them down on the plantation once they had seen Mobile?

The slave's preference was easily understood. Not only was urban life more congenial, but the alternative was especially grim. Solomon Northup found that every Negro sharing his Washington pen "dreaded the thought of being put into the cane and cotton fields." [11] Douglass, too, remembered that it was "a source of deep consternation" to him and his friends in Maryland that "we should be hurried away to the cotton fields and rice swamps, of the sunny south." [12] A sympathetic Northern traveler caught both the white and Negro perspectives when he observed that "The atmosphere of the city is too life-giving, and creates thought. It is the doom of them all to be sent back to the gloom of the plantation cabin." [13]

II

The cause of slavery's difficulty in the city was the nature of urban society itself. In the countryside physical isolation comprised one dimension of a successful discipline. Another was the simple division between master and slave, with virtually no other important element. The distinction between field hand and house servant, while important to the Negroes involved, constituted no significant fracture in the system. Treatment and comforts might vary, privileges could be more extensive, and everyday tasks quite different, but no area of independence was thus created. Indeed, a house servant often fell more directly under the eye of his owner than the black in the field. Nor did the overseer create a new interest among the whites. Employed by the master, usually a short-term resident, living apart from the colored quarters, and only occasionally a confidant of the owner, the overseer had at most a marginal influence on the structure.

Between black and white the social distance was immense. Slaves were confined to primitive work at worst or acquired rudimentary skills at best. Their contacts with whites were few and seldom lasting. An occasional visitor sometimes broke the isolation; nearby white families were seen just often enough to be recognized; overseers came and went. Except for the infrequent trip to town or a neighboring farm, the possibilities of outside stimuli scarcely existed. Even on small plantations or farms, the contacts with the surrounding world were circumscribed. Indeed, without other slaves about he was deprived of even the most elementary association. Rural life had always involved some social remoteness; for the plantation slave, isolation, next to his servitude, was the most compelling fact of life.

The cities, on the other hand, developed more complex structures. Both white and Negro communities included many different parts, and in the larger places a highly sophisticated system evolved with almost endless groupings and distinctions. This fragmentation, which, of course, characterized urban life nearly everywhere, had a special significance for slavery. It meant that the great gap between owner and chattel would be filled with all kinds of diverse elements, inevitably disturbing the institution's ordinary relationships. The Louisiana planter who so feared town life saw this process clearly. "The distance is so vast between slave and master" under bondage, he argued, that in the city "the interval is filled up immediately by corrupting influences." And the slaveholder was helpless. He could perceive "the evil of his slave without being able to prevent it," since it sprang from the intractable nature of urban life itself.[14]

III

The most obvious added ingredient in the urban scene was the free Negro. He was, to be sure, also a rural resident, but the distance and detachment of the countryside greatly diluted his influence on slavery. Often living in a remote spot, sometimes as a yeoman, more often a hired hand, he was bound to have a modest role. His opportunity there moreover was limited. Without resources he found it hard to buy land; without many others of his own kind his social life was sparse. Hence he gravitated toward the metropolis.

Freedmen constituted the most highly urbanized group in Dixie. By 1860 they outnumbered slaves ten to one in Baltimore and 9209 to 1774 in Washington. In the deep South, too, their numbers grew with each census. New Orleans always had a considerable contingent; on the eve of the Civil War it exceeded 10,000. Yet even the places which had tried hardest to limit their free colored population could not alter the trend. Charleston had 1475 in 1820 and over 3200 in 1860, while Mobile's figures in the same span were 183 and 817. Across the South nearly a third of the free blacks were found in the larger urban centers. The report of a visitor in 1836 that "the emancipated negroes generally leave the country, and congregate in the cities and larger towns" was a common observation.[15]

The free Negro's position in Southern towns was always precarious, occupying, as one Southerner put it, "a sort of uncertain and undefined position in our midst." [16] His color suggested servitude, but his status secured a portion of freedom. Hence he suffered many of the inhibitions of his slave brothers while enjoying some privileges denied them. His advantages over the slave were considerable. He could marry, have children, and enjoy something of a normal family life. He could own property, have the right to his earnings, and engage in a few trades forbidden the enslaved. Though the situation was never favorable to either domestic tranquillity or economic advancement, there was at least a measure of independence. And, most crucial of all, in the privacy of the home could be found a seclusion from the constant surveillance of the white world.

Free Negroes learned quickly not to count on much beyond this. "We know full well," the New Orleans *Picayune* wrote with candor, "that the pretence of any real freedom being designed or expected for these negroes is but a sham." [17] In the streets the distinction among colored people was not clear; in the courts the free were sometimes only fined while the slaves were whipped; and legislation increasingly covered all blacks with only nominal regard for status. City ordinances usually handled both categories in a single section. An 1832 Baltimore ordinance dealing with Negro discipline set forth the crucial identification: "such free negro or mulatto shall be subject to the same punishment, and be liable in every respect to the same treatment and penalty as slaves" and "be guilty of, and convicted of, any offense for which slaves are now punishable." [18]

Despite these obstacles, the free colored of every city struggled to establish a meaningful associational life. They formed congregations and erected churches, established schools and aid societies, and organized improvement projects aimed at bringing some of the better things of life to their members. Occasionally this activity became elaborate, the Negro equivalent of fashionable white life. The Bonneau Literary Society in Charleston, for example, met Wednesday evenings at nine "to further progress in Literary Improvement ... and the Improvement of our Mental Faculties," [19] while in New Orleans the famous masked balls were carefully planned to emulate the subtlest pretensions of the city's first citizens.

To a few Southerners the presence of free Negroes created no great problem. Indeed, a state legislator from New Orleans called "the better class of our free colored population ... a powerful check on the turbulence of the more vicious of our slaves." Another, Charles Gayarré, saw them as "sober and industrious mechanics, quiet and useful citizens who are susceptible of noble sentiments and virtues." [20] Similarly, the preamble to a Maryland statute could refer to Baltimore's free blacks as "honest, industrious and peaceable colored persons" as it widened their privileges to form associations for the care of "the destitute of their own color." [21] And a Savannah resident went so far as to say that the "true policy of safety" in the South required emancipation for deserving slaves, since the local experience evidenced the "uniformly quiet conduct" of freedom. [22]

But the common judgment went the other way. A Louisville editor in 1851 came close to the nearly universal view when he stated bluntly that "the free negro question is the most insoluble of all the social problems of the day, and stands as a practical sarcasm on all the theories of abolition and emancipation." [23] A Richmond memorial containing the signature of John Marshall elaborated the ordinary indictment. They numbered "not an eighth part of the inhabitants; yet it would be hazarding little to say that half the criminals tried in the City for the offense of larceny, are free persons of color." In addition, the petitioners said, "their idleness is proverbial; they live, few know in what way, and fewer still know where; their rate of increase far exceeds even that of the slaves, and in a higher degree that of the whites; and whatever energy can be spared from annoying both classes, appears to be expended in multiplying their own number." [24] And a New Orleans editor called the full roll when he spoke of "the absolute idleness, the thriftlessness, the laziness, the dishonesty, the drunkenness, the proneness to vagrancy and vice of the negro when free from all the restraints of servitude." [25]

The central complaint, however, had less to do with the wretchedness of free Negro life, or even with their high crime rate, than with their influence on slaves. Living amongst bondsmen, yet without masters, carrying by color the stigma of servitude, yet without its most humiliating features, shut off from white society, yet released from the confinements of slavery, the free blacks were always a disturbing factor. "They are a plague and pest in the community," the *New Orleans Daily Picayune* asserted, because they brought "the elements of mischief to the slave population." [26]

"The superior condition of the free persons of color," a memorial of Charleston citizens argued, "excites discontent among our slaves, who continually have before their eyes, persons of the same color, many of whom they have known in slavery, and with all of whom they associate on terms of equality." The slave saw these blacks "freed from the control of masters, working where they please, going whither they please, and spending money how they please." He thus became "dissatisfied" and "pants after liberty." [27]

But this envy did not split the colored community. "There is an identity of interest between the slave and the free person of color," the Charleston citizens continued, "whilst there is none between the latter class and the whites." And this identity was sustained by many elements: "they are associated by color, connected by marriages, and by friendships. Many of the free negroes have parents, brothers, sisters and children, who are slaves." In case of an insurrection, the document warned, "they would have every inducement to join it." [28]

"The intercourse of free negroes with slaves," wrote a New Orleans paper, "is just as mischievous" as letting loose abolitionists among them. . . . If they do not render the slave insubordinate, they make him vicious." This "fact" was "so well understood that in the country" planters could only "with difficulty effect the emancipation of their slaves," and the law usually required that newly liberated slaves be removed from the state.[29] "It is the saucy and insolent air of the *free* negroes," a St. Louis police report declared, "which is most dangerous to the slave population." [30] Whatever the precise formulation of the argument, Southern town dwellers could agree that their free colored residents rendered control over their slaves increasingly difficult.

IV

They could also agree that there were some whites who were almost as unsettling to the system as freed blacks. These people had found a place at the edge of slavery where their economic life was enmeshed in the irregular relationships bred by the system in its urban environment. Some were grocers who sold to slaves; others ran shops which catered to a colored clientele; still others were ministers who organized Negro churches and sought to bring religion to the enslaved. Port merchants, too, could be included, since their trade brought ships with mixed crews into the harbor. Less easily identified, but also important, were whites sporadically connected with the informal life of town blacks. These interests were obviously quite different, but all developed a stake in the loose form of bondage which evolved in the cities.

The activity of some was illegal because it involved dealing with slaves who did not have the proper papers or permissions. Even ministers tended to allow bondsmen and free blacks to run the colored churches without the careful supervision required by law. And the association of whites in the demi-world of the Negro's night life violated both custom and law. Yet the interstices of slavery were so wide that these relations became a normal part of the functioning of the institution. Despite everything municipal officials could do, there were more whites in this position in the 1850's than ever before. Thus, there arose a white element whose influence, like the presence of free blacks, weakened the system of restraints and exclusions on which slavery rested.

The grocers and the grog-shop operators had the most obvious and deepest stake in the loose enforcement of police regulations. Nearly all dealt occasionally with slaves, and many depended on the trade. Though traffic in any goods was frowned upon, it was the sale of liquor that lay at the center of the controversy. Nearly all whites disliked this commerce; the master because it "led to the corruption of our servants and the loss of property," and others because it resulted in "the unrestrained intercourse and indulgence of familiarities between black and white." In short, the trade created conditions "destructive of the respect and subserviency which our laws recognize as due from the one to the other and which form an essential feature in our institutions." [31]

In every city the suppression of the traffic became a major issue. A Charleston grand jury considered it so important that it proposed that "unprincipled white men" who "interfere between the slave and the owner or employer" ought to be deprived of all civil rights including suffrage. The suggestion was shrewd because it was political power which in the last instance protected the illicit trade. Whenever the public be-

came outraged, the "grocers" acted in concert to control the
city government and the police. "The Mayor & Marshall you
are aware," wrote a leading Savannah public figure to a
friend, "regulate the shopkeepers politically by *not* regulating
them as to the Law." [32] Earlier, in 1828, a blue-ribbon citizens
committee had tried to crack down and pushed the issue into
an election of councilmen. A "Grocer's Ticket" immediately
entered the field. Scorning the reformers as "(would-be) gentlemen" and dubbing their program "*pious tampering*," they
carried the fight to the voters.[33] The outcome appeared inconclusive, but the ordinance which the committee wanted
strengthened remained unchanged. In subsequent years the
initial observation of the reform group remained a fact of life
in Savannah: "shop keepers in the country can be effectively
broken up by the enforcement of the State laws, while one in
the city may even yet, before an ordinary jury, justify his act
under the present ordinances." [34] A decade later, the grocers,
again facing opposition from reformers, easily swept to vic-
tory under the banner of "Friends of Civil Freedom." [35]

The same question erupted in Charleston politics in 1834-
35, when a new state law was at issue. The editor of the
Courier summarized the legislation, which embodied a change
of emphasis rather than a reversal of long-standing policy.
The older statutes, he explained, were designed "to lessen the
danger of depredation on the property of owners by making
it highly penal to purchase from, or traffic with their slaves.
The main object of the new law, is to prevent slaves from being corrupted in their habits, and ruined in their constitutions
by the use of intoxicating liquors." [36] Passage of the new regulations followed a vigorous drive by many prominent Charleston people.

The grocers quickly moved to protect themselves. They
not only argued their own case in saying that the law would

drive out a "hardy and hard-working class" but identified themselves with other interests as well. Since the shops would have to shut down, landlords would be deprived of their rent. Thus, "the loss would fall on a class least able to sustain it—namely, widows and orphans, whose sole income in a great number of cases, arises from this species of property." More subtly, and more significantly, they linked themselves to the entire middle-class by saying that, if the grocers and their kind disappeared, then "society in the South shall contain two classes—the master and the slave—the province of one of which shall be to command and the other to obey." [37] The law remained; so too did the problem; and so too did the grocers.

The shopkeepers often found an ally in those responsible for breaking up the traffic—the police. As early as 1822 a memorial of prominent Charleston residents declared that the City Guard "as now organized, are of little benefit to the city," because "most of them are shop-keepers or retailers of spiritous liquors to the negroes. It is therefore their interest and it is notorious that this interest induces them to permit such of the negroes as are their customers, to pass unmolested through our streets after the bell has rung and the watch has set." [38] In Savannah's election of 1850 Dr. Richard Arnold discovered what this coalition could do. In the campaign he charged "the shopkeepers openly proclaimed that they had a Mayor who suited them very well, and that if elected I would fine every shop-keeper a hundred dollars who might be convicted of breaking the ordinances." On election day the troops moved into action. When the polls opened, the City Guard marched "*en masse* with tickets marked by their officers.... The day was then before them to electioneer and bully." When the returns came in he could conclude sadly, "Dr. Wayne's shopkeepers were too strong." [39]

V

The role of the ministers proved more complicated. In stimulating the religious activity of Negroes, they felt they were discharging a public as well as a Christian duty. Believing that a pious slave was a well-behaved, docile, and obedient servant, most felt that the oftener he could be within earshot of the Word of God, the better for master and slave. Yet the elaborate regulations surrounding colored congregations tended to inhibit rather than encourage an enlarged spiritual life. Hence clergymen tended to bend if not break the law. Their control was formal rather than close; their attendance at meetings casual rather than constant.

But any movement to shut up the churches brought white ministers to the defense of the blacks. "*There is not* . . . sufficient room for their accommodation in the galleries of other churches," five beleagured Methodist clergymen in Mobile contended, "besides their presence there would be regarded by many as a great evil particularly in the church of which the subscribers are members." The Negroes would moreover regard the action "as a grievance" and "suffer great *injury* in their spiritual interests, an injury that would be irreparable." Pledging "our word and standing in the community . . . that all future *instruction* shall be unexceptional and all *meetings* of colored people under our *direction lawful*," they urged the city council to "take no step to abridge the *present* religious privileges of the blacks in Mobile." [40] Elsewhere the story was the same. White ministers, believing in the necessity of religious instruction to the Negroes, tried to temper the enforcment of laws against colored congregations. Except in Charleston in the 1820's they proved uniformly successful.

A handful of lawyers in every city also discovered an interest in a lax system of slavery. They operated in the crucial intersection of slavery and freedom—the granting of emancipation papers. The complaint of a St. Louis man explained the practice and detailed the danger. The law permitted a Negro who claimed freedom to bring the case to court. "This is but right, rational and humane," "Topaz" admitted, "but the liberty has become abused, at least in St. Louis, by the ruthless encouragement of those who left-handedly profit by such suits." It worked like this: "Tom wants his freedom, and sallies in quest of legal advice; he states his case, and right or wrong, is flattered to proceed. Pleased with his prospects, he brags to Dick, who after a little scratching of the bump of his reminiscences, takes a notion he has a right to freedom too." Then the hope spreads through the black community. "Fired with untried hope, Dick flies to Ned . . . Ned catches flame and communicates it to Big Bill—Big Bill to little Jim, and little Jim to everything that wears wool." Soon discipline everywhere flags. The slave "grumbles at his master's commands—neglects his duties, and takes his chastisement with the sullen insolence of one who thinks he shall shortly be able to set the white man at defiance." [41]

The lawyer's clients might be slaves whose manumission depended on the action of a municipal body when certain conditions and technicalities were under question. In New Orleans the number was so large that a committee of the city council asserted that everyone was "well aware" there were "persons who speculate and deal" in emancipation papers and made good money at it.[42] Another transaction involved replacing lost documents or establishing the fact that a black was not a runaway. Everywhere a few lawyers discovered a stake in the untidy organization of urban slavery.

Even some masters developed such an interest. Employers of large numbers of slaves in commercial or industrial enterprises increasingly preferred not to house blacks on their own property, and this attitude in turn loosened one of the most intimate bonds. Others found hiring out their slaves profitable and permitting them to live out convenient. These expedients, of course, put a heavy responsibility on public discipline. Yet many owners resented the interference from public authorities that followed. "While loud in their complaints" about lax discipline, a New Orleans editor observed wryly, some masters were "only willing to have every slave not their own arrested." When the police "execute the law vigorously and their heavy hand falls . . . many interfere and by their remonstrances with the officers, dampen their energy and destroy their zeal in the special discharge of their duty." [43]

In a conflict between masters and municipal authority, owners often appeared as advocates of leniency. Before the magistrate they sometimes preferred to pay a fine rather than to surrender their slave for a correction by the jailer. Frequently they complained that the elaborate public discipline confused the bondsmen. "They cannot distinguish why their master has no power to give them his consent to go out and spend an evening with a friend without the fear of the guard house hanging over his head," "A Slave Owner" in Mobile declared. Attacking the entire city code, he concluded with a curious touch of anarchy: "It is human nature, the more stringent the laws the worse they are." [44] Hence even masters occasionally found themselves advocates of a more relaxed regime than local officials believed necessary.

VI

In the metropolis the worlds of bondage and freedom overlapped. The line between free blacks and slaves became hopelessly blurred. Even whites and blacks found their lives entangled in some corners of the institution of slavery. No matter what the law said or the system required, this layer of life expanded. Though much of it was subterranean, at points it could be easily seen. The mixed balls, the numberless grog and grocery shops, the frequent religious gatherings, and the casual acquaintances in the streets were scarcely private. Physical proximity bred a certain familiarity that most residents came to expect. To be sure, when a Richmond officer saw "a white man, walking arm and arm with a black man," he demanded "to know the why and wherefore of such a cheek and jowl business." [45] But occasional friendships that transcended the deference of slavery raised few eyebrows.

What did bother townspeople, however, was the evidence that beyond these visible contacts lay a world of greater conviviality and equality. In this nether world blacks and whites mingled freely, the conventions of slavery were discarded, and the worst fears of Southerners became realized. Not only did the men find fellowship without regard to color in the tippling shops, back rooms, and secluded sheds, but the women of both races joined in. Such mixing engaged a good deal of the private conversation of white people in cities, but its public manifestations were usually found in only police reports and the major's court.

In Mobile, for instance, "two couples, embracing two males and two females, the former in both instances colored, and the latter white," came before the judge on the charge of "amalgamation." They had been found in a bedroom with "only one garment on apiece." One of the women was the "notorious Hoosier Ann"—a certain Ann Fuller—who was no stranger to the police.[46] This episode was not unusual. Five days later, Nancy Bohanan, another white, was picked up for running an "assignation house." "The principal frequenters to this infamous den" were "negro cab drivers, none of whose names or ownerships could be sworn to." [47] Not long after, Mrs. Eliza Crowe, the widow of a "very respectable tailor," came before the court accused of being with two colored men in her house with "the door locked." [48] And three days later Julia McCarthy "was found laying on the same bed with a well known negro driver of a baggage wagon." [49]

The Richmond newspapers usually carried brief notices of similar matters "too delicate to dwell on." Yet on occasions they printed a fuller story, especially when some reform seemed appropriate. "Yesterday two youthful white girls, not of uncomely features or shape," ran the court reporter's account in 1859, "were brought before the crowd's gaze" for "having been caught pandering for lucre's sake to the passions of negroes. These females, depraved in every sense of the word, are named Betty Moore and Mary Brown." They were sent to jail "for want of $100 bail." The writer thought "the place for such creatures should be a house of reform where they could be kept for a period at industrious pursuits." [50]

Hugh Kelly, who lived in Indiana but commuted to Louisville, rented a house and for more than a year "made free with a negro woman, the property of one of our citizens." The affair became common knowledge in the neighborhood until the police caught him "between a straw and feather bed" and gave him three months.[51] Other blacks had better protection than Kelly. When a "handsome" Negro woman came before New Orleans officials for an illicit alliance, "at least forty respectable persons came to the Recorder's office to offer themselves as bail," and she was later released when no witnesses appeared.[52]

This social underworld encompassed every possible combination of color and status. The cases brought before New Orleans officials in a few months in the 1850's illustrate this. "A slave girl and a white man," ran a typical newspaper account, "were arrested for violating some of the more prominent of the Ten Commandments." [53] "Frank, a slave, and Mary Ann Kirvella were arrested for living in a room on Burgundy Street, in contravention of existing ordinances of good morals," another recorded.[54] In the Third District, outside the Old Quarter, "two white women have recently been discovered ... living with negro men," the *Daily Delta* noted with dismay, "in open violation of all social rules. One of them was a runaway slave." [55] Another item suggested the wide compass of these associations: "A young and tolerably good-looking woman of the pave, Brigit Smith, and one of the ugliest of the ugly negro men, named Jack, were brought before Recorder Caldwell this morning ... for what —we will not say." [56]

Indeed few racial issues produced so much explosiveness. "No subject, political or otherwise, brought forth such a number of persons in many years as this," the *New Orleans Daily Delta* admitted in 1860 in the midst of the "Martin Affair." Thomas J. Martin, a free Negro, had been the city's most sought-after music teacher for twenty years. He had written a successful popular song as well as some serious compositions. In the course of this career, it was belatedly discovered, he had also seduced twenty women—most of them white. After his arrest 2000 people poured into Lafayette Square to protest his transgressions and demand punishment. The newspaper noted that the matter went "much deeper than the first blush would indicate." Moreover, "to trifle with this subject" would be "aiding and abetting of a mischief, a wrong that should be discountenanced by every true Southern man." "Let the amalgamationists say what they want," the editor concluded, but the question was more than "a trifle, a fiarro." [57]

There can be no doubt of the wide extent of this miscegenation. Visitors often commented on it; the newspapers complained about it; the court records teem with it. Even Governor Hammond, who defended the South in general against the charge of racial mixing, admitted its prominence in the cities. The clandestine nature of these attachments makes a more precise generalization risky, but the fear, if not the fact, of "amalgamation," "miscegenation," and "mixing" plainly increased in the decades before 1860. Few defenders, much less advocates, appeared. The public stigma and the hostility of the law made it clear why: those who practiced it did not preach it.

New Orleans, with its large population of free and enslaved blacks, had the most famous demi-world in Dixie. The celebrated masked balls and the casual acceptance of colored mistresses seemed to reflect its Spanish and French roots. Yet that explanation is too facile. The rural areas of Louisiana, some of which reflected similar origins, did not develop the same mores; and, more persuasively, other cities with quite different beginnings did. Actually what visitors noticed about New Orleans was true of urban life throughout the South.

VII

Northern cities, too, had their disorganized elements who left a trail across police blotters, court records, and poorhouse lists. There, too, community leaders, somewhat bewildered by the spread of undisciplined low life, sought some way to introduce system and stability. But, important as this was to civic leaders elsewhere, in the South the problem was greatly complicated by the existence of slavery. On the one hand, the institution required a high degree of order, the careful regulation of Negro affairs, and a fixed status for bondsmen. On the other hand, the city demanded fluidity, a constant re-allocation of human resources, and a large measure of social mobility. Initially, it appeared as though slavery could provide the discipline town life seemed to need. In the long run, however, the force of urbanization loosened the restraints of bondage, smudged the distinctions of status among Negroes, and at points pierced the racial walls of Dixie's cities.

This antithesis was early felt by some municipal leaders.

Since slavery was presumed to be an established part of Southern town life for any foreseeable future, none talked about incompatibility. Instead, the dominant race sought to solve it with ordinances, the orderly development of a legal hiring-out system, and a plentiful police force in case of trouble. Yet the acids of urbanization continually eroded the discipline on which bondage rested. Though the disintegration was often hard to gauge, those close to the problem knew it was happening.

To arrest the attrition and handle its consequences, Southern cities moved along three lines. One involved the sale of young male blacks into the countryside. This removed one of the most disturbing elements from the urban scene while meeting a constant demand for field hands in the cotton and cane regions. A second was the tightening of emancipation procedures to stop the accumulation of free Negroes in towns. A third was to develop racial arrangements which took into account the new situation and which embodied most of the features later identified as segregation.

The sale of the men into the cotton and cane country was never an official policy. After the Vesey affair a Charleston spokesman recommended the thinning of the Negro population as a deliberate program, and the *Richmond Enquirer* advocated "reducing surely but quietly, the number of our slaves" following Turner's uprising.[58] But to force owners to this course never seemed feasible. Likewise, the widespread interest in attracting white immigrants to Southern cities to replace black labor, even as domestic servants, was not easy to implement. And the high demand for field hands in the new areas furnished a convenient rationale for action that was only partially economic in motivation.

Despite these difficulties the tendency to sell men into the country was pronounced. It was, in fact, the theme of John S. C. Abbott's diary of his Southern trip in 1859. "The slaves in the cities, working in the midst of the conversation of white men, listen eagerly, and gain some information," he noted. "This has alarmed their masters, and they are sending them off, as fast as possible, to the plantations where, as in a tomb, no sight or sound of knowledge can reach them." [59] An examination of real estate conveyances in New Orleans, which list the names and residences of both buyer and seller, confirms the observation. The persistent imbalance between the sexes characteristic of urban Negro populations reveals the same tendency. Perhaps, however, the wry observation of the *Daily Crescent* in 1853 describes best the situation: "The whole number of slaves in New Orleans does not exceed 16,-000, of which the greater portion are women and children." [60]

While Dixie's towns sloughed off their male bondsmen, they also moved to reduce the number of free Negroes in their midst. This policy involved a change in strategy, for initially emancipation was used as part of a sophisticated control system. "The object of design of such permission," wrote the mayor of New Orleans' Third Municipality, "is to offer a reward to such slaves as would demean themselves correctly, be respectful to the white population or render important services to the state or to their masters." Another object was "to encourage the slave population in imitating the good example and following in the footsteps of those who by an honest, active, and useful conduct have succeeded in obtaining their freedom." [61] But everywhere the fear of increasing the number of liberated blacks, no matter how well-behaved, overcame the advantages of the selected manumission program. A chorus rose which demanded not only restriction but absolute prohibition.

The case of New Orleans was illustrative, because its policy encompassed both the widest leniency for most of the antebellum years and an absolute ban on the eve of war. Through most of the period, under Louisiana law, city councils could grant freedom on petition, and they did so on a substantial scale. In the four years between 1846 and 1850 the First Municipality alone emancipated 321 blacks, while the Second Municipality manumitted at a rate of about 75 annually. The grounds were usually "long important and faithful services" and most carried the notation, "without being compelled to leave the state." [62] Masters wishing to let their slaves go generally got a sympathetic hearing from officials. But not all requests were granted. When, for example, Sara Connor's petition came up for action, a police report disclosed that a few months earlier she had been picked up "in a house on St. John street, dancing, in company with sixteen colored girls, mostly slaves, and about ten or twelve white men." The committee decided that Sara was liberated enough already.[63]

New Orleans' liberal practice obscured somewhat the increasing hostility to emancipation of any kind in Louisiana. The 1830 law required the newly freed Negro to leave the state within thirty days; in 1852 the right to manumit was taken from city officials and given to the legislature. Flooded with petitions, worried about the influence of the unbonded on the slaves, and concerned about rumored insurrections, the state government in 1857 forbade manumission under any conditions. Two years before, a legislator had expressed the tighter attitude: "if slavery is not an evil ... why should we emancipate under any circumstances in the State of Louisiana?" [64] In 1859 provisions were made for free blacks to choose a master and return to bondage.

Other cities exercised less control over emancipation than New Orleans, but the tendency everywhere was the same. When an owner manumitted, his slave was to be removed quickly from the state. Free colored people from the outside could not become residents, and even Negro sailors arriving in port temporarily on business were kept onboard ships or confined in jail. Though petitions to state legislatures often brought relief, the possibility became more remote with each passing decade. By 1860 the percentage of free Negroes among the South's urban population had dropped considerably.

VIII

While Southern cities increasingly moved to reduce their colored population, both slave and free, they also developed a new system of racial deference more appropriate to urban life than slavery in its traditional form. As the institution of slavery encountered mounting difficulties and, as its control over the blacks weakened, another arrangement was devised which maintained great social distance within the physical proximity of town life. Increasingly public policy tried to separate the races whenever the surveillance of the master was likely to be missing. To do this, the distinction between slave and free Negro was erased; race became more important than legal status; and a pattern of segregation emerged inside the broader framework of the "peculiar institution."

In a sense this tendency was always present, though the reliance on traditional controls obscured its importance. The heart of the established system was, of course, the subordination of the slave to his owner. The wide discretion vested in the master made day-to-day discipline almost a private matter. But in the cities a public etiquette was needed to govern the relations of races when the blacks were beyond the supervision of their owners. Increasingly that etiquette required the separation of black and white without regard to legal status. Beginning in only a few areas, the arrangement spread to include the most important public aspects of life.

Taverns, restaurants, and hotels were always off-limits to the Negroes. The laws against trading with slaves, of course, covered all these areas, and their location in the business part of town prevented much laxity. Free blacks fell under the same ban, though by custom rather than by law. In public conveyances this discrimination appeared again. Richmond's ordinances, to cite but one case, prohibited Negroes from "driving, using or riding in any Hackney coach or other carriage for hire unless in the capacity of a servant." [65] In New Orleans the street railway kept separate cars for blacks. And encoachments on this arrangement met with physical exclusion. In 1833, for instance, when "certain colored persons wishing to go to the lake, took possession of the cars appropriated to white people," the conductor evicted them.[66]

Public grounds, however, presented an even clearer case. Savannah's 1827 ordinances, for example, excluded "negroes, mullattoes, or other colored persons" from "the public promenade in South Broad street, or on that leading from thence to the Hospital." And the preamble said why: "for the purpose of protecting the Citizens while engaged in recreation upon the Public Walks, from molestation or intrusion of improper persons." [67] A section of Richmond's Negro code was entitled "What place slaves not to Walk or be in." The segregated areas included "the grounds adjacent to the City Spring, City Hall, or Athenaeum," as well as "any of the places known as city grounds" and "any public burying ground for white persons." The law relented if the slave accompanied his owner as employer, but the prohibition of free blacks was absolute.[68]

Charleston's regulations kept colored people off the "enclosure of the Garden at White Point" and forbade them "to walk on the East or South Batteries." [69] If attending white children, and if they had a ticket, slaves could enter. Even this variation, however, brought criticism. "It now takes from four to two wenches, *with their attendents*, to take one baby in the air," one white wrote indignantly, while taxpayers are "jostled by a succession of darkies" each of whom has "a detachment of 'little niggers' at her heels." [70]

These measures simply excluded the blacks without providing alternative facilities. It was otherwise in the case of jails, hospitals, and cemeteries. Here the separation was careful and complete, if sometimes painfully contrived. Also, wherever Negroes shared public buildings with whites their quarters were set apart. The division was sometimes by room, at other times by floor. But in every case the segregation was clear and unmistakable.

Prisons presented few problems. Either the blacks had a special jail or they were assigned to a designated section of the same building. Some separate jails had the whipping post in a nearby yard; others, such as Charleston's, adjoined workhouses where colored inmates toiled on tough tasks or kept the treadmill going. When gangs were sent to work on the street or other public projects, officials maintained the same distinction. The New Orleans city council was so anxious in this regard that it furnished different colored clothes for Negro and white prisoners employed on municipal projects.[71]

The same principle governed the organization of poorhouses. The care of the indigent slave, of course, fell to the owner, but free Negroes were the city's responsibility. If the "mandate of the law, the counsel of true wisdom and policy, as well as the dictates of justice and humanity," made them "the fit and rightful objects of poor relief," as a Charleston report observed, it was also "conceded" that they should be "provided for in a place different and separated from . . . the white poor." "The distinction of castes must be strictly and broadly pursued in slaveholding communities," the committee explained.[72] In Baltimore, where the numbers were much greater, a similar practice developed. In the 1830's some mixing occurred because of a continuing space shortage. By 1841, however, the trustees could say that "the colored and white inmates are in general kept separate from each other." Two years later, a new building permitted the removal of white women from the female yard, and thus the Negroes were left with a "comfortable hospital and eating room ... instead of their being confined exclusively to the garret rooms of the west wing." [73]

Hospitals, too, maintained the pattern. It was most obvious when the institution was initially built for slaves exclusively. Each city had at least one of these. But most also established hospitals which admitted both races to separate quarters and facilities. Usually a wing, or in the case of Louisville, the basement, was set aside for the blacks.[74] Even in times of emergency, when additional structures were taken over for hospital use, health officials did not abandon the practice.

Cultural and recreational enterprises were also segregated when they did not exclude Negroes entirely. Theaters provided special galleries for colored persons which were often approached through special entrances. Lyell found the upper tiers of boxes at the New Orleans Opera House assigned to Negroes.[75] Another visitor reported, "Some of them were pointed out to me as very wealthy; but no money can admit them to the pit, or to the boxes." [76] Others, like Thomas L. Nichols, put a different construction on the segregation, when he referred to the "portion of the house devoted to ladies and gentlemen of colour" where "no common white trash was allowed to intrude." [77] But the fact of separation had been part of official policy since the beginning. As early as 1816 an ordinance established the practice: "It shall not be lawful for any white person to occupy any of the places set apart for people of color; and the latter are likewise forbidden to occupy any of those reserved for white persons, at any public exposition or theatre." [78]

On the stage, of course, no intrusion was permitted. When a Northern newspaper reported that a colored actress had performed in New Orleans, the *Bee* retorted indignantly: "We beg leave to contradict and unequivocally this remark. No negress ever has been, or ever will be permitted to appear on the stage of New Orleans. We are a slave-holding state, and whatever may be the pretended philanthropy of our Northern brethren in relation to our conduct, we possess too much self-respect to submit to any such degrading exhibition." [79] The prohibition on reading and writing, of course, put libraries off-limits.

Negroes remained as segregated in death as in life. Funerals increasingly became wholly colored affairs. The law usually required a white minister at the service, and the master and the family sometimes attended, but a petition by Richmond's blacks to the state legislature indicated the reality. The Negroes noted that a new statute, passed in 1832, prohibited slaves and free Negroes from officiating at funerals. As a consequence, they lamented, "many coloured human beings are inter'd like brutes, their relatives and friends being unable to procure white ministers to perform the usual ceremony in the burial of the dead." Eleven clergymen joined in the memorial arguing that the "pressing engagements of white ministers left no time for this function." [80]

The body was finally interred in a segregated cemetery. Sometimes a congregation would set aside space in its church yard for colored members. No doubt, too, though the evidence is scarce, a faithful slave would on rare occasions be buried in the master's plot. But the bulk of urban Negroes, slave and free, rested ultimately in places confined to their own race. Every city maintained at least one extensive "burial ground for negroes," and most churches kept separate cemeteries for black and white. A Charleston directory for 1856 lists fifteen colored graveyards, two owned by the town, one by the Brown Fellowship Society, and the rest by Negro or white congregations.[81] Nowhere else were there so many, but everywhere the distinction was maintained. And New Orleans, with mathematical precision, divided its facilities into three parts: one-half for whites, one-quarter for slaves, and one-quarter for free blacks.[82]

IX

Religious organizations quickly developed segregated facilities without the help of municipal officials and the law. Nearly all Protestant denominations, especially those with large black contingents, either put their colored members in separate galleries during regular services or established special churches for them. This arrangement covered not only Sunday gatherings but prayer meetings during the week and Bible classes as well. The system, however, stemmed less from white design than Negro preference, for whenever the opportunity appeared colored worshippers patronized their own congregations. A Savannah preacher recorded the normal experience in 1819: "There was one side of the gallery [in his church] appropriated for their use, and it was always the most thinly seated part of the church; while there were two respectably large colored churches in the city, with their pastor, and deacons, and sacraments, and discipline, all of their own." [83]

Colored churches, of course, reflected the tendency toward segregation even more clearly. Distrusted by whites, enthusiastically supported by Negroes, they represented the ambiguity of race relations under slavery. Whites developed elaborate devices to keep the races apart in public places and to seal off their own slaves from others in private life; but religious activity fell between these situations. Masters, often considering it a family affair, sought a compromise under one roof. Negroes, on the other hand, finding social as well as spiritual satisfaction by themselves, flocked to separate congregations. Except for some Catholic churches and a few

Protestant ones, this combination made Sunday morning one of the most segregated moments of the week.

Slaves were excluded from schools by the legislation against teaching them to read and white, but the pattern of segregation applied to free blacks. Not only could they not attend white classes, but they had to make their own arrangements for education. Even these schools had uncertain careers, being subject to police interference and legal prohibitions as well as financial difficulties. After the Vesey episode, the Charleston grand jury wanted to remove all Negro teachers in private schools, which would have shut them down altogether. "As the Blacks are most carefully excluded from all schools kept by *white* persons, where their persons would be considered as a sort of contamination both by the master and scholars," an English visitor observed, "this bill of the Grand Jury will deprive them at once of all instruction." Indeed, he concluded, "Although they do not avow it (for even the most hardened are sometimes sensible to public shame)," it was "their real object and intention." [84] If some slaves managed to bootleg a little learning in a free colored school, no black was ever knowingly admitted to a white one.

This exclusion did not, however, exempt Baltimore's large free Negro population from paying the public school tax. As early as 1839, 55 colored leaders asked the mayor to grant them relief, since "coloured people are not at all interested in the public schools directly or indirectly." Failing in that, five years later they asked for "two schools in different sections of the city" for their own children. In 1850, 90 Negroes were joined by 126 whites in another petition. Noting that the blacks "are taxed for the support of public schools, into which, for obvious reasons, their children cannot be admitted," it argued that "the true instinct of the white population, as well as the colored, will be promoted by the instruction of the children . . . in such elements of learning as may prepare them ... with usefulness and respectability, [for] those humble stations in the community to which they are confined by the necessities of their situation." The solution lay in establishing schools for the 20,000 Negro residents. The city refused on the ground that the state would withdraw money from Baltimore's "school fund" if any went to Negro schools.[85]

X

Law and custom sanctioned the segregation of races in public places and accommodations as well as in churches and schools. To disentangle white and black in employment and housing was a different matter. Yet the significant fact is that such a separation took place increasingly often in the last few decades before the Civil War. Under the pressure of white craftsmen, Negroes were pushed out of one line of work after another. With the weakening of the reins of slavery, bondsmen found housing away from their owners and generally in areas of accumulating colored population. Both movements were far from complete, but the tendency was unmistakable.

In employment the clearest manifestation of segregation was the exclusion of blacks, slave and free, from the better jobs. A memorial of Charleston's City Council to the state legislature expressed both the difficulties and the objects of the policy. Noting that "slavery is so interwoven with the constitution of our Society that even if our interests permitted it would be impossible to eradicate it," the petitioners argued that it was "necessary to fix as far as possible the grade of employments" for slaves and "to exclude them by Legislative enactment from all others." [86] Charleston's own ordinances prohibited teaching slaves "in any mechanic or handicraft trade," though the wording was vague and its enforcement almost impossible.[87]

In Savannah the restrictions were more precise. No Negro could be apprenticed "to the trade of Carpenter, Mason, Bricklayer, Barber or any other Mechanical Art or Mystery." [88] Later, cabinetmaker, painter, blacksmith, tailor, cooper, and butcher were added to the list.[89] Georgia excluded blacks from "being mechanics or masons, from making contracts for the erection . . . or repair of buildings." [90] Though no two cities had the same categories, all tried to keep colored workers out of the higher skills. The fact that practice often belied the law simply underlined the significance of the intent.

If slaves and blacks were still found in many of the better crafts in 1860, they had been pushed out of many of the lesser-skilled jobs. In Baltimore whites took the carting and draying business from them by 1830.[91] A few years later, a visitor could report that "the Irish and other foreigners are, to a considerable extent, taking the place of colored laborers and of domestic servants." [92] In 1823 the City Council of New Orleans directed the mayor "to hire white labor for the city works, in preference to negroes." [93] Two decades later, some prominent citizens there described the extent of the attrition: "Ten years ago, say they, all the draymen of New Orleans, a numerous class, and the cabmen, were colored. Now they are nearly all white. The servants of the great hotels were formerly of the African, now they are of the European race." [94] Even in the home, the displacement occurred with the customary racial rationale. "We have all times spoken against the impropriety of having white and black servants in homes in the South," the *Richmond Enquirer* explained, "especially so in in any capacity where slaves or negroes may be inclined to consider themselves on a par of equality with white servants." [95]

John S. C. Abbott, who toured the South in 1859, found

this tendency pronounced everywhere. In Mobile, for instance, he was "surprised to see how effectually free labor seems to have driven slave labor from the wharves and streets." The Irish and Germans, he noted, did the outside work, while white girls moved into domestic service. When he saw New Orleans, he commented, though no doubt with exaggeration, that "hardly a colored face is to be seen on the levee, and the work is done by the Germans and the Irish. . . . Indeed, now, New Orleans and Mobile seem but little more like slave cities than do Philadelphia and New York." [96]

Though the process varied in Dixie's cities and Negroes hung on in many skills, "job busting" became a normal tactic for the growing white labor force faced with traditional colored employment practices. As the black population dropped, white newcomers moved in and took over craft after craft. Occasionally accompanied by violence and usually with official sanction, slave and free colored workers were shunted into the most menial and routine chores. In 1830 Negroes, both slave and free, had been used in a wide variety of employments; by 1860 the number of possibilities had shrunk markedly. The movement toward segregation, so noticeable in other aspects of urban life, was rapidly invading employment.

In housing the same trend was perceptible, though less advanced. The spread of the "living out" system, both in its legal and irregular form, gave slaves some choice of residence. Since the urge to leave the enclosure reflected the freedom from surveillance it entailed, slaves sought spots as removed from whites as possible. For most this meant a retreat to the outer edges of the city or beyond the municipal line altogether. There was seldom any escape from all whites, but there were parts of town with clusters of colored inhabitants. By the 'forties and 'fifties it was apparent in most places that Negroes were settling on the periphery of the cities.

Savannah is a good illustration of this process. The central portion had always been the commercial heart of town. Immediately around it and stretching southward, the substantial and the wealthy built their houses. The best addresses bore the names of eight or ten squares directly away from the wharf toward Forsyth Park. The western and southern edges became the sites for the low-income whites and increasingly for the free colored as well. As slaves moved away from the master's yards, they headed for these areas.

The 1848 census, which listed slaves from their actual place of residence rather than from their master's addresses, revealed the concentrations. Old Oglethorpe Ward on the west had 1327 Negroes to 999 whites. In the same place there were only five brick houses to 451 wooden ones. To the east, Carpenter's Row, Trustees Gardens, and Gilmerville showed the same tendency with fewer numbers. There 300 blacks lived with 182 whites; none of the 127 houses was brick. Significantly enough, Currytown on the southeast edge of the city showed the same characteristics—Negro majorities and wooden dwellings. Elsewhere in Savannah, the figures ran the other way, with white preponderance and large numbers of brick homes.

The movement to the periphery was increasingly common, though in some towns colored concentrations grew up more haphazardly in small enclaves or strips in out-of-the-way places. And the centers of Negro life, formal and informal, followed the people. Colored churches, especially those established after 1840, sought locations in these neighborhoods. Grocery stores and dram shops, too, settled there. Even the cemeteries were put near the living. In Savannah's case, for example, four Negro churches, three Baptist, and one Methodist, were on the west side, while another served the east side. The central city had none. Of 174 "grocers" 101 did business in the outer residential wards, West Broad alone accommodating 19.[97] In Charleston the convergence was on the northern border and the Neck beyond.

In no case did anything like full residential segregation emerge. Few streets, much less blocks, were solidly black. Everywhere some whites occupied nearby dwellings. Still the inclination to cluster here, to concentrate there, was more marked by 1860 than in 1820. The separation apparent in other areas of life was slowly insinuated into housing.

Thus, even before slavery had been abolished, a system of segregation had grown up in the cities. Indeed, the whites thought some such arrangement was necessary if they were to sustain their traditional supremacy over the Negroes. The countryside provided enough room to give meaning to racial separation. The master could be physically quite removed from his blacks, though sharing the same plantation or farm. And together both were isolated from others. In cities these spatial relationships were quite different. Both races were thrown together; they encountered each other at every corner, they rubbed elbows at every turn; they divided up, however inequitably, the limited space of the town site. Segregation sorted people out by race, established a public etiquette for their conduct, and created social distance where there was proximity. Urban circumstances produced this system long before the destruction of slavery itself.

Of course, the complete separation of races was impossible in the city, and the practice differed from place to place. In some towns, public conveyances remained mixed; in others Negroes were not excluded from all public grounds; in still others housing continued scrambled. Yet every city developed its own arrangement expressed in the contrived separation of colored and white in countless ways. Though never total, the segregation was so extensive that Negroes were never permitted to forget their inferior position.

XI

The rising incidence of segregation was another index of the increasing weakness of slavery in the cities. Rooted in the white's need for discipline and deference, it developed to take up the slack in the loosening system. It provided public control to replace dwindling private supervision of the master over his slave. To do this, the difference between free and enslaved Negroes had to be narrowed, depriving free blacks of part of their freedom even while permitting a wider latitude to bondsmen. To most whites, however, there seemed no alternative. The old system no longer really controlled; the walls no longer really confined; the chains no longer really held.

The decline of slavery in the cities was the central fact of race relations in the South's cities in the ante-bellum decades. It was also a fact that conditioned Negro life in subsequent generations, for it meant that, when emancipation finally did come, most of the colored population would be in the countryside rather than in cities. Accustomed only to routine tasks, imbruted by the severe limitations of plantation existence, and unused to managing their own affairs, they became free under the most difficult of circumstances.

If the Negro population in the cities had grown in the same proportion as the whites, there would have been present an invaluable pool of potential leadership, for there many blacks, even under slavery, had begun to develop the most important tools of citizenship. There they acquired some skills and learned the rudiments of reading and writing. There, too, many had commenced to manage their own affairs, and in churches they developed a capacity for organization. In short, the metropolis nourished the literacy and self-reliance needed in a free system.

Observers generally agreed on the other hand that rural blacks plainly bore the mark of their servitude. "The field-hand negro is, on the average, a very poor and bad creature," Olmsted wrote sadly, "much worse than I supposed before I had seen him and grown familiar with his stupidity, indolence, duplicity, and sensuality. He seems to be but an imperfect man, incapable of taking care of himself in a civilized manner." [98] House servants were presumably in a favored condition, but their contacts usually were only somewhat wider, their self-reliance seldom encouraged, and their horizons not appreciably better.

Olmsted found quite the opposite in the cities. "Slaves can never be brought together in denser communities but their intelligence will be increased to a degree dangerous to those who enjoy the benefit of their labor," he observed. "Hundreds of slaves in New Orleans must be constantly reflecting and saying to one another, 'I am as capable of taking care of myself as this Irish hod-carrier, or this German market-gardner; why can't I have the enjoyment of my labor as well as they? I am as capable of taking care of my own family as much as they of theirs; why should I be subject to have them taken from me by those other men who call themselves our owners?'" And the speculation no doubt extended to the next generation: "'Our children have as much brains as the children of these white neighbors of ours, who not long ago were cooks and waiters at the hotel, why should they be spurned from the school rooms? I helped build the school house, and have not been paid for it. One thing I know, if I can't have my rights, I can have my pleasures; and if they won't give me wages I can take them.'" [99]

Olmsted saw this distinction more clearly than most. But visitors from the North, travelers from abroad, in fact, masters and slaves, also understood the difference. It was an uncomfortable fact for the whites. To them it presaged a wider freedom for the Negro, with all the uncertainties and perhaps chaos that would follow. Hence the response of owners and officials was to tighten rather than adjust, to expel rather than emancipate, to segregate rather than liberate. At the end the "free air of the city" was being increasingly denied to a higher and higher proportion of blacks.

The full significance of the de-urbanization of the Negro under slavery was apparent only much later. Emancipation found him located primarily in the least dynamic area of American life. Capable of simple tasks, familiar only with rural routine, largely illiterate, and unused to managing his own affairs, he faced a long road to full freedom. Ultimately that road carried him to the city. Though confronted by both discrimination and segregation, he could find there the numbers and leadership which could one day spring him loose from the confinements of an earlier bondage.

The recovery of the metropolis began before the First World War. The depression slowed the pace somewhat, but a second global conflict produced an irresistible urban undertow. Colored families had abandoned the land by now or were pushed off it by machines and new techniques. By the thousands each day they flocked to the cities both North and South. There, often amid squalor and deprivation, they began the dramatic rally of forces that would dissolve the walls which for three centuries had kept them outside the promised land of equal rights.

Significantly, among the datelines which reported the new phase of the story were New Orleans, Mobile, Savannah, Charleston, Richmond, Louisville, and St. Louis. A new generation of Negroes pushed aside older leadership and took to the lunchrooms and streets as well as the courts in a drive to desegregate the public life of the South. Though Dixie resisted everywhere, the first breakthrough appeared in the urban areas. Parks, buses, public facilities, and a few schools opened first; commercial enterprises, restaurants, and hotels grudgingly followed. Moreover, the rise of Negro voting in the major cities gradually provided a stable base for further successes.

The characteristic focus of the movement was the churches. Like their ante-bellum predecessors, they were more than religious centers, encompassing in a unique way the whole range of organized Negro life in the city. Their ministers spoke not merely for their own congregations but for the colored community as a whole. And standing in a long Christian and Southern tradition, they commanded respect among important white groups in the city. In the churches the people gathered, heard speeches, and bolstered their morale. Boycotts were planned, discipline established, even demonstrations started from the same sanctuaries. Ironically now, the pattern of social organization born in slavery became the vanguard of a new freedom.

Bibliographic Essay

THE HISTORIAN who examines any aspect of the institution of slavery enters an area of intense and continuous interest by scholars. Even before the Civil War slavery demanded the attention of serious commentators both within the United States and abroad. Because the conflict itself centered upon the issue and left deep and permanent scars on the nation, every generation of historians has found in the South's "peculiar institution" a topic of enduring importance and relevance. It has excited some of our best minds and produced some of our best scholarship.

The two most important books treat slavery from quite different perspectives, but taken together they provide a convenient summary of what historians know and think about the system. Ulrich Bonnell Phillips's *American Negro Slavery; A Survey of the Supply, Employment and Control of Negro Labor As Determined by the Plantation Régime*, published in 1918, was the standard work for more than a generation. Though based on extensive research and careful scholarship, its conclusions were marred by the author's racial assumptions. In 1956 *The Peculiar Institution; Slavery in the Ante-Bellum South* by Kenneth M. Stampp substantially revised Phillips's account by including much new material and writing from the view that "slaves were merely ordinary human beings, that innately Negroes *are*, after all, only white men with black skins, nothing more, nothing less."

While these two historians have written the fullest and most

comprehensive studies, others have widened our understand-
ing by putting slavery in broader contexts. Allan Nevins, for
example, produced the best brief description of the institution
while tracing the origins of the Civil War in the *Ordeal of the
Union*. Stanley Elkins opened new and stimulating questions
by probing the relationship between slavery and its general
institutional setting in both the United States and Latin
America. In this book, *Slavery; A Problem in American Institutional and Intellectual Life*, he experimented with the application of modern concepts of personality to enslaved Negroes
of an earlier time. John Hope Franklin examined slavery as a
crucial phase in the history of the American Negro in *From
Slavery to Freedom; A History of American Negroes*.

In addition, hundreds of monographs have studied the system intensively on a state or regional level. Indeed, there is
scarcely a state in the Old South which is without a competent
survey. And some specialized topics have been handled with
special distinction. For instance, Frederic Bancroft's *Slave-
Trading in the Old South* and Howell Meadoes Henry's *The
Police Control of the Slave in South Carolina* remain standard
accounts even after a generation of research into the same
problem. Moreover, innumerable articles have provided indispensable information on such important subjects as the incidence of slaveholding, the profitability of slavery, and the
position of the free Negro on the edge of the institution. In
short, the historian who writes about slavery quickly learns
he is not engaged in a pioneering enterprise. The trail along
the way is well marked and the footprints clear and often big.

Yet this rich tradition of scholarship generally assumed
slavery to be a rural institution, or, as Phillips's subtitle indicated, a system of labor "determined by the plantation regime." Ironically, his chapter on "town slaves" constitutes an
unusual recognition of the urban dimension of this problem.
But almost without exception the emphasis rested on the

countryside. Hence historians sought their evidence in plantation records, family manuscripts, the economics of cotton-
growing, the price of slaves, and the occupation of the new
lands in the Mississippi valley and the Southwest.

In writing this book, I have had to find clues elsewhere;
what was essential for traditional histories proved only occasionally appropriate for this one. The most important of the
conventional sources were travelers' accounts and slave narratives. Both, of course, pose special problems for historians.
Visitors usually spent only a few days in each city, talked to
a limited number of people, and came to the South with fixed
views on the Negro and slavery. But some, like Frederick Law
Olmsted, convey an enormous amount of information as well
as many perceptive insights. Slave recollections, when au-
thentic, contain all kinds of invaluable material. And since a
large portion of these narratives concerned Negroes who
lived for at least some time in cities, they were often useful
in this study.

For the most part, however, the material for this volume
came from the cities themselves. Court records, police dockets,
real-estate conveyances, and tax and assessment books provide essential official information about masters and slaves as
well as many glimpses into the workings of the system. The
minutes of the city councils, municipal ordinances, and the
reports of special committees often dealt with slavery and the
control of Negroes. Grand jury presentments proved especially useful because they sometimes became "state of the
city" messages, viewing this question in relation to many
others. State archives contained the enactments of the legislatures, messages by governors, reports of committees, and
petitions by private citizens and municipalities which dealt
with race and slavery.

But it would not have been possible to tell this story without the voluminous files of early local newspapers. Every

city had several, both dailies and weeklies, which provide indispensable narratives of events in each place. Moreover, their advertisements and announcements often reveal a great deal of everyday information usually not preserved in any other way.

There are no urban analogues of the plantation records which provided the basic materials for Phillips, Stampp, and others. Only a handful of diaries deal with the treatment of city slaves, and even in these the concern is peripheral. Some account books give data on hiring out or the slave trade. Church records pertain to a crucial area of Negro life, and the occasional papers of Negro societies illuminate a neglected area of colored activity. In addition, scattered across the South or gathered in special archives are manuscript collections which yield important, if scanty, information.

The physical environment helped shape the nature of urban slavery. Enough remains of the historic centers of these towns to give a sense of the spatial relationships in which the system operated. Some sketches, a few maps, occasional drawings by fire-insurance companies, and real-estate plats add some precision to these impressions. Business directories and yearbooks include addresses and locations which make it possible to reconstruct the distribution of commercial buildings and public facilities.

In short, the material for this study is found on every hand in Southern cities. Because of this diversity, it seemed more appropriate to indicate the sources and their location in the notes than to append a formal and lengthy bibliography.

Notes

Chapter One

1. *Louisville Daily Journal*, February 22, 1848.

2. Samuel Walker, "The Diary of a Louisiana Planter, Elia Plantation," Typescript, Tulane University Library.

3. Frederick Law Olmsted, *A Journey Through Texas; Or a Saddle-Trip on the Southwestern Frontier; with a Statistical Appendix* (N.Y., 1857), 37.

4. Frederick Douglass, *My Bondage and My Freedom* (N.Y., 1855), 147-8.

5. *De Bow's Review*, XXIX (1860), 613-14.

6. Frederick Law Olmsted, *The Cotton Kingdom* (N.Y., 1861), I, 291. See also Charles Lyell, *A Second Visit to the United States of North America* (London, 1855), II, 91.

7. Joseph H. Ingraham, *The Sunny South; a Southerner at Home* (Philadelphia, 1860), 338.

8. John Adam Paxton, *The New Orleans Directory and Register* (New Orleans, 1822), 46.

9. William Gilmore Simms, *Letters; Collected and Edited by Mary C. Simms Oliphant, Alfred Taylor Odell and T.C. Duncan Eaves* (Columbia, S.C., 1952), I, 35.

10. *De Bow's Review*, I (1846), 44.

11. Albert J. Pickett, *Eight Days in New Orleans* (n.p., 1847), 19.

12. Ingraham, *Sunny South*, 338.

13. *De Bow's Review*, II (1846), 53.

14. G.W. Cable, "New Orleans," in the *Tenth Census of the United States, Report on the Social Statistics of Cities* (Washington, 1887), XIX, 256. (Hereafter cited as Tenth Census of U.S., *Social Statistics of Cities*, XIX.)

15. Howard Horace Justice, *Diary, 1857-1859*, MSS. (Duke University Library, Durham, N.C.).

16. Adam Hodgson, *Remarks During a Journey Through North*

America in the Years 1819, 1820, and 1821, in a Series of Letters (N.Y., 1823), 156.

17. See for example, Frederick Law Olmsted, *A Journey in the Seaboard Slave States, With Remarks on Their Economy* (N.Y., 1856), 565; Francis and Theresa Pulszky, *White, Red, Black Sketches of American Society in the United States During the Visit of Their Guests* (N.Y., 1853), II, 113.

18. *Niles' Register*, April 6, 1822.

19. *Mobile Commercial Register*, November 7, 1833; September 30, 1835.

20. All the census figures are taken from the Tenth Census of U.S., *Social Statistics of Cities*, XIX, 191.

21. Olmsted, *Seaboard Slave States*, 567.

22. Hiram Fuller, *Belle Brittan on a Tour, at Newport and Here and There* (N.Y., 1858), 112.

23. Ingraham, *Sunny South*, 504.

24. Olmsted, *Seaboard Slave States*, 405; William Cullen Bryant, "A Tour in the Old South," *Prose Writings of William Cullen Bryant*, ed. by Parke Godwin (N.Y., 1884), II, 36.

25. *Savannah Republican*, November 20, 1851; May 16, 1844.

26. Quoted in the *Savannah Republican*, November 20, 1851.

27. *Report of R.D. Arnold, Mayor of the City of Savannah, for the Year Ending September 30th, 1860, Etc.* (Savannah, 1860), 26.

28. Joseph Bancroft, *Census of the City of Savannah* (Savannah, 1848, 2nd. ed.), 3.

29. Quoted in *Savannah Republican*, April 28, 1853.

30. C.G. Parsons, *Inside View of Slavery; or a Tour Among the Planters* (Boston, 1855), 23.

31. *De Bow's Review*, I (1846), 44.

32. This virtual stagnation led to several local censuses by city officials. Their findings, however, only substantiated the dreary figures of the national count. See particularly those of 1824 and 1848. *Charleston Courier*, August 7, 1824; J. L. Dawson and H.W. DeSaussure, *Census of the City of Charleston, South Carolina for 1848* (Charleston, 1849).

33. *Charleston City Gazette and Commercial Daily Advertiser*, September 20, 1824.

34. *Charleston Courier*, May 29, 1845.

35. *Charleston Courier*, November 29, 1844.

36. *Charleston City Gazette and Commercial Daily Advertiser,* July 24, 1829.

37. James Stirling, *Letters from the Slave States* (London, 1857), 250.

38. Frederick Law Olmsted, *A Journey in the Back Country* (N.Y., 1860), 280.

39. Kathleen Bruce, *Virginia Iron Manufacture in the Slave Era* (N.Y., 1931), 100ff.

40. Olmsted, *Seaboard Slave States,* 19. For the same view by a British traveler, see Stirling, *Letters,* 335.

41. *Richmond Enquirer,* May 16, 1828.

42. Quoted in the *Richmond Enquirer,* July 30, 1839.

43. Tenth Census of the U.S., *Social Statistics of Cities,* XIX, 79.

44. *Louisville Daily Democrat,* August 31, 1858.

45. Richard C. Wade, *The Urban Frontier, The Rise of Western Cities, 1790-1830* (Cambridge, Mass., 1959), 13ff.

46. Louis C. Hunter, *Steamboats on the Western Rivers, An Economic and Technical History* (Cambridge, Mass., 1949), 37.

47. Gabriel Collins, *Louisville Directory for the Year 1836* (Louisville, 1836), vii.

48. Gabriel Collins, *Louisville Directory for the Year 1843-4* (Louisville, 1843), G.

49. Tenth Census of the U.S., *Social Statistics of Cities,* XIX, 122.

50. Olmsted, *A Journey Through Texas,* 22.

51. *Missouri Republican,* January 8, 1855.

52. *De Bow's Review,* XVII (1854), 397.

53. Tenth Census of the U.S., *Social Statistics of Cities,* XIX, 567.

54. Hunter, *Steamboats on Western Rivers,* 644-5.

55. Tenth Census of the U.S., *Social Statistics of Cities,* XIX, 576.

56. Charles Keemle (ed.), *The St. Louis Directory for the Year, 1838-1839* (St. Louis, 1838), x; Wyatt Winton Belcher, *The Economic Rivalry Between St. Louis and Chicago, 1850-1880* (N.Y., 1947), 46.

57. J. Benwell, *An Englishman's Travels in America, His Observations of Life and Manners in the Free and Slave States* (London, 1853), 113.

58. Adolph B. Benson (ed.), *America of the Fifties: Letters of Fredrika Bremer* (N.Y., 1924), 96.

59. Robert Russell, *North America, Its Agriculture and Climate; Containing Observations on the Agriculture and Climate of Canada, the United States, and the Island of Cuba* (Edinburgh, 1857), 151.

60. The Charleston figures are somewhat complicated by the annexation of the "Neck," a suburb, in 1850 which enlarged the city's population but did not alter the percentages appreciably.

61. Unless otherwise indicated, these population figures are taken from the federal censuses, manuscript returns.

62. The family unit is a better index of the extent of slaveholding than individual whites, for everyone in the household was a master in the operative sense of the word, even though legal ownership was lodged in the head of the family. Use of this larger unit raises the incidence of slaveholding both on the countryside and in the cities.

63. City of Richmond, Personal Property Tax, 1840, 1850, 1860, MSS., Virginia State Library, Richmond.

64. In addition to the federal censuses, see *List of the Tax Payers of the City of Charleston for 1860* (Charleston, 1861).

65. Richmond, Personal Property Tax, 1820, 1830, 1840, 1850, 1860.

66. Eighth Census, 1860, Louisiana, III.

67. *List of Tax Payers of the City of Charleston for 1860.*

68. Richmond, Personal Property Tax, 1860. Mobile, too, had its share of large owners, James Saunders with 125, Duke W. Goodman with 105, John O. Cumings Jr. with 128, William Moore with 69, and 44 others with over twenty proved that as late as 1860 extensive holdings were not unknown there. Eighth Census, 1860, Slaves, Alabama, IV. Even in cities where the regime of bondage seemed to be dying, a few still kept many Negroes. A. Throckmorton, of Louisville, reported 82 in 1840, while Jonathan Cochran listed 52 and James Breckenridge 46. Sixth Census, 1840, Kentucky, VI. Farther west eleven St. Louisans held over a score, though none had many more than that.

69. Eighth Census, 1860.

70. Eighth Census, 1860.

71. Among Baltimore's slave population women outnumbered men 1541 to 677. Eighth Census, 1860.

72. Kenneth M. Stampp, *The Peculiar Institution, Slavery in the Ante-Bellum South* (N.Y., 1956), 28.

73. Ibid., 28.

Chapter Two

1. *Richmond Daily Dispatch*, August 18, 1853.
2. Quoted in Olmsted, *Back Country*, 301.
3. *New Orleans Bee*, October 13, 1835.

4. Alfred Pairpont, *Uncle Sam and His Country* (London, 1857), 219.

5. *Charleston Courier*, May 22, 1832.

6. Charleston City Council, Memorial to the State Legislature, MSS., South Carolina Archives Division, Columbia, S.C.

7. Lyell, *Second Visit to the United States*, I, 222.

8. Samuel A. Cartwright, "Ethnology of the Negro or Prognathous Race," *The New Orleans Medical and Surgical Journal*, XIV (1857), 155.

9. *Louisville Daily Democrat*, January 11, 1853.

10. *New Orleans Daily Delta*, June 3, 1858.

11. Douglass, *My Bondage*, 144.

12. Joseph Bancroft, *Census of the City of Savannah*, 8, 13.

13. *Census of the City of Charleston for the Year of 1848*, 29-34.

14. *Charleston Courier*, September 12, 1850.

15. *New Orleans Daily Picayune*, September 2, 1852.

16. Richmond, Personal Property Tax, 1860.

17. William Cullen Bryant, *Prose Writings*, ed. by Parke Godwin, II, 25.

18. Ibid., 25-6.

19. Alexander MacKay, *The Western World* (London, 1849, 2 vols.), II, 74.

20. Joseph Clarke Robert, *The Tobacco Kingdom; Plantation, Market, and Factory in Virginia and North Carolina, 1800-1860* (Durham, N.C., 1938), 204.

21. Russell, *North America*, 152.

22. Charles Weld, *A Vacation Tour in the United States and Canada* (London, 1855), 313-14.

23. Olmsted, *Seaboard Slave States*, 102.

24. Henry Box Brown, *Narrative of Henry Box Brown, Who Escaped from Slavery* (Boston, 1849), 41.

25. U.S. Eighth Census, 1860, Slaves, Virginia, IV.

26. Robert, *Tobacco Kingdom*, 208.

27. *Richmond Enquirer*, January 13, 1825.

28. For the most detailed discussion of Anderson and the Tredegar Iron Works see Bruce, *Virginia Iron Manufacture in the Slave Era*, Chapters IV, V, and especially VI; for other iron manufacturers see Chapter VIII.

29. *Richmond Enquirer*, May 29, 1847. For the same judgment twenty years earlier see also October 9, 1827.

30. U.S. Seventh Census, 1850, Slave Inhabitants, Louisiana, IV.

31. *New Orleans Bee*, June 2, 1836.

32. Pulszky, *Red, White, Black*, II, 98; the Sixth Census listed the Gas Light and Banking Company with 25 slaves.

33. Quoted in the *New Orleans Daily Delta*, January 15, 1859.

34. *New Orleans Daily Crescent*, September 19, 1859.

35. U.S. Eighth Census, 1860, Slaves, South Carolina, II; Richmond, Personal Property Tax, 1860.

36. U.S. Sixth Census, 1840, Louisiana, IV.

37. Thomas Nichols, *Forty Years of American Life* (N.Y., 1937), 355.

38. *Mobile Evening News*, May 9, 1855.

39. James Stuart, *Three Years in North America* (N.Y., 1833, 2 vols.), II, 68.

40. James Rudd, *Account Book, 1830-1860*, MSS., I (Filson Club, Louisville).

41. Edward Abdy, *Journal of a Residence and Tour in the United States of North America, from April, 1833, to October, 1834* (London, 1835, 3 vols.), II, 244.

42. The extent of hiring out cannot be estimated with any reliability. De Bow once asserted that there were nearly as many "non-slaveholding slave-hirers" as there were slaveholders. His figure for 1850 was 158,974 compared to 186,551 owners. This figure probably did not include an employer who hired on a short-term basis. But by any calculation the practice was widespread. See John S.C. Abbott, *South and North; or Impressions Received During a Trip to Cuba and the South* (N.Y., 1860), 201n-2n.

43. In Mobile, however, "the universal custom was," as a judge asserted, ". . . to pay only for a full month of twenty-six working days, unless . . . a special contract to the contrary." Helen Tunnicliff Catterall (ed.), *Judicial Cases Concerning American Slavery and the Negro* (Washington, D.C., 4 vols.), III, 199.

44. C. W. and A. Thruston to James Brown, January 1, 1832, MSS., C. W. Thruston Papers, *Slavery Documents, 1823-1845*, R. C. Ballard Thruston Collection (Filson Club, Louisville).

45. Quoted in *De Bow's Review*, XXVI (1859), 600.

46. *Police Code, or Collection of the Ordinances of Police Made by the City Council of New Orleans* (New Orleans, 1808), 250.

47. *Digest of the Ordinances and Resolutions of the Corporation of New Orleans* (New Orleans, 1817), 222.

48. *Digest of Ordinances of the City Council of Charleston, From the Year 1783 to July 1818, Etc.* (Charleston, 1818), 182.

49. *Digest of Ordinances of the City Council of Charleston, From the Year 1783 to Oct. 1844* (Charleston, 1844), 21.

50. *A Digest of All the Ordinances of the City of Savannah ... which were in Force on the 1st January 1858* (Savannah, 1858), 417-18.

51. *The Code of Ordinances of the City of Mobile, Etc.* (Mobile, 1859), 174.

52. *Report of R. D. Arnold, Mayor of Savannah, 1860,* 26.

53. *Charleston Courier,* August 31, 1849.

54. Charleston, *Digest of Ordinances, 1818,* 187-8.

55. Savannah, *Digest of Ordinances, 1858,* 418.

56. New Orleans, *Digest of Ordinances, 1817,* 226.

57. Charleston, *Digest of Ordinances, 1818,* 172, 188. The ordinance was first enacted in 1815.

58. *Mobile Commercial Register,* May 30, 1826.

59. New Orleans, *Digest of Ordinances, 1817,* 226.

60. Mobile, *Digest of Ordinances, 1858,* 174; Charleston, *Digest of Ordinances, 1818,* 189.

61. Mobile, *Digest of Ordinances, 1817,* 189; *Digest of Ordinances, 1837,* 136.

62. *Missouri Gazette,* March 28, 1821.

63. *Louisville Daily Democrat,* December 20, 1855.

64. *Richmond Enquirer,* January 18, 1855.

65. *Richmond Enquirer,* July 11, 1845.

66. *Richmond Enquirer,* December 30, 1831.

67. *Richmond Enquirer,* December 20, 1832.

68. *Richmond Enquirer,* January 3, 1833.

69. *Richmond Enquirer,* February 23, 1836.

70. *New Orleans Daily Picayune,* April 24, 1857.

71. *New Orleans Daily Crescent,* April 24, 1851.

72. *New Orleans Daily Picayune,* July 3, 1853.

73. *New Orleans Daily Picayune,* December 31, 1853.

74. *New Orleans Daily Delta,* July 19, 1854; *New Orleans Daily Picayune,* May 30, 1856.

75. *New Orleans Daily Picayune,* September 6, 1843.

76. *New Orleans Daily Picayune,* February 5, 1858.

77. *New Orleans Daily Picayune,* July 22, 1857.

78. *Louisville Daily Democrat,* December 19, 1858.

79. *Louisville Daily Democrat*, January 11, 1853.

80. *Louisville Daily Democrat*, February 10, 1851.

81. For some examples see, *Louisville Daily Democrat*, February 15, 1854; January 4, 1854; December 19, 1858.

82. New Orleans City Council, Resolution, June 7, 1820, *Digest of Ordinances*, 1831, 145.

83. New Orleans City Council, Resolution, October 19, September 11, 1823, *Proceedings of the Council Meetings*, Typescript, New Orleans Public Library.

84. Council of the First Municipality of the City of New Orleans, Journal, March 22, 1841.

85. Charleston, Ordinance, October 13, 1806, *Digest of Ordinances*, *1818*, 223; Richmond, Minutes of Common Council, January 24, 1820, MSS., City Hall, Richmond.

86. *Savannah Republican*, August 27, 1842.

87. *Savannah Republican*, May 31, 1851.

88. *Savannah Republican*, June 24, 1826.

89. R.Y. Hayne, *Report of the Proceedings of the City Authorities of Charleston During the Past Year ... 1837; With Suggestions For the Improvement of the City* (Charleston, 1837), 14.

90. *Richmond Enquirer*, January 6, 1858.

91. John Berkley Grimball, *Diaries, 1832-1883*, MSS. (Southern History Collection, University of North Carolina Library).

92. Russell, *North America*, 151.

93. Bruce, *Virginia Iron Manufacture in the Slave Era*, 245n.

94. *Richmond Enquirer*, January 5, 1859.

95. Rudd, *Account Book, 1830-1860*.

96. C. W. Thruston Papers, *Slavery Documents, 1823-1845*; C. W. Thruston to John O'Fallon, February 1, 1828, MSS.

97. *Missouri Gazette*, November 29, 1817.

98. Commissioner of Public Roads and Streets of New Orleans, Record Books of First Municipality, 1839-1843, MSS., City Archives, Public Library.

99. James Redpath, *The Roving Editor; or Talks with Slaves in the Southern States* (New York, 1859), 183.

100. Nehemiah Adams, *A South-Side View of Slavery; or, Three Months at the South in 1854* (Boston, 1854), 76.

101. Quoted in the *Savannah Republican*, February 3, 1859.

102. Douglass, *My Bondage*, 318, 328.

103. Charles Ball, *Slavery in the United States: A Narrative of the Life and Adventures of Charles Ball, a Black Man, Etc.* (Lewistown, Pa., 1836), 391.

104. *Louisville Public Advertiser*, June 24, 1820.

105. *Charleston Courier*, September 12, 1850.

106. *Savannah Republican*, October 28, 1845.

107. South Carolina Legislature, "Bill to Amend the Act for Better Government of Slaves and Free Persons of Color," December 8, 1845, MSS., South Carolina Archives Division.

108. *Charleston Courier*, September 12, 1850.

109. *Missouri Republican*, July 19, October 4, 1824.

110. *Missouri Republican*, December 20, 1833.

111. *St. Louis Observer*, November 5, 1835.

112. Charleston, Ordinance, October 28, 1806, *Digest of Ordinances, 1818*, 185.

113. South Carolina Committee on Colored People, Report, December 7, 1858, MSS., South Carolina Archives Division.

114. *Charleston City Gazette and Commercial Daily Advertiser*, October 26, 1824.

115. South Carolina Committee on Colored People, Report, December 7, 1858, MSS.

116. Petition of the Mechanics and Workingmen of the City of Charleston to the Senate of South Carolina, November 16, 1858, MSS., South Carolina Archives Division.

117. Quoted in the *Savannah Republican*, February 3, 1859.

118. *Savannah Republican*, October 28, 1845.

119. South Carolina Committee on Colored People, Report, December 7, 1858, MSS., South Carolina Archives Division.

120. Ibid.

121. Rudd, *Account Book, 1830-1860*.

122. Thomas Jones, *Experience and Personal Narrative of Uncle Tom Jones: Who was Forty Years a Slave* (Boston, n.d.), 25.

123. Philo Tower, *Slavery Unmasked: Being a Truthful Narrative of a Three Years' Residence and Journeying in Eleven Southern States: To Which is Added the Invasion of Kansas, Including the Last Chapter of Her Wrongs* (Rochester, 1856), 111.

124. George Lewis, *Impressions of America and American Churches* (Edinburgh, 1845), 177.

125. Douglass, *My Bondage*, 328-9.

126. Tower, *Slavery Unmasked*, 226.

Chapter Three

1. *De Bow's Review,* X (1851), 623.

2. Stampp, *Peculiar Institution,* 294.

3. Housing was so peripheral to slave life on the plantation that historians have paid little attention to it. For example, Stampp allots it only a few pages and Phillips nowhere treats it systematically. Stampp, *Peculiar Institution,* 292-5; Ulrich B. Phillips, *American Negro Slavery* (N.Y., 1918), 279, 289, 298, 310.

4. Many of these structures still stand, permitting an inspection of the old shell of the dwellings, though not its ante-bellum furnishings. In addition, real estate transfers sometimes included sketches of buildings which provide contemporary confirmation of their estimated size. In St. Louis an insurance map of 1870 gives the outside measurements, though not room sizes, of this housing. See for example, block 119, plots 520, 518, 615 in C.T. Aubin, *A. Whipple & Co's. Insurance Map of St. Louis, Mo.* (n.p., 1870).

5. U.S. Census, 1840.

6. *Census of the City of Charleston...For the Year 1848,* 20.

7. *List of the Tax Payers of the City of Charleston for 1860* (Charleston, 1861).

8. *Report of the Committee of the City Council of Charleston, Upon the Epidemic Yellow Fever of 1858* (Charleston, 1859), 19.

9. Charleston Grand Jury, Presentment, March Term, 1856, MSS., South Carolina Archives Division.

10. Carlton H. Rogers, *Incidents of Travel in the Southern States and Cuba. With a Description of the Mammoth Cave* (N.Y., 1862), 247.

11. Many local historians trace this early Southern architecture, with the residences on the street and yards or piazzas behind, to Spanish or French influences. Yet this explanation does not account for the appearance of the same scheme in cities quite removed from that background.

Nor was this design characteristic of only downtown residences. In the 1840's Robert Playfair, for example, described housing in Louisville away from the commercial areas as "elegant" and "situated in gardens and pleasure grounds, with apartments diverging behind from the main building for the slave servants." Robert Playfair, *Recollections of a Visit to the United States and British Provinces of North America in the Years 1847, 1848, and 1849* (Edinburgh, 1856), 190.

12. *Fire Insurance Map*, 1870 (Louisiana State University Library). For St. Louis see Aubin, *Insurance Map of St. Louis, Mo.*

13. On the edge of town where lots were large, the tendency was to put the Negro quarters at the rear of the premises.

14. Robert C. Allen, *Survey of Charleston, 1851*, MSS., 2 vols. (South Carolina Historical Society, Charleston).

15. Camille N. Dry, *Pictorial St. Louis, The Great Metropolis of the Mississippi Valley, A Topographical Survey Drawn in Perspective A.D. 1875*, designed and edited by Richard J. Compton (St. Louis, 1876); see especially plates 3, 22, 44.

16. Rev. Dr. [James Henley] Thornwell, *A Review of Rev. J.G. Adger's Sermon on the Instruction of the Colored Population* (Charleston, 1847), 13.

17. Bancroft, *Census of the City of Savannah ... 1848*, 7.

18. Quoted in "Petition of Certain Citizens of Charleston to Prohibit the Introduction of Slaves Merely for Sale and for Certain Other Amendments of the Law in Relation to Slaves," 1847, MSS. (South Carolina Archives Division).

19. *Digest of the Ordinances of the City Council of Charleston, From the Year 1783 to July, 1818; Etc.* (Charleston, 1818), October 28, 1806.

20. New Orleans, Ordinances, October 8, 1817.

21. *Mobile Mercantile Advertiser*, July 14, 1837.

22. *St. Louis Observer*, November 5, 1835.

23. Richmond, Ordinances, December 22, 1857.

24. Louisville City Journal, April 28, 1828, MSS. (City Hall, Louisville).

25. *Missouri Republican*, December 20, 1853.

26. *Savannah Republican*, January 25, 1847.

27. *Charleston Courier*, September 23, 1845.

28. *Mobile Daily Advertiser*, November 4, 1851.

29. *Mobile Daily Advertiser*, November 5, 1851.

30. *Mobile Daily Advertiser*, November 8, 1851.

31. *Mobile Register and Journal*, July 10, 1847.

32. *Mobile Evening News*, January 17, 1856. For other representative views see also January 10, 21, 28, 1856.

33. *Mobile Daily Advertiser*, July 8, 1857.

34. *Mobile Register and Journal*, July 10, 1847.

35. Parsons, *Inside View of Slavery*, 25.

36. James Stuart, *Three Years in North America* (N.Y., 1833), II, 68, 132.

37. *Richmond Enquirer*, August 31, 1853.

38. For example, see Louisville, Ordinances, October 31, 1853.

39. Henry Box Brown, *Narrative of Henry Box Brown, Etc.* (Boston, 1849), 51.

40. *Charleston Courier*, May 11, 1835.

41. *Charleston Courier*, October 24, 1839.

42. *Charleston Courier*, December 17, 1839.

43. *Mobile Daily Advertiser*, November 18, 1857.

44. *Mobile Register and Journal*, July 10, 1847.

45. *Richmond Enquirer*, August 31, 1853.

46. *Savannah Republican*, May 5, 1832.

47. *Louisiana Courier*, January 22, 1831.

48. *Census of the City of Charleston . . . For the Year 1848*, v.

49. Ibid., 2.

50. *Charleston Courier*, September 22, 1845.

51. Charleston Grand Jury, Presentment, March Term, 1856, MSS., South Carolina Archives Division.

52. *Charleston Courier*, October 1, 1825.

53. *Mobile Evening News*, January 17, 1856.

54. Bruce, *Virginia Iron Manufacturing*, 254.

55. *Richmond Daily Dispatch*, October 25, 1852.

56. *Richmond Enquirer*, August 10, 1853.

57. Richmond, Ordinances, December 22, 1857.

58. This aspect of Negro housing in St. Louis, Louisville, and Lexington is briefly described but overestimated in Wade, *The Urban Frontier*, 221.

59. These lanes were never considered alleys, and the city council consistently barred any commercial traffic through them. See for example, Savannah, Minutes of the City Council, April 15, 1847, MSS., City Hall, Savannah.

60. Parsons, *Inside View of Slavery*, 23.

61. Mary Scott Saint-Amand, *A Balcony in Charleston* (Richmond, 1941), 133.

62. U.S. Census, 1840.

63. Bancroft, *Census of the City of Savannah*, 8.

64. *Charleston Courier*, August 7, 1824.

65. *Census of the City of Charleston For the Year 1848*, 8.

66. U.S. Census, 1860.

67. Council of the First Municipality of the City of New Orleans, *Journal*, 1847, 3b.

68. Council of the Second Municipality of the City of New Orleans, *Proceedings*, March, 1847, City Archives, New Orleans Public Library.

69. U.S. Census, 1860.

70. *Mobile Commercial Register*, December 13, 1833.

71. Mobile, *Assessment Book, 1854*, MSS., Mobile City Hall.

72. *Richmond Enquirer*, October 26, 1854.

73. City of Baltimore, *Assessment Book, 1823-1835, 1852-1859*, MSS., City Archives, Baltimore City Hall.

74. John B. Jegle, *John B. Jegle's Louisville, New Albany, Jeffersonville, Shippingport and Portland Directory for 1845-1846, Etc.* (Louisville, 1845), 9. The highest incidence of slaveholding was the Sixth Ward. This was a relatively high income neighborhood where the homes were large and well-built; many were still standing in 1958.

75. *Savannah Republican*, May 5, 1832.

76. Parsons, *Inside View of Slavery*, 23.

77. William Chambers, *Things As They Are in America* (Philadelphia, 1854), 271-2.

78. *Louisiana Courier*, January 23, 1831.

Chapter Four

1. *Charleston Courier*, September 22, 1845.

2. *Charleston Courier*, May 1, 1827. The patrol system in country areas was never quite as satisfactory as "T.R." indicated. Especially at times of rumored slave unrest, public complaints were numerous. In 1856, a Richmond editorial called attention to the fact that "out of the cities we have no organized means of protection against a sudden emergency." He warned that "every day develops some fresh scheme of revolt among the slaves of Western and Southern states and some better arrangements should be made." *Richmond Enquirer*, December 16, 1856.

3. *The Religious Instruction of the Black Population...A Discussion Etc.* (Charleston, 1847), 13, 14.

4. *The True American*, October 15, 1839.

5. *New Orleans Daily Picayune*, September 16, 1840.

6. *New Orleans Daily Delta*, June 12, 1846.

7. Both the petition and the rejoinder of the white ministers are in the City of Mobile, Municipal Papers, Reports, 1840, MSS., Mobile City Hall.

8. *Richmond Enquirer*, August 17, 1859.

9. *Louisiana Gazette*, May 10, 1820.

10. *New Orleans Bee*, November 8, 1837.

11. *New Orleans Daily Delta*, November 19, 1853.

12. *Savannah Republican*, February 19, 1836.

13. *Mobile Evening News*, December 9, 1854.

14. *Louisville Daily Democrat*, March 17, 1858.

15. *Richmond Enquirer*, November 30, 1853.

16. Charleston Grand Jury, Presentment, January Term, 1859, MSS., South Carolina Archives Division.

17. *Savannah Republican*, August 29, 1839.

18. *New Orleans Daily Delta*, September 10, 1854.

19. *Richmond Enquirer*, September 22, 1853.

20. Three whites were brought into court on a single day for gambling with slaves in their homes. See *Richmond Enquirer*, August 26, 1853. The fines ranged from $5 to $15.

21. *Louisville Daily Democrat*, May 12, 1852.

22. *Mobile Evening News*, December 18, 1854.

23. *Mobile Evening News*, December 24, 1854.

24. *Richmond Enquirer*, August 26, 1853.

25. *Louisiana Advertiser*, April 11, 1834.

26. *Mobile Daily Advertiser*, August 27, 1851.

27. *Mobile Daily Advertiser*, November 14, 1851.

28. *Richmond Enquirer*, September 20, 1853.

29. *Charleston Courier*, September 22, 1845.

30. Memorial of the City Council of Charleston, 1826, MSS., South Carolina Archives Department.

31. "Slavery as a Moral Relation," *Southern Literary Messenger*, XVII (1851), 403.

32. Stirling, *Letters from the Slave States*, 295.

33. Lyell, *Second Visit*, I, 267.

34. Douglass, *My Bondage*, 155.

35. Benjamin Drew (ed.), *The Refugee, or the Narratives of Fugitive Slaves in Canada* (Boston, 1856), 181.

36. Thomas Pinckney, *Reflections, Occasioned by the Late Disturbances in Charleston* (Charleston, 1822), 9.

37. *The True American*, November 6, 1839.

38. *Mobile Daily Advertiser*, February 14, 1858.

39. A South Carolinian, *A Refutation of the Calumnies Circulated Against the Southern and Western States, Respecting the Institution and Existence of Slavery, Etc.* (Charleston, 1822), 55.

40. Olmsted, *Back Country*, 444.

41. Basil Hall, *Travels in North America, in the Years 1827 and 1828* (Edinburgh, 1829), III, 168.

42. L. Moreau Lislet (ed.), *A General Digest of the Legislature of Louisiana: Passed from the Year 1804 to 1827, Inclusive* (New Orleans, 1828, 2 vols.), I, 103.

43. Herbert B. Adams, *The Life and Writings of Jared Sparks* (Boston, 1893), I, 433f.

44. Hall, *Travels*, 167.

45. Douglass, *My Bondage*, 148.

46. Stirling, *Letters*, 288.

47. Louis Hughes, *Thirty Years a Slave, From Bondage to Freedom* (Milwaukee, 1897), 9.

48. Charleston, Ordinance, August 8, 1807.

49. New Orleans, Ordinance, October 8, 1817.

50. See for instance, *Charleston Courier*, December 14, 1855; August 25, 1856; September 18, 1857.

51. Charleston, Ordinance, July 29, 1825.

52. *Charleston Mercury and Morning Advertiser*, September 24, 1822.

53. Karl Bernhard, Duke of Saxe-Weimar-Eisenach, *Travels Through North America, during the Years 1825 and 1826* (Philadelphia, 1828, 2 vols.), II, 9, 10.

54. J.D.B. De Bow, *The Industrial Resources Etc. of the Southern and Western States* (New Orleans, 1853, 3 vols.), II, 249.

55. Ironically the complaining master in this instance wanted to be less rigid than the law required and could not explain to his slave why he could not be so. *Mobile Evening News*, January 4, 1856.

56. Olmsted, *Back Country*, 444.

57. Louis Fitzgerald Tasistro, *Random Shots and Southern Breezes, Containing Critical Remarks on the Southern States and Southern Institutions, with Some Serious Observations on Men and Manners* (N.Y., 1842), II, 135.

58. Chambers, *Things As They Are in America*, 272.

59. Stuart, *Three Years*, II, 231.

60. Arthur Cunynhame, *A Glimpse at the Great Western Republic* (London, 1851), 264.

61. Louisville, Trustees Book, February 5, 1822.

62. Louisville, Trustees Book, September 15, 1826.

63. Louisville, Trustees Book, June 10, 1825.

64. Robert V. Hayne, *Report of the Proceedings of the City Authorities of Charleston, During the Past Year, Ending September 1st, 1837; With Suggestions for the Improvement of the City* (Charleston, 1837), 10.

65. Charleston, Ordinances, August 13, 1822.

66. William P. Niles, *Mayor's Report on City Affairs* (Charleston, 1857), 20.

67. Richmond Common Council, Minutes, September 18, 1833; Richmond, Ordinances, September 20, 1833.

68. *Richmond Enquirer*, November 19, 1857.

69. *Report of R.D. Arnold, Mayor of Savannah, 1860.*

70. C.M. Waterman, *General Message of Mayor C. M. Waterman to the Common Council of the City of New Orleans, October 1st, 1857* (New Orleans, 1857), 33.

71. *New Orleans Daily Delta*, January 7, 1853.

72. *Louisville Daily Advertiser*, November 7, 1822.

73. *New Orleans Bee*, quoted in *New Orleans Delta*, January 7, 1853.

74. *Charleston Courier*, July 27, 1837.

75. *Charleston Courier*, October 8, 1842.

76. Niles, *Mayor's Report on City Affairs*, 17.

77. *Louisville Public Advertiser*, November 10, 1827.

78. *St. Louis Observer*, November 5, 1835.

79. *Mobile Mercantile Advertiser*, September 12, 15, 22, 1835.

80. *Census of the City of Charleston . . . for the Year 1848*, 52. Charleston's legal system, however, also illustrated the confusion over some categories of Negro crime. "The Magistrate's Court has jurisdiction over the crimes and misdemeanors committed by free negroes and slaves, and extends to life. The Court is regulated by Statutes of the State, and has jurisdiction throughout the Parishes of St. Philips and St. Michaels, embracing within these limits the City of Charleston. The only class of persons who can be criminally tried before this Court is that of persons of color, and the trial is by a jury of freeholders," 52. Negroes accused in the Vesey plot were tried before such a court. But more routine matters went before the mayor.

81. H.L. Pinckney, *A Report Containing a First Review of the Proceedings of the City Authorities, from September, 1838, to First August, 1839* (Charleston, 1839), 46.

82. *Mobile Daily Advertiser*, November 4, 1851.

83. *Mobile Evening News*, May 28, 1855.

84. *Mobile Evening News*, March 5, 1855.

85. *Mobile Evening News*, March 10, 1855.

86. *Mobile Daily Advertiser*, July 12, 1857.

87. *Mobile Daily Advertiser*, July 9, 1857; *Mobile Evening News*, December 11, 1854; November 21, 1854.

88. *Mobile Evening News*, January 12, 1855.

89. *Mobile Evening News*, November 24, 1854; January 18, 1855.

90. *Louisville Daily Democrat*, December 20, 1858.

91. *Louisville Daily Democrat*, December 22, 1858. See also City of Louisville, Order Books of the City Court, MSS., City Hall Annex, Louisville.

92. *Louisville Daily Journal*, May 29, 1850.

93. *Louisville Daily Journal*, February 2, 1850; January 18, 1850.

94. Quoted in William Goodell, *The American Slave Code in Theory and Practice* (N.Y., 1853), 173.

95. Drew, *The Refugee*, 7.

96. The following discussion is drawn from Richmond, Ordinances, December 22, 1857.

97. Mobile's Code contained a more detailed, but more common definition: "The term 'negro' includes mulatto, free persons of color and all persons of mixed blood descended on the part of the father or mother from negro ancestors, to the third generation inclusive, though one ancestor of each generation may have been a white person." *The Code of Ordinances of the City of Mobile, with the Charter and an Appendix*, compiled by Alexander McKinstry (Mobile, 1854), 78.

98. For a discussion of these regulations see Chapters Two and Three.

99. Douglass, *My Bondage*, 147.

Chapter Five

1. Marianne Finch, *An Englishwoman's Experience in America* (London, 1853), 295.

2. Bancroft, *Census of the City of Savannah*, 7.

3. Saint-Amand, *A Balcony in Charleston*, 133.

4. Richard H. Shryock (ed.), *Letters of Richard A. Arnold, M.D., 1808-1876, Mayor of Savannah, Georgia, First Secretary of the American Medical Association*. Papers of Trinity College Historical Society, XVIII-XIX (Durham, N.C., 1929), 118.

5. Charleston Grand Jury, Presentment, March Term, 1856, MSS., South Carolina Archives Division.

6. Their masters were each fined $10 "for *their* neglect." *Mobile Daily Advertiser*, November 5, 1851. Italics are mine.

7. Louisville, Ordinances, October 31, 1853.

8. Stuart, *Three Years*, II, 73. Courting, too, had its hazards. "Caesar went to see his lady-love last night, but was indiscreet enough to venture on the pleasant mission without a pass." He spent the night at the Guard House and got 20 lashes in the morning. *Mobile Daily Advertiser*, July 12, 1859.

9. Adams, *A South-Side View of Slavery*, 82.

10. Garnett Duncan to Orlando Brown, Louisville, April 10, 1841, MS. *Orlando Brown Papers* (Filson Club, Louisville).

11. Duncan to Brown, Louisville, December 19, 1841. *Brown Papers*.

12. Adams, *A South-Side View of Slavery*, 85.

13. Ibid., 82, 83.

14. Ibid., 85.

15. U.S. Census, 1820.

16. *Census of the City of Charleston ... for the Year 1848*, 6.

17. U.S. Census, 1820; 1860.

18. See for example, Louisville in 1840. U.S. Census, 1840.

19. U.S. Census, Richmond, 1860. Bondsmen were enumerated in this census by owner or employer; slave housing was not as concentrated as these figures suggest.

20. U.S. Census, Mobile, 1840.

21. See Chapter One for a more detailed account of this imbalance.

22. *De Bow's Review*, VII (1849), 494.

23. The courts, however, did crack down on white women and Negro men whenever found together. See Chapter Nine.

24. Mary Boykin Chesnut, *A Diary from Dixie*, ed. Ben Ames Williams (Boston, 1961), 21-2.

25. Olmsted, *Seaboard Slave States*, 601-2.

26. Justis, *Diary*, September 26, 1859, MSS.

27. Herbert A. Kellar, "A Journey Through the South in 1836; Diary of James D. Davidson," *Journal of Southern History*, I (1935), 361.

28. By a Resident, *New Orleans As It Is*, 41.

29. Olmsted, *Seaboard Slave States*, 595.

30. Stampp, *Peculiar Institution*, 351.

31. Peter Randolph, *Sketches of a Slave Life, or Illustrations of the 'Peculiar Institution'* (Boston, 1855), 59.

32. Olmsted, *Seaboard Slave States*, 102.

33. Stirling, *Letters*, 263.

34. For Negro clothing on the plantation see Stampp, *Peculiar Institution*, 289-92.

35. Olmsted, *Seaboard Slave States*, 27-8.

36. Adams, *A South-Side View of Slavery*, 30.

37. Olmsted, *Seaboard Slave States*, 28.

38. *Southern Patriot and Commercial Advertiser*, September 12, 1822.

39. The full extent of this discrepancy is perhaps embodied in an episode in Richmond when a free Negro was brought before the municipal court on a charge of stealing clothes from a slave. *Richmond Enquirer*, September 8, 1853.

40. *New Orleans Bee*, February 5, 1855.

41. *New Orleans Daily Delta*, November 4, 1851.

42. *Savannah Republican*, June 6, 1849.

43. *Southern Patriot and Commercial Advertiser*, September 12, 1822.

44. *Southern Patriot and Commercial Advertiser*, September 12, 1822.

45. Charleston Grand Jury, Presentment, October 1822, MSS., South Carolina Archives Division.

46. Charleston Grand Jury, Presentment, October 1822, MSS., South Carolina Archives Division.

47. Harriet Beecher Stowe, *Uncle Tom's Cabin; or Life Among the Lowly* (Boston, 1852); Dolphin Books, Doubleday and Company, Inc. (Garden City, N.Y., n.d.), 117, 212, 402.

48. Stowe, *Uncle Tom's Cabin*, 391, 2.

49. Pinckney, *Reflections*, 30.

50. Phillips, *Life and Labor in the Old South*, 197.

51. Stampp, *Peculiar Institution*, 282.

52. Thornwell, *A Review of Rev. J. B. Adger's Sermon on Instruction of the Colored Population*, 5.

53. Charles Dickens, *American Notes* (N.Y., 1893), 159-60.

54. New Orleans, Ordinances, October 8, 1817.

55. *Richmond Enquirer*, August 18, 1853.

56. *Richmond Enquirer*, August 10, 1853.

57. Kenneth Stampp attacks very convincingly the tradition of robust, healthy slaves toiling in the fields under a hot sun and flourishing in the heat and the labor. "A tradition with less substance to it," he asserts, "has seldom existed." See the entire section on health. *Peculiar Institution*, 295-321.

58. Dr. A.P. Merrill in *De Bow's Review*, XX (1856), 621.

59. *Savannah Republican*, November 2, 1858.

60. *Charleston Courier*, November 30, 1839.

61. *Savannah Republican*, October 5, 1858.

62. Bennett Dowler, *Tableau of the Yellow Fever of 1853, with Topographical, Chronological, and Historical Sketches of the Epidemics of New Orleans Since Their Origins in 1796, Illustrative of the Quarantine Question, In Cohen's New Orleans Directory ... For 1854* (New Orleans, 1854), 38.

63. Bennett Dowler, "Yellow Fever in Charleston in 1858," *The New Orleans Medical and Surgical Journal*, XVI (1859), 597. See also an interesting table on yellow fever deaths in Charleston between 1819 and 1839 in the *Charleston Courier*, November 30, 1839.

64. Dowler, *Tableau of the Yellow Fever of 1853*, 38.

65. *Richmond Enquirer*, September 18, 1832.

66. *Richmond Enquirer*, September 25, 1832.

67. *Richmond Enquirer*, September 28, 1832.

68. *Richmond Enquirer*, October 23, 1832.

69. *Report of the Committee of the City Council of Charleston, Upon the Epidemic Yellow Fever, of 1858* (Charleston, 1859), 19-20.

70. *Report of the Committee ... Upon the Epidemic Yellow Fever*, 20.

71. Shryock (ed.), *Letters of Richard A. Arnold*, 70.

72. William Harden, *Recollections of a Long and Satisfactory Life* (Savannah, 1934), 47.

73. Karl Bernhard, *Travels*, II, 132.

74. William Dosite Postell, *The Health of Slaves on Southern Plantations* (Baton Rouge, 1951), 138-9.

75. Postell, *Health of Slaves on Southern Plantations*, 139.

76. *Richmond Enquirer*, December 30, 1854.

77. *Richmond Enquirer*, September 18, 1832.

78. *Charleston Courier*, March 3, 1855.

79. *Richmond Enquirer*, March 20, 1860.

80. Mobile, Ordinances, 1858.

81. Mobile, Municipal Papers, *Report of the Hospital for April 1 to November 11th, 1856*, MSS., Mobile City Hall.

82. "Bill for the Circus Street Hospital for the Medical Treatment and Attendance for Slave Joachin, 1856," MS., Kuntz Collection, Tulane University.

83. *De Bow's Review*, IV (1847), 286.

84. Baltimore, "Report of Consulting Physician," Ordinances, 1829, Appendix, xxiii.

85. Baltimore, "Report of the Board of Health," Ordinances, 1851, Appendix, 238. This explanation is not wholly convincing because as early as 1827 the board of doctors engaged in a general campaign for vaccination noted that "a small number only of those who refused the vaccination were coloured persons." Baltimore, "Report of the Board of Health," Ordinances, 1828, Appendix, 26.

86. Ethan Allen Andrews, *Slavery and the Domestic Slave-Trade in the United States* (Boston, 1836), 45. See also his mortality figures for slaves, free blacks, and whites, 44.

87. *Niles' Register*, April 16, 1825.

88. *Niles' Register*, January 16, 1830.

89. Lester B. Shippee (ed.), *Bishop Whipple's Southern Diary 1843-1844* (Minneapolis, 1937), 112-13.

90. Douglass, *My Bondage*, 144, 147.

91. Robert J. Turnbull, quoted in A South Carolinian, *A Refutation of the Calumnies Circulated Against Southern and Western States*, 58.

Chapter Six

1. Quoted in Olmsted, *Seaboard Slave States*, 592.

2. *Savannah Republican*, February 3, 1859.

3. Quoted in the *Savannah Republican*, February 3, 1859.

4. *Mobile Register and Journal*, July 10, 1847.

5. *Mobile Daily Advertiser*, February 16, 1858.

6. *Mobile Daily Advertiser*, February 27, 1858.

7. *Mobile Daily Advertiser*, November 4, 1851.

8. *Louisville Daily Focus*, March 5, 1831.

9. *Richmond Enquirer*, November 26, 1853.

10. *Mobile Evening News*, December 14, 1854.

11. *New Orleans Bee*, November 8, 1837.

12. *Charleston Courier*, October 20, 1848.

13. *Southern Recorder* (Milledgeville, Georgia), August 6, 1822.

14. *Charleston Courier*, September 20, 1845.

15. *New Orleans Bee*, June 22, 1855.

16. *Mobile Daily Advertiser*, July 8, 1857.

17. *Charleston Courier*, April 25, 1834.

18. *Mobile Evening News*, December 9, 14, 1854.

19. For aspects of this campaign see *Mobile Commercial Advertiser*, July 9, 16, 22, 1857.

20. See for example, *Mobile Daily Advertiser*, January 20, 1857.

21. *New Orleans Daily Picayune*, October 6, 1858.

22. *New Orleans Daily Picayune*, October 6, 1858.

23. Committee on Colored Population, Report, December 1, 1846, MSS., South Carolina Archives Division.

24. *City Council* v. *Seeba*, 4 Strobhart 319, January 1850. Catterall, *Judicial Cases*, II, 415.

25. *Charleston Courier*, March 17, 1835.

26. *Charleston Courier*, March 6, 1835.

27. *Charleston Courier*, March 14, 1835.

28. *Charleston Courier*, December 7, 1837.

29. *Charleston Courier*, October 20, 1848.

30. *Charleston Courier*, May 2, 1859.

31. *Louisville Daily Focus*, March 2, 5, 1831.

32. *Charleston Courier*, March 13, 1835.

33. *Savannah Republican*, February 19, 1836.

34. *Charleston Courier*, October 13, 1826.

35. *Charleston Courier*, October 20, 1848.

36. *Richmond Enquirer*, August 17, 1859.

37. S. A. Cartwright, "Philosophy of the Negro Constitution," *The New Orleans Medical and Surgical Journal*, IX (1853), 198.

38. *Savannah Republican*, August 29, 1839. A typical entry in the court reporter's pad in Richmond included the notation: "A couple of slaves were treated to a whipping...for making the night hideous while under the influence of liquor." Four days later: "Alexander, a slave of E. Pinkillon, found drunk and spread out obnoxiously in Theater alley, was ordered '25.'" *Richmond Enquirer*, July 29, August 3, 1858.

39. *New Orleans Daily Delta,* October 13, 1858.

40. Charleston Grand Jury, Presentment, May Term, 1846, MSS., South Carolina Archives Division.

41. Charleston Grand Jury, Presentment, May Term, 1851, MSS., South Carolina Archives Division.

42. Quoted in Olmsted, *Seaboard Slave States,* 593. Olmsted said that though this complaint came from the *New Orleans Crescent,* he had "heard, or seen in the journals, at Richmond, Savannah, Louisville, and most other large manufacturing, or commercial towns of the South" the same sentiment.

43. *Mobile Register and Journal,* July 10, 1847.

44. *Louisiana Gazette,* October 21, 1820.

45. *Charleston Courier,* March 6, 1835.

46. *New Orleans Bee,* November 8, 1837.

47. *New Orleans Daily Delta,* September 10, 1854.

48. *Richmond Enquirer,* September 23, 1853.

49. *The Religious Instruction of the Black Population. The Gospel to be Given to Our Servants. A Sermon Preached in Several Protestant Episcopal Churches in Charleston on Sundays in July, 1847, by Rev. Paul Trapier, in Charleston S.C. Etc.* (Charleston, 1847), 14.

50. "Public Proceedings, relating to Calvary Church, and the Religious Instruction of Slaves; with an Appendix, &c.," *The Charleston Gospel Messenger, and Protestant Episcopal Register,* XXVII (July, 1850), 118.

51. *Proceedings of the Meeting in Charleston, S.C., May 13-15, 1845, on the Religious Instruction of the Negroes together with the Report of the Committee and the Address to the Public* (Charleston, 1845), 7.

52. *The Religious Instruction of the Black Population,* 2.

53. "Public Proceedings, relating to Calvary Church, and the Religious Instruction of Slaves," 118.

54. Thornwell, *A Review of Rev. J.B. Adger's Sermon on the Instruction of the Colored Population,* 12, 13.

55. Abbott, *South and North,* 75-6.

56. *Missouri Republican,* June 13, 1835; Olmsted, *Back Country,* 109; *Seaboard Slave States,* 266.

57. Olmsted, *Back Country,* 187-96.

58. Petition of Slaves and Free Negroes for Church, Petitions of the City of Richmond to the State Legislature, December 23, 1823, MSS., State Library, Richmond.

59. Lyell, *A Second Visit*, I, 208.

60. *Richmond Enquirer*, May 28, 1857. The next year the First Baptist Church set up an extensive new program, see *Richmond Enquirer*, July 7, 1858.

61. Daniel R. Hundley, *Social Relations in Our Southern States* (N.Y., 1860), 350-51; Jeffrey R. Brackett, *The Negro in Maryland, A Study of the Institution of Slavery* (Baltimore, 1889), 206.

62. G. Collins, *The Louisville Directory for the Year 1843-44* (Louisville, 1843), 192.

63. City of Louisville, Journal of the City Council, MSS., December 28, 1835. The official latitude was almost enlarged when a move to strike out "orderly" lost, four votes to three.

64. *New Orleans Sunday Delta*, January 4, 1857.

65. *New Orleans Daily Picayune*, May 21, 1858; *New Orleans Daily Delta*, October 13, 1860. One of the colored churches in the Second District had over 1100 communicants. Rainey, *Myatt & Co's. Directory*, 1857, n.p.

66. *An Account of the Late Intended Insurrection Among a Portion of the Blacks of this City. Published by the Authority of the Corporation of Charleston* (Charleston, 1822, 3rd ed.), 30, 22-3.

67. *The Religious Instruction of the Black Population*, 7.

68. *The Religious Instruction of the Black Population*, 2, 8.

69. L.P. Jackson, "Religious Instruction of Negroes, 1830-1860, With Special Reference to South Carolina," *Journal of Negro History*, XV (1930), 100-102.

70. Charles Colcock Jones, *Suggestions on the Religious Instruction of the Negroes in the Southern States* (Philadelphia, n.d.), 59.

71. Olmsted, *Seaboard Slave States*, 24.

72. Olmsted, *Seaboard Slave States*, 405-6.

73. *Southern Patriot* (Charleston), September 19, 1835.

74. Lillian Foster, *Wayside Glimpses, North and South* (N.Y., 1860), 109.

75. W.C. Bryant, *Letters of a Traveller; or Notes of Things Seen in Europe and America*, 94.

76. Petition of the Free People of Color to the Virginia State Legislature, Dec. 17, 1834, MSS., Virginia State Library, Richmond.

77. *Public Proceedings Relating to Calvary Church and the Religious Instruction of Slaves* (Charleston, 1850), 40.

78. Lyell, *Second Visit*, II, 15.

79. Finch, *An Englishwoman's Experience in America*, 299.

80. Thornwell, *Review of J. B. Adger's Sermons on Religious Instruction*, 13.

81. Pinckney, *Reflections*, 9.

82. Stirling, *Letters*, 295.

83. Stirling, *Letters*, 296.

84. Foster, *Wayside Glimpses, North and South*, 94.

85. Lyell, *Second Visit*, I, 267.

86. Noah Davis, *A Narrative of the Life of Noah Davis* (n.p., 1859), 35.

87. Douglass, *My Bondage*, 155, 319.

88. Drew, *The Refugee*, 180-81.

89. William W. Brown, *Narrative of William W. Brown, A Fugitive Slave* (Boston, 1848), 27; Randolph, *Sketches of Slave Life*, 58.

90. *The Southern Literary Messenger* expressed this conventional ante-bellum Southern sentiment in 1851 when it contended that "the movements of the abolition party have made it a measure of police essential to the tranquility, nay to *the existence* of Southern society, to prevent the general instruction of negroes in the arts of reading and writing." "Slavery as a Moral Relation," *Southern Literary Messenger*, XVII (1851), 403.

91. City of Charleston, Ordinances, Dec. 20, 1800.

92. Petition to the House of Representatives of South Carolina by 147 Charlestonians, October 11, 1820, MSS., South Carolina Archives Division.

93. Memorial of the City Council of Charleston to the State Legislature of South Carolina, 1826, MSS., South Carolina Archives Division.

94. *Richmond Enquirer*, January 21, 1832.

95. *Louisville Daily Democrat*, January 5, 1857.

96. *New Orleans Daily Delta*, March 9, 1859.

97. *New Orleans Daily Delta*, March 13, 1859.

98. *New Orleans Daily Delta*, October 9, 1859.

99. *De Bow's Review*, XII (June, 1852), 692.

Chapter Seven

1. *Savannah Republican*, February 9, 1843.

2. Rennick V. Chloe, *Reports of Cases Argued and Decided in the Supreme Court of the State of Missouri from 1840 to 1842* (Fayette, Mo., 1843), VII, 197.

3. Drew, *The Refugee*, 257-8.

4. G.E. Stephens to J.C. White, Aboard U.S. Steamer Walker, Pensacola, Florida, January 8, 1858, MS. (Moorland Room, Howard University, Washington, D.C.)

5. *New Orleans Bee*, July 2, 1836.

6. *Savannah Republican*, May 23, 1843.

7. *Richmond Enquirer*, November 28, 1853.

8. *Mobile Daily Advertiser*, July 11, 1857.

9. *Mobile Daily Advertiser*, September 8, 1859.

10. *Mobile Daily Advertiser*, October 4, 1851.

11. *Mobile Daily Advertiser*, October 27, 1859.

12. *Savannah Republican*, May 23, 1843.

13. *Louisiana Advertiser*, April 14, 1834.

14. For a typical comment on the favorable side, see Karl Bernhard's characterization of a Charleston jail as "remarkable neatness." *Travels*, II, 9.

15. *New Orleans Bee*, July 13, 1837.

16. New Orleans, Council of the First Municipality, Journal, January 11, 1841, City Archives, Public Library.

17. *Louisville Public Advertiser*, October 30, 1834.

18. In bankruptcy cases, of course, the opposite occurred. Slaves might remain in jail until the courts disposed of the property. Mrs. Bremer ran across a group of women slaves in a New Orleans jail who claimed to have been there for two years. Bremer, *Letters*, 272-4.

19. Quoted in Olmsted, *Back Country*, 96.

20. Shippee (ed.), *Bishop Whipple's Diary*, 108.

21. *Richmond Enquirer*, August 29, 1859.

22. *Richmond Enquirer*, August 5, 1858.

23. Charleston Grand Jury, Presentment, May Term, 1846, MSS., South Carolina Archives Division.

24. *Charleston Courier*, July 28, 1837.

25. James Watkins, *Struggles for Freedom: or the Life of James Watkins, Formerly a Slave in Maryland, U.S.; Etc.* (Manchester, 1860), 22.

26. Richmond, Minutes of the Hustings Court, February 19; March 23; May 3; June 8; August 25; October 22, 1825, MSS., Richmond City Hall.

27. *Mobile Evening News*, December 26, 1854; January 6, 9, 12; March 10; July 23, 1855.

28. *Charleston Courier*, April 6, 1837.

29. See, for example, the case of "slave Sophia Ann" in the *New Orleans Daily Delta*, October 23, 1850.

30. Richmond, Minutes of the Hustings Court, March 12, 1825; see also March 23, May 3, August 13, November 12, December 16, 1825, MSS., Richmond City Hall.

31. Richmond, Minutes of the Hustings Court, March 2, 1835.

32. *Charleston Courier*, July 29, 1837.

33. *Charleston Courier*, July 27, 1837.

34. *Charleston Courier*, July 27, 1837.

35. *Charleston Courier*, July 29, 1837.

36. *Charleston Courier*, July 28, 1837.

37. Randolph, *Sketches*, 59.

38. Bernhard, *Travels*, II, 40.

39. *Charleston Mercury and Morning Advertiser*, September 24, 1822.

40. Bernhard, *Travels*, II, 10.

41. Hall, *Travels in North America*, III, 167.

42. *Missouri Republican*, May 24, 1824.

43. Sutton Account Books, 1821, MSS. (Missouri Historical Society, St. Louis).

44. *Richmond Enquirer*, September 7, 1846. It may be that the editor was a little optimistic, because the report also stated that Giles "would occasionally catch the eye of some of his sable acquaintances, and speak and nod to them with a smirking smile," and at the final moment he gave "a hearty and cheerful farewell."

45. *Charleston Courier*, June 28, 1847.

46. Douglass, *My Bondage*, 148.

47. J. S. Schirmer, *Diary*, MSS. (South Carolina Historical Society, Charleston).

48. Frederic Bancroft, *Slave-Trading in the Old South* (Baltimore, 1931), 312.

49. This trend was particularly marked in the 'thirties. See, for example, City of New Orleans, Conveyor's Office, Conveyances, XVIII (May 3, 1834-May 4, 1835) for a day-to-day recording of sales, including a description of the slave, the state from which he came, and the name and address of the new owner.

50. Bancroft, *Slave-Trading in the Old South*, 315.

51. Treasurer of the City of New Orleans, Census of Merchants, First District, I, MSS., 1854.

52. Treasurer of the City of New Orleans, Census of Merchants, Third District, III, MSS., 1854.

53. D.E. Everett, *Free Persons of Color in New Orleans, 1803-1856* (Unpublished Doctoral Dissertation, Tulane University, 1952), 209. There were over 4000 in 1845-6, and less in 1834-5. See volumes XXXIV and XVIII of City of New Orleans, Conveyances, Conveyor's Office.

54. *New Orleans Daily Delta*, October 27, 1848.

55. *New Orleans Daily Delta*, October 4, 1850.

56. *New Orleans Daily Delta*, June 9, 1850.

57. *New Orleans Daily Delta*, June 25, 1854.

58. *New Orleans Daily Delta*, November 6, 1849.

59. L.A. Chamerovzow (ed.), *Slave Life in Georgia: A Narrative of the Life, Sufferings, and Escape of John Brown, A Fugitive Slave Now in England* (London, 1855), 111-13.

60. Charles MacKay, *Life and Liberty in America* (N.Y., 1859), 200.

61. Pulszky, *Red, White, Black*, II, 100.

62. Bancroft, *Slave-Trading in the Old South*, 333-4.

63. Bancroft, *Slave-Trading in the Old South*, 97n-98n.

64. Bancroft, *Slave-Trading in the Old South*, 175n-177n, 222ff, 298-300.

65. Bancroft, *Slave-Trading in the Old South*, 122, 128ff, 139.

66. Bancroft, *Slave-Trading in the Old South*, 406.

67. *Savannah Republican*, January 20, 1857. The house mentioned was Dickinson, Hall, & Co.

68. *Richmond Enquirer*, October 27, 1857.

69. Richmond source quoted in *Savannah Republican*, January 21, 1851.

70. Bancroft, *Slave-Trading in the Old South*, 190ff.

71. Bancroft, *Slave-Trading in the Old South*, 337-8.

72. John R. White, *Account Books*, MSS., Chinn Collection (Missouri Historical Society, St. Louis).

73. M. Greiner, Comp., *The Louisiana Digest, Embracing the Laws of the Legislature of a General Nature Enacted from the Year 1804 to 1841, Etc.* (New Orleans, 1841), 520.

74. New Orleans, Ordinances, March 30, 1929.

75. New Orleans, Ordinances, April 15, 21, 1829; November 12, 1830.

76. New Orleans, Ordinances, January 27, 1835; June 15, 1841.

77. *A Digest of the Ordinances and Resolutions of the Council of Municipality No. Three of the City of New Orleans* (New Orleans, 1846), December 7, 1836; January 11, 1846.

78. New Orleans, Council of the Second Municipality, Ordinances, December 9, 1845.

79. Council of the Second Municipality of New Orleans, December 2, 1845.

80. *Louisville Daily Journal*, October 21, 1833.

81. City of Mobile, *The Code of Ordinances of the City of Mobile, With the Charter and an Appendix* (Mobile, 1859).

82. Richmond, Ordinances, June 20, 1836.

83. Memorial of the City Council of Charleston to the South Carolina Senate, November 26, 1839, MSS., South Carolina Archives Division; Report of the Committee of the Judiciary on the Memorial of the City Council Praying That All Sales of Slaves at Auction in Charleston Be Made at the Slave Mart About to be Established by the City Council, 1839, MSS., South Carolina Archives Division.

84. Charleston, Ordinances, November 20, 1837.

85. Charleston, Ordinances, May 21, 1841.

86. Charleston, Ordinances, January 31, 1842.

87. Shippee (ed.), *Bishop Whipple's Diary*, 89.

88. Quoted in Olmsted, *Seaboard Slave States*, 32.

89. Randolph, *Sketches of Slave Life*, 59.

90. Brown, *Narrative of William W. Brown*, 31, 64.

Chapter Eight

1. A South Carolinian, *A Refutation of the Calumnies Circulated Against the Southern and Western States*, 55.

2. Abbott, *South and North*, 124.

3. A South Carolinian, *A Refutation of the Calumnies Circulated Against the Southern and Western States*, 58.

4. Adams, *A South Side View of Slavery*, 62, 16, 18.

5. S.A. Cartwright, "Ethnology of the Negro or Prognathous Race," *The New Orleans Medical and Surgical Journal*, XIV (1857), 154-5.

6. *New Orleans Daily Picayune*, July 23, 1839.

7. *New Orleans Daily Delta*, October 17, 1851.

8. *Charleston Courier*, June 22, 1854.

9. *New Orleans Daily Picayune*, August 2, 1839.

10. Petition of John Jones, October 1840, MSS., South Carolina Archives Division.

11. *Mobile Register and Journal*, December 4, 1843.

12. *New Orleans Daily Crescent*, June 23, 1853.

13. James Buckingham, *The Slave States of America* (London, 1842), I, 571.

14. Mayor of the City of New Orleans, Message, November 14, 1834 (Journal of City Council).

15. South Carolina Association, Petition to the South Carolina Legislature, 1830 (?), MSS., South Carolina Archives Division.

16. *Savannah Republican*, January 25, 1847.

17. Richmond, Minutes of the Common Council, January 13, 1833; *New Orleans Daily True Delta*, January 10, 1856; *New Orleans Bee*, December 1, 1837.

18. New Orleans, Ordinances, August 20, 1813.

19. *Charleston Courier*, November 3, 1830.

20. *Louisville Public Advertiser*, September 10, 1832.

21. *Louisville Public Advertiser*, August 16, 1832.

22. *New Orleans Daily Picayune*, November 19, 1843.

23. *New Orleans Daily Picayune*, December 15, 1843.

24. *Charleston Courier*, September 30, 1828.

25. *Charleston Courier*, March 15, 1831; two years later his master was still advertising for him and still presumed him to be in the city, *Charleston Courier*, March 20, 1833.

26. *Charleston Courier*, March 11, 1834.

27. *Charleston City Gazette and Commercial Daily Advertiser*, August 25, 1823; *Charleston Courier*, August 25, 1823.

28. *New Orleans Daily Picayune*, August 28, 1837.

29. *Richmond Enquirer*, September 23, 1825.

30. *Charleston Courier*, April 16, 1830.

31. *New Orleans Daily Delta*, June 29, 1859.

32. *New Orleans Daily Delta*, April 8, 1857.

33. *Richmond Enquirer*, July 19, 1853.

34. *Richmond Enquirer*, July 29, 1858.

35. G. Stith, *Message of the Mayor to the Common Council*, October 11, 1859.

36. *New Orleans Daily Delta*, August 3, 1859.

37. Baltimore, Ordinances, 1838, 492.

38. Baltimore, Ordinances, 1855, Appendix, 340.

39. *States Rights and Free Trade Evening Post* (Charleston), March 18, 1833.

40. *Charleston Courier*, July 13, 1829.

41. *Charleston City Gazette and Commercial Daily Advertiser*, August 25, 1824.

42. *Charleston Courier*, August 29, 1824.

43. *New Orleans Daily Delta*, November 9, 1858.

44. *New Orleans Daily Delta*, June 22, 1859.

45. *New Orleans Daily Delta*, May 14, 1856.

46. *New Orleans Daily Delta*, December 1, 1850; *New Orleans Bee*, August 4, 1852.

47. Ninian Edwards to William Carr Lane, September 21, 1828, MSS. (Missouri Historical Society).

48. For example, see *Louisville Public Advertiser*, November 12, 1831; January 9, 1833.

49. *Louisville Public Advertiser*, January 2, 1835.

50. *Louisville Public Advertiser*, September 12, 1833.

51. *Charleston Courier*, April 16, 1830.

52. *Charleston City Gazette and Commercial Daily Advertiser*, January 4, 1823.

53. *Mobile Commercial Register*, June 14, 1828; March 10, 1826; September 27, 1828.

54. *New Orleans Daily Picayune*, September 14, 1839.

55. *New Orleans Daily Picayune*, April 10, 1842.

56. *New Orleans Daily True Delta*, February 16, 1854.

57. *New Orleans Daily Picayune*, December 8, 1840; *New Orleans Daily True Delta*, January 1, 1854.

58. *Richmond Enquirer*, November 26, 1833. For the background of the complaint see the petition of "Sundry Citizens" against the "repeated instances which have occurred in this City of negroes running away from their owners and employers." Richmond, Minutes of the Common Council, September 18, 1833.

59. *De Bow's Review*, XI (1851), 331-3.

60. *Richmond Enquirer*, February 15, 1855.

61. *Richmond Enquirer*, November 26, 1833.

62. *Savannah Republican*, January 25, 1847.

63. *New Orleans Daily Delta*, October 7, 1854.

64. *New Orleans Daily Picayune*, October 6, 1858.

65. *New Orleans Bee*, May 2, 1850.

66. *Missouri Republican*, October 20, 1835.

67. *Missouri Republican*, May 20, 1836.

68. *Louisville Daily Journal*, August 20, 1850.

69. *New Orleans Daily Picayune*, March 8, 1856.

70. *Savannah Republican*, June 6, 1849.

71. *Memorial of the Citizens of Charleston to the Senate and House of Representatives of the State of South Carolina* (Charleston, 1822).

72. *New Orleans Daily Crescent*, December 31, 1856.

73. *Mobile Mercantile Advertiser*, September 1, 1835.

74. Ezekial Butler to Ben Thomas, Baltimore, September 21, 1831, MSS. (Bureau of Archives, City Hall, Baltimore).

75. *Mayor's Correspondence*, MSS. (Bureau of Archives, City Hall, Baltimore).

76. Lionel H. Kennedy and Thomas Parker, *An Official Report of the Trials of Sundry Negroes, charged with an Attempt to raise an Insurrection in the State of South-Carolina: preceded by an Introduction and Narrative; and in an Appendix, a Report of the Trials of Four White Persons, on Indictments for attempting to Excite the Slaves to Insurrection. Prepared and Published at the Request of the Court. By Lionel H. Kennedy & Thomas Parker* ... (Charleston, 1822), iii.

77. *Official Report*, 50.

78. A postscript to the publication revised this original version slightly, asserting that Devany actually told his young master the information first, but the free Negro subsequently advised him to go directly to his master. The editors concluded that this added information "places the fidelity of the slave ... on much higher ground." *Official Report*, "Extracts," 4.

79. *Official Report*, 51.

80. *Official Report*, 51.

81. *Official Report*, 3ff.

82. Ana Hayes Johnson to Elizabeth E. W. Haywood, Charleston, June 23, 1822, MS., *Ernest Haywood Papers* (Southern Historical Collection, University of North Carolina Library).

83. "A Colored American," *The Late Contemplated Insurrection in Charleston, S.C., with the Execution of Thirty-Six of the Patriots, Etc.* (N.Y., 1850), 7.

84. *Southern Patriot and Commercial Advertiser*, September 12, 1822.

85. Ana Hayes Johnson to Elizabeth E. W. Haywood, Charleston, July 18, 1822, MSS. Ernest Haywood Papers.

86. Ana Hayes Johnson to Elizabeth E. W. Haywood, Charleston, July 18, 1822, MSS. Ernest Haywood Papers.

87. Ana Hayes Johnson to Elizabeth E. W. Haywood, Charleston, July 27, 1822, MSS. Ernest Haywood Papers.

88. *Official Report*, vi.

89. *Official Report*, iii, vii.

90. L. Kennedy, Thomas Parker, William Drayton, Nathaniel Heyward, J.R. Pringle, H. Deos, Robert J. Turnbull, to Governor Thomas Bennett, July 24, 1822, MSS., South Carolina Archives Division.

91. Petition for the Pardon of Monday Gell, Charleston Drayton and Harry Haig to the Governor of South Carolina, July 24, 1822, MSS., South Carolina Archives Division.

92. *Official Report*, 183.

93. Bacchus, the Slave of Benjamin Hammett, *Confession*, William and Benjamin Hammett Papers, MSS. (Duke University Library).

94. Petition of B. Belknap of the City of Charleston to the Senate and House of Representatives, November 14, 1822, MS., South Carolina Archives Division.

95. Report of the Committee on the Memorial of the City of Charleston, Senate Committee, December 14, 1822, MSS., South Carolina Archives Division.

96. *Charleston Courier*, August 12, 1822.

97. *Charleston Courier*, August 24, 1822.

98. *Southern Patriot and Commercial Advertiser*, July 19, 1822.

99. Memorial of the City Council of Charleston to the Senate of the State of South Carolina, 1822, MSS., South Carolina Archives Division.

100. Thomas Pinckney, *Reflections, Occasioned by the Late Disturbances in Charleston. By Achates* [*pseud.*] (Charleston, 1822), 5.

101. Pinckney, *Reflections*, 23.

102. Benwell, *An Englishman's Travels in America*, 178.

103. John R. Godley, *Letters from America* (London, 1844, 2 vols.), II, 207.

104. Stuart, *Three Years*, II, 275.

105. "A Colored American," *The Late Contemplated Insurrection in Charleston, S.C.*, 5ff.

106. U.S. Census, 1820.

107. Pinckney, *Reflections*, 10.

108. The *Official Report* contained the conventional view. "Few if any domestic servants were spoken to, as *they* were distrusted." *Official Report*, 26. Pinckney's contention suggests that he did not wholly trust the analysis of the court even if he believed in the existence of the plot.

109. Pinckney, *Reflections*, 6, 7, 8, 9.

110. *Official Report*, 21.

111. Pinckney, *Reflections*, 9.

112. *Acts and Resolutions of the General Assembly of the State of South-Carolina Passed in December, 1820* (Columbia, 1821), 22-4.

113. "A Colored American," *The Late Contemplated Insurrection in Charleston, S.C.*, 5.

114. *New Orleans Daily Crescent*, January 23, 1853.

Chapter Nine

1. *Richmond Enquirer*, November 29, 1853.

2. Finch, *An Englishwoman's Experience in America*, 300.

3. Abbott, *South and North*, 112-13.

4. Walker, "Diary of a Louisiana Planter."

5. *Louisville Public Advertiser*, November 30, 1835.

6. Quoted in *De Bow's Review*, XXVI (1859), 600.

7. Abbott, *South and North*, 124.

8. *De Bow's Review*, XXIX (1860), 615.

9. Douglass, *My Bondage*, 235.

10. Lyell, *Second Visit*, I, 209.

11. Solomon Northup, *Twelve Years a Slave; Narrative of Solomon Northup, A Citizen of New York, Etc.* (Auburn, 1853), 62.

12. Douglass, *My Bondage*, 176.

13. Abbott, *South and North*, 138-9.

14. Walker, "Diary of a Louisiana Planter."

15. Andrews, *Slavery*, 43.

16. Quoted in Everett, *Free Persons of Color in New Orleans*, 191.

17. Quoted in Everett, *Free Persons of Color in New Orleans*, 197.

18. Baltimore, Ordinances, March 14, 1832.

19. *Brown Fellowship Society Papers*, September 6, 1833, MSS. (Possession of Mae Purcell, Charleston).

20. Quoted in Everett, *Free Persons of Color in New Orleans*, 131.

21. Baltimore, Ordinances, 1846, 156.

22. *Savannah Republican,* May 6, 1823.

23. *Louisville Daily Democrat,* August 5, 1851.

24. Petition of the Colonization Society of Virginia to the Virginia State Legislature, Dec. 20, 1831, MSS., Virginia State Library, Richmond.

25. *New Orleans Bee,* April 16, 1858.

26. *New Orleans Daily Picayune,* March 8, 1856.

27. *A Documentary History of American Industrial Society,* II, 108-9.

28. *A Documentary History of American Industrial Society,* II, 109.

29. *New Orleans Daily Delta,* December 12, 1856.

30. *St. Louis Daily Pennant,* July 9, 1840.

31. Presentation of the Charleston Grand Jury, May Term, 1846, MSS., South Carolina Archives Division.

32. Shryock (ed.), *Letters of Richard A. Arnold,* 39.

33. *Savannah Republican,* September 3, 1829.

34. *Savannah Republican,* July 8, 1829.

35. *Savannah Republican,* August 29, 30, September 4, 1839.

36. *Charleston Courier,* April 8, 1834.

37. *Charleston Courier,* March 6, 1835.

38. *A Documentary History of American Industrial Society,* II, 113.

39. Shryock (ed.), *Letters of Richard A. Arnold,* 46, 39.

40. City of Mobile, Papers, Reports, 1840, MSS., Mobile, City Hall.

41. *Missouri Argus,* January 20, 1837.

42. Council of the First Municipality of New Orleans, *Journal,* June 9, 1851, MSS., New Orleans, City Hall.

43. *New Orleans Daily Picayune,* October 6, 1855.

44. *Mobile Evening News,* January 4, 1856.

45. *Richmond Enquirer,* August 30, 1853.

46. *Mobile Daily Advertiser,* October 15, 1859.

47. *Mobile Daily Advertiser,* October 20, 1859.

48. *Mobile Daily Advertiser,* November 10, 1859.

49. *Mobile Daily Advertiser,* November 13, 1859.

50. *Richmond Enquirer,* August 17, 1859.

51. *Louisville Daily Democrat,* March 10, 1847.

52. *New Orleans Daily Delta,* August 24, 1855.

53. *New Orleans Daily Delta,* July 13, 1852.

54. *New Orleans Bee,* January 24, 1854.

55. *New Orleans Daily Delta*, July 25, 1852.

56. *New Orleans Daily Delta*, July 16, 1851.

57. *New Orleans Daily Delta*, June 26, 1860.

58. *Richmond Enquirer*, October 25, 1831.

59. Abbott, *South and North*, 124. For further discussion see also 74, 112-13, 139, 175, 190, 321.

60. *New Orleans Daily Crescent*, June 23, 1853.

61. Council of the Third Municipality of the City of New Orleans, *Journal*, January 31, 1848, MSS., City Archives, New Orleans.

62. Council of the First Municipality of the City of New Orleans, *Slaves Emancipated*, MSS., City Archives, Public Library; New Orleans City Council, *Record of Emancipation*, 1846-1851, MSS., Public Library, New Orleans.

63. Council of the Second Municipality of the City of New Orleans, Proceedings, April 1, 1851.

64. Quoted in Everett, *Free Persons of Color in New Orleans*, 154. For an earlier expression of the mounting opposition to routine emancipation see the report of the Judiciary Committee of the Council of the First Municipality of New Orleans in 1851 when its chairman complained that the full "body" often acted "very harshly" toward petitions for emancipation. June 9, 1851, Journal, MSS., City Archives, Public Library, New Orleans.

65. Richmond, Minutes of the Common Council, January 13, 1833.

66. The Negroes resisted this affront and "went away and armed themselves." They later returned to take a few shots at the conductor. *Niles' Register*, August 24, 1833.

67. Savannah, Ordinances, August 2, 1827.

68. Richmond, Ordinances, December 22, 1857.

69. Charleston, Ordinances, July 30, 1838.

70. *Charleston Courier*, July 28, 1841.

71. New Orleans, Ordinances, October 8, 1817.

72. *Report on the Free Colored Poor of the City of Charleston* (Charleston, 1842), 10.

73. Baltimore, Ordinances, 1841, Appendix, 98.

74. See, for example, Karl Bernhard, *Travels*, II, 132.

75. Lyell, *Second Visit*, II, 94.

76. Pulszky, *Red, White, Black*, II, 101.

77. Thomas L. Nichols, *Forty Years of American Life* (London, 1864), II, 279.

78. New Orleans, Ordinances, June 8, 1816.

79. *New Orleans Bee*, October 13, 1837.

80. Petition of the Free People of Color to the Virginia State Legislature, Dec. 17, 1834.

81. *Charleston City Directory*, 233.

82. New Orleans, Ordinances, March 5, 1835.

83. Quoted in Albert M. Shipp, *A History of Methodism in South Carolina* (Nashville, 1884), 426.

84. William Blane, *An Excursion Through the United States and Canada* (London, 1824), 220.

85. City of Baltimore, Petition to the Mayor, January 20, 1839; Petition to the City Council, January 30, 1844; Petition to the Mayor, February 7, 1850; Report of Joint Committee on Colored Schools, February 20, 1850; MSS. Bureau of Archives (City Hall, Baltimore).

86. Memorial of the City Council to the Legislature of South Carolina, 1826, MSS., South Carolina Archives Division.

87. Charleston, Ordinances, October 28, 1806.

88. Savannah, Minutes of the Council, October 15, 1822, MSS., City Hall, Savannah.

89. Savannah, Ordinances, November 11, 1831.

90. Quoted in Lyell, *Second Visit*, II, 81.

91. *Genius of Universal Emancipation*, January 12, 1828.

92. Andrews, *Slavery*, 73.

93. New Orleans, Proceedings, September 13, 1823.

94. Lyell, *Second Visit*, II, 125. John Milton Mackie found the same thing in Mobile; *From Cape Cod to Dixie and the Tropics* (N.Y., 1864), 158. Though the book bears a later date, this trip took place before the war.

95. *Richmond Enquirer*, August 27, 1857.

96. Abbott, *South and North*, 112, 113.

97. *Directory for the City of Savannah to Which is Added a Business Directory for 1860* (Savannah, 1860), 176-7.

98. Olmsted, *Back Country*, 432.

99. Olmsted, *Seaboard Slave States*, 591.

Appendix

THIS APPENDIX has been compiled from official censuses of the United States government. The figures listed here, despite their apparent precision, are only approximately correct. Generally the statistics for white population are more accurate than those for colored residents. Moreover, those for free Negroes are somewhat better than those for slaves. These figures nevertheless are useful in showing various relationships and general trends.

No city had an accurate count of its slave population in these decades. Usually the census taker relied on the master to enumerate his Negroes. Since most towns had a tax on slaves, there was some inducement to minimize holdings. At any rate, official figures never erred on the large side. In addition, the cities always had a large floating population of Negroes; some were runaways, others had a status that was in doubt. In either case, they were happy to avoid being counted. Hence, official figures always underestimated the number of slaves and colored inhabitants in Southern urban centers.

POPULATION OF MAJOR SOUTHERN CITIES 1820-1860

BALTIMORE, MD.

	Total	White	Free Negro	Slave
1820	62,738	48,055	10,326	4,357
1830	80,620	61,710	14,790	4,120
1840	102,313	81,147	17,967	3,199
1850	169,054	140,666	25,442	2,946
1860	212,418	184,520	25,680	2,218

CHARLESTON, S.C.

	Total	White	Free Negro	Slave
1820	24,780	10,653	1,475	12,652
1830	30,289	12,828	2,107	15,354
1840	29,261	13,030	1,558	14,673
1850	42,985	20,012	3,441	19,532
1860	40,522	23,376	3,237	13,909

LOUISVILLE, KY.

	Total	White	Free Negro	Slave
1820	4,012	2,886	93	1,031
1830	10,341	7,703	232	2,406
1840	21,210	17,161	619	3,430
1850	43,194	36,224	1,538	5,432
1860	68,033	61,213	1,917	4,903

MOBILE, ALA.[1]

	Total	White	Free Negro	Slave
1820	2,672	1,653	183	836
1830	3,194	1,647	372	1,175
1840	12,672	8,262	541	3,869
1850	20,515	12,997	715	6,803
1860	29,258	20,854	817	7,587

NEW ORLEANS, LA.

	Total	White	Free Negro	Slave
1820	27,176	13,584	6,237	7,355
1830	29,737	12,299	8,041	9,397
1840	102,193	59,519	19,226	23,448
1850	116,375	89,459	9,905	17,011
1860	168,675	144,601	10,689	13,385

[1] The Mobile returns for 1820 are for Mobile county.

NORFOLK, VA.

	Total	White	Free Negro	Slave
1820	8,478	4,618	599	3,261
1830	9,814	5,130	928	3,756
1840	10,920	6,185	1,026	3,709
1850	14,326	9,075	956	4,295
1860	14,620	10,290	1,046	3,284

RICHMOND, VA.

	Total	White	Free Negro	Slave
1820	12,067	6,445	1,235	4,387
1830	16,060	7,755	1,960	6,345
1840	20,153	10,718	1,926	7,509
1850	27,570	15,274	2,369	9,927
1860	37,910	23,635	2,576	11,699

ST. LOUIS, MO.[2]

	Total	White	Free Negro	Slave
1820	10,049	8,014	196	1,810
1830	14,125	11,109	220	2,796
1840	16,469	14,407	531	1,531
1850	77,860	73,806	1,398	2,656
1860	160,773	157,476	1,755	1,542

SAVANNAH, GA.

	Total	White	Free Negro	Slave
1820	7,523	3,866	582	3,075
1830	7,776			
1840	11,214	5,888	632	4,694
1850	15,312	8,395	686	6,231
1860	22,292	13,875	705	7,712

WASHINGTON, D.C.

	Total	White	Free Negro	Slave
1820	13,247	9,606	1,696	1,945
1830	18,826	13,367	3,129	2,330
1840	23,364	16,843	4,808	1,713
1850	40,001	29,730	8,158	2,113
1860	61,122	50,139	9,209	1,774

[2] The St. Louis returns for 1820 and 1830 are for St. Louis county.

WHITE POPULATION BY SEX

	BALTIMORE		CHARLESTON	
	Male	*Female*	*Male*	*Female*
1820	23,922	24,133	5,323	5,330
1830	30,025	31,685	6,326	6,502
1840	38,841	42,306	6,827	6,203
1850	70,873	69,793	10,238	9,774
1860	88,613	95,907	11,714	11,662

	LOUISVILLE		MOBILE	
	Male	*Female*	*Male*	*Female*
1820	1,824	1,062	1,105	548
1830	4,843	2,860	1,094	553
1840	9,272	7,889	5,655	2,607
1850	19,468	16,756	7,022	5,975
1860	31,299	29,914	11,509	9,345

	NEW ORLEANS		NORFOLK	
	Male	*Female*	*Male*	*Female*
1820	8,266	5,318	2,187	2,431
1830	7,357	4,942	2,483	2,647
1840	34,903	24,616	2,886	3,299
1850	51,792	37,667	4,196	4,879
1860	75,252	69,349	4,870	5,420

	RICHMOND		ST. LOUIS	
	Male	*Female*	*Male*	*Female*
1820	3,492	2,953	4,837	3,177
1830	3,981	3,774	6,424	4,685
1840	5,435	5,283	8,830	5,577
1850	7,783	7,491	42,367	31,439
1860	12,396	11,239	83,350	74,126

	SAVANNAH		WASHINGTON	
	Male	*Female*	*Male*	*Female*
1820	2,106	1,760	4,786	4,820
1830			6,579	6,788
1840	3,235	2,653	8,196	8,647
1850	4,409	3,986	14,526	15,204
1860	7,590	6,285	24,323	25,816

FREE NEGRO POPULATION BY SEX

| | BALTIMORE | | CHARLESTON | |
	Male	*Female*	*Male*	*Female*
1820	4,363	5,963	623	852
1830	6,165	8,625	814	1,293
1840	7,261	10,706	583	975
1850	10,832	14,610	1,355	2,086
1860	10,346	15,334	1,247	1,990

| | LOUISVILLE | | MOBILE | |
	Male	*Female*	*Male*	*Female*
1820	50	43	83	100
1830	117	115	172	200
1840	300	319	250	291
1850	698	840	286	429
1860	862	1,055	355	462

| | NEW ORLEANS | | NORFOLK | |
	Male	*Female*	*Male*	*Female*
1820	2,432	3,805	229	370
1830	3,246	4,795	356	572
1840	8,438	10,788	410	616
1850	3,999	5,906	364	592
1860	4,472	6,217	358	678

| | RICHMOND | | ST. LOUIS | |
	Male	*Female*	*Male*	*Female*
1820	532	703	100	96
1830	837	1,123	80	140
1840	860	1,066	267	264
1850	1,075	1,294	742	656
1860	1,142	1,434	785	970

| | SAVANNAH | | WASHINGTON | |
	Male	*Female*	*Male*	*Female*
1820	224	358	750	946
1830			1,342	1,787
1840	262	370	1,949	2,859
1850	264	422	3,398	4,760
1860	323	382	3,858	5,351

SLAVE POPULATION BY SEX

BALTIMORE

	Male	Female
1820	1,968	2,389
1830	1,658	2,462
1840	1,169	2,030
1850	947	1,999
1860	677	1,541

CHARLESTON

	Male	Female
1820	5,695	6,957
1830	6,777	8,577
1840	6,334	8,339
1850	8,631	10,901
1860	6,563	7,346

LOUISVILLE

	Male	Female
1820	495	536
1830	1,135	1,271
1840	1,383	2,047
1850	2,410	3,022
1860	1,968	2,935

MOBILE

	Male	Female
1820	449	387
1830	611	564
1840	1,901	1,968
1850	3,212	3,591
1860	3,871	3,716

NEW ORLEANS

	Male	Female
1820	2,709	4,646
1830	3,369	6,028
1840	9,795	13,653
1850	6,818	10,193
1860	5,382	8,003

NORFOLK

	Male	Female
1820	1,453	1,808
1830	1,579	2,177
1840	1,498	2,211
1850	1,677	2,618
1860	1,331	1,953

RICHMOND

	Male	Female
1820	2,171	2,216
1830	3,288	3,057
1840	3,953	3,556
1850	5,307	4,620
1860	6,636	5,063

ST. LOUIS

	Male	Female
1820	987	823
1830	1,365	1,431
1840	696	835
1850	1,266	1,390
1860	556	986

SAVANNAH

	Male	Female
1820	1,325	1,750
1830		
1840	1,978	2,716
1850	2,949	3,282
1860	3,602	4,110

WASHINGTON

	Male	Female
1820	880	1,065
1830	1,021	1,309
1840	649	1,064
1850	733	1,380
1860	574	1,200

Index